4D Leadership

4D Leadership
Competitive advantage through vertical leadership development

Dr Alan Watkins

KoganPage

LONDON PHILADELPHIA NEW DELHI

First published in Great Britain and the United States in 2016 by Kogan Page Limited

2nd Floor, 45 Gee Street
London EC1V 3RS
United Kingdom
www.koganpage.com

1518 Walnut Street, Suite 1100
Philadelphia PA 19102
USA

4737/23 Ansari Road
Daryaganj
New Delhi 110002
India

© Complete Coherence Limited, 2016

ISBN   978 0 7494 7464 5
E-ISBN   978 0 7494 7465 2

British Library Cataloguing-in-Publication Data

A CIP record for this book is available from the British Library.

Library of Congress Cataloging-in-Publication Data

Names: Watkins, Alan, 1961- author.
Title: 4D leadership : competitive advantage through vertical leadership
    development / Alan Watkins.
Other titles: Four D leadership.
Description: London ; Philadelphia : Kogan Page Limited, 2016. | Includes
    bibliographical references and index.
Identifiers: LCCN 2015036070 | ISBN 9780749474645 | ISBN 9780749474652 (ebk)
Subjects: LCSH: Leadership. | Executive ability. | Strategic planning.
Classification: LCC HD57.7. W3787 2016 | DDC 658.4/092–dc23 LC record available at
http://lccn.loc.gov/2015036070

Typeset by Graphicraft Limited, Hong Kong
Print production managed by Jellyfish
Printed and bound by CPI Group (UK) Ltd, Croydon, CR0 4YY

CONTENTS

Coherence:
The secret science
of brilliant leadership

'The approaches in this book have helped me remain in the present.
In life, sometimes your inner voice can be nervous, worried and unhappy...
learning to operate from a position of inner peace and calmness, to be present,
is transformational.'
John Browett, CEO, Monsoon

'It makes sense that if you want to perform at your best you should know
the key drivers of how that is possible. If you don't, you will be at a distinct
disadvantage. Fortunately for me I met Alan Watkins, and now everyone can
benefit when they read this book.'
Michael Drake, Managing Director, TNT Express – AMEA

Every business leader faces innumerable challenges every working day, each one
taking their toll on precious energy levels and the ability to respond and react
positively in a commercial environment. *Coherence* uncovers the fundamental
issues that can limit a leader's effectiveness and ability to lead, and provides the
reader with unique solutions, from the biological to the behavioural, designed to
improve business results. Problems today cannot be solved with yesterday's level
of thinking. CEOs fail and leaders burn out because our thinking has not sped up
or powered up. Dr Alan Watkins not only recognizes that leaders have the
potential for limitless processing power, but shows them how to access it, taking
them back to fundamentals and, quite literally, to the heart of who we are and
how we function successfully. By showing leaders how to be 'younger, smarter,
healthier and happier', *Coherence* gives every decision maker the power to make
brilliant decisions under pressure and achieve sustainable success at every level.

ISBN: 978 0 7494 7005 0
Published by Kogan Page

Introduction

In the rolling hills of the English countryside I stood in an oak-panelled library of a boutique hotel overlooking the championship golf course with 12 Executive Board members of a very successful multi-national organization. Every one of them was looking very confused.

I was seeking to explore with them the multi-dimensional nature of leadership. Initially I'd asked the group to write on the flip chart what they do all day. This question was easy and the executives quickly filled a whole page with things like, strategy; marketing plan; performance management; drive top line revenue; cost management to deliver the bottom line; goal setting; define metrics for measuring initiative outcomes, and so on. Asking executives to make a list of what they 'do' all day is pretty straightforward because they live in the objective rational world of 'action', 'task' and 'to do lists'. In fact 'doing' is what most executives think about virtually all the time. This is not what was causing the bewilderment. What had stumped them was a different question – 'Can you write down everything that happens on the inside of you every day, the interior phenomena?'

The assembled group were extremely smart, highly experienced business professionals and yet it appeared that they didn't even understand the question never mind have a lucid answer. I decided to prompt them a little. 'What about that strange phenomenon called "thinking" that you may have noticed', I joked. Each group wrote 'thinking' on the flip chart but then looked baffled again. So I prompted them a second time. 'Perhaps you've also heard of this weird thing called "feeling"?', I teased. 'Ah yes, of course', someone replied. A couple of groups even started to write down a list of specific feelings before I reminded them they were all the same phenomenon and there were no bonus points for naming specific feelings. Again the conversation foundered and they couldn't come up with any other answers. 'OK, never mind that, turn the page and write down everything that happens between you and other people.' Again the confusion returned, albeit slightly less. A couple of groups got a few answers out. 'Do you mean things like trust and empathy?' 'Yes, that's right', I encouraged. But after three or four words the groups dried up and the page remained almost empty.

When placing the flip chart pages next to each other it was abundantly clear to everyone in the room that their individual and collective executive focus was almost exclusively on the dimension of 'doing'. The other two dimensions of 'being' or 'relating' were virtually empty. When I suggested what some of the answers for the interior phenomenon could be – identity, morality, virtue, consciousness, self, ethics, ego – they all immediately realized that actually there were a lot of things they could have said but these concepts just didn't occur to them spontaneously. Likewise when I reviewed some of the interpersonal concepts such as rapport, team working, alignment, mythology, belonging, culture and values they again recognized the concepts.

I have repeated this exercise on numerous occasions with different executive teams with the same result. In business we are 'Human Doings' not 'Human Beings'. Most leaders and executives spend almost all their time focused on what they need to do in their business and spend very little time thinking about who they are being or how they are interacting with others. In business the focus is virtually always on their outside tangible world and not their inside world. This is interesting because if you ask most leaders whether they think their moral compass alters what they 'do' they admit that morality and ethics make a massive difference to their actions and behaviour. And yet this interior landscape is almost exclusively ignored.

When asked if the strength of relationships in a team alter that team's ability to get things done most leaders will again agree wholeheartedly. Interpersonal dynamics make a significant difference to the outcome of any strategy or plan. And yet again this interpersonal landscape is so often minimized, ignored or dismissed as irrelevant. They are not fully aware of the multi-dimensional nature of leadership or that there are other dimensions other than just 'doing' that are vital to commercial success. As a result most leaders completely miss the rich rewards inherent in these other dimensions. This book is an exploration of these various dimensions which, when properly understood, can create disruptive, long-term competitive advantage and allow us to genuinely future proof our businesses.

The three dimensions

In *Coherence: The secret science of brilliant leadership* (Watkins, 2014), I explained how integral philosopher Ken Wilber organized the entire human experience into the three dimensions: namely the objective 'IT'; the subjective 'I' and the interpersonal 'WE' dimensions.

FIGURE 0.1 Ken Wilber's original AQAL model as it applies to business

I	IT
(individual interior) Self and consciousness – invisible (ie thinking, feeling, emotions and awareness)	(individual exterior) Action and system (visible behaviour)
WE	**ITS**
(collective interior) Culture and worldview	(collective exterior) Social system and environment

There are hundreds of theories on just about everything – including leadership. Wilber set out to see if it was possible to construct a 'theory of everything' (2001). What he found was that most of the major theories tended to focus on just one quadrant and all of the theories whether relating to leadership, management practice, philosophy, psychology, spirituality, ecology or frankly any academic discipline, could all be placed within his four quadrant map of reality. This four box model, as originally described, separates the interior from the exterior landscape of human experience for both the individual and the collective. As such it describes individual leaders and teams as well as the interior and exterior reality of each (see Figure 0.1).

Wilber's objective is to provide a framework that will allow us to understand the complexity of the modern world and ultimately to create an integral theory that, more than any other single theory, is more inclusive and more accurately explains reality.

Working with leaders from multiple market sectors all over the world we've adapted Wilber's four quadrant model slightly by rotating it anti-clockwise one quarter turn, making it three-dimensional and putting the leader at the centre of what we call the Enlightened Leadership Model. We found that this is more in tune with how leaders see their own landscape (see Figure 0.2).

Since 2010 myself and my colleagues have successfully 'road-tested' the Enlightened Leadership Model with 500 Global CEOs including 70 per cent of the FTSE 100, the best CEOs in India and China plus luminaries in the Fortune 500 (Tappin and Cave, 2010; Tappin, 2012). We specifically

FIGURE 0.2   The Enlightened Leadership Model

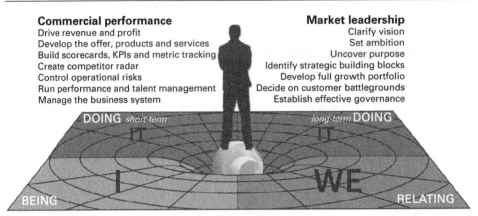

Commercial performance
Drive revenue and profit
Develop the offer, products and services
Build scorecards, KPIs and metric tracking
Create competitor radar
Control operational risks
Run performance and talent management
Manage the business system

Market leadership
Clarify vision
Set ambition
Uncover purpose
Identify strategic building blocks
Develop full growth portfolio
Decide on customer battlegrounds
Establish effective governance

DOING *short-term*   *long-term* DOING

IT   IT

I   WE

BEING   RELATING

Personal performance
Step change quality of thinking
Develop boundless energy
Uncover personal purpose

People leadership
Identify organizational 'Way' and evolve organizational culture
Develop integrated fellowship and high performing team
Clarify personal leadership qualities

investigated whether the model did represent reality for these leaders and whether they were paying attention to anything that was not included in this model. They're not – every single meeting they were having, every single moment of every single day, every type of activity they were engaged in, everything they were paying attention to dropped neatly into one of these four quadrants.

At first glance this may appear like another piece of useless academic theory and you may be thinking to yourself 'So what? What has this got to do with leadership or business or helping me get the results I need?' The answer is that it has everything to do with it. When you know that nothing exists outside this model then every situation, challenge or scenario you face immediately falls into one or a combination of these four quadrants, or more succinctly the three dimensions of 'I' ('being', bottom left-hand quadrant); 'WE' ('relating', bottom right-hand quadrant); or 'IT' ('doing', top right- and top left-hand quadrants). And this distinction can significantly improve your chances of finding appropriate and effective solutions.

This model offers us a very powesrful way of looking at complex issues, including leadership so we can appreciate why they are working and why they are not working. Furthermore this model has been thoroughly embraced by our clients because it better explains what they are actually experiencing in business than any other leadership approach they have found.

Leaders stand at the centre of their 'gravity grid' looking out into their business and the environment that they operate in. Business leaders live and die by their results so it makes sense that leaders are looking out into the external, objective world of 'IT' and what they are actually doing. Expectations are sky high and life at the top can be short lived for those that don't deliver. It's little wonder that most leaders spend the vast majority of their time focusing on the external world of 'IT' – either the front left quadrant where the focus is on short-term commercial performance or the front right quadrant where the focus is on longer-term market leadership. Either way, business leaders and senior executives live their entire corporate life in the dimension of 'IT' because IT is what they are judged on.

As we seek to compete in a world characterized by ever increasing volatility, uncertainty, complexity and ambiguity (VUCA), most leaders are struggling to meet and surpass ever increasing targets. In an effort to improve performance and grow the business, leaders are still competing almost exclusively in the dimension of 'IT'. They may for example seek greater operational efficiency or shift strategy, they may decide to enter a new market, develop a new product or engage in mergers and acquisitions – all these manoeuvres are traditional routes to greater growth and all belong in the dimension of 'IT'. Whilst there are still many improvements to be made in this dimension it is becoming increasingly difficult to differentiate just by focusing on what you are 'doing' and trying to 'do it better' than your competitors. Such commercial advantages are pretty hard to identify and expensive to come by. But 'IT' is not the only dimension. We just don't realize it because we hardly ever look behind us.

Disruptive competitive advantage

Over our left shoulder, and out of normal vision, is the inner, subjective personal performance world of 'I' and over our right shoulder is the inter-personal people leadership world of 'WE'. And what we have witnessed over the last 20 years is that it is possible to step change individual, team and organizational performance relatively easily and cheaply, through some minor albeit targeted modifications in the largely ignored dimensions of 'I' and 'WE'.

Unfortunately too many of us, especially seasoned business executives, are still convinced that driving results and business growth is basically all about goals, targets and plans in the external dimension of 'IT' and the awareness of the potential of the other dimensions is minimal.

But just think about it for a moment ... Do you perform better when you are angry and frustrated or focused and passionate? If you receive bad news just before attending an important meeting do you find yourself distracted for the entire day or are you able to push it aside and press on unaffected? How we are 'being' fundamentally changes not only what we are 'doing' but also how well we are 'doing it'. Similarly, when the business operates from within silos and cross-functional relationships are based on transactions rather than trust achieving productive outcomes becomes much harder. The quality of relationships between different divisions or even individuals within the same division also influences our ability to get things done. Values and maturity can also totally change leadership behaviour. Relationships and team work is essential in business and a team is always more productive if the people in the team respect and understand each other. Yet when we try to improve our business we invest nearly all of our time and energy into changing organizational structures, re-engineering process, re-working strategy and re-ordering our 'to do' list of priorities and not on forensically dissecting the nature of human relationship and how we can step change the quality of our connections with those around us. Such matters are often dismissed as 'touchy-feely' nonsense, too difficult or largely irrelevant. Plus in our rush to 'get on with things' we don't often engage in self-reflection. As a result, the dimensions of 'I' and 'WE' are almost exclusively ignored.

If we are to reap the competitive advantage inherent in the multi-dimensional nature of reality described by the Enlightened Leadership Model we must appreciate that our efforts in the rational, objective world are actually built on the subjective, internal world of 'I' (physiology, emotions, feelings and thoughts) and that the success of what we want to build requires high-quality relationships, a high performance culture, great teams that trust each other and our connectivity with customers and staff in the interpersonal world of 'WE'. Only then can we create sustainable positive impact in the objective external world of 'IT'. Ultimately it doesn't matter if the strategy is brilliant and the short-term results look good, if no one likes, trusts or respects the leader they will never unlock the discretionary effort of the workforce required to implement the strategy anyway and failure becomes more likely.

1D vs 4D

Having spent their careers largely focused on the short-term dimension of 'IT' most business leaders are already very proficient in many of the tasks within the world of 'doing'. They are often so busy 'doing' that they may have lost touch with their 'being'. To compound the error few have really cultivated the ability to connect on a deeper level in the dimension of 'relating'. As a result very few are bringing all of themselves to work and end up living a partial, fragmented and one-dimensional life. For most of us being labelled one-dimensional would be an insult but in this context we are literally talking about the number of dimensions we are actively aware of and can operate in proficiently. It is not an insult – merely an observation of the human condition.

When we only bring a small fragment of our true potential to the table we and others only experience a small fragment of what we are truly capable of. Obviously if we only bring a piece of ourselves, perhaps the piece we feel is appropriate or expected and leave the rest at home, then we can never be truly authentic as leaders. Powerful, authentic leaders always bring all of who they are to the party – that's what makes them powerful and authentic.

One-dimensional expression will always deliver a sub-optimal outcome. But it's not just business people who sell themselves short. Some people choose to turn their back on the world of 'doing', disenfranchised with the greed, avarice and inequality in what they see as a grabbing capitalist world full of ego and self-serving individuals. Instead they pursue a more 'noble' life of inner contemplation and spiritual development. They have effectively turned inward to the interior world of 'I'. They often reject what business stands for and passionately denounce the materialism often incumbent in commercial activity. They may be highly evolved with a highly honed degree of spiritual insight but as one CEO put it to me recently, such individuals may live to 120 years old but who have they helped and what difference have they really made in the world beyond themselves? Such a mono-focused interior exploration is every bit as one-dimensional as the single-minded business leader who focuses exclusively on the external world of 'doing' at the expense of his health, relationships and environment.

Similarly, some people, often those in the caring professions, not-for-profit organizations or the service industries often choose to immerse themselves in the interpersonal world of 'WE' and dedicate their lives to service of one sort or another. These individuals often put others' needs before their own to such an extent that they become ill. They fail to sufficiently look after their own 'being', sacrificing what they may need in the service of others. There for everyone else but not themselves. This is a fairly common phenomenon in mothers who can lose their identity only to discover 20 years later when their children leave home that they no longer know who they are beyond the role of 'mother' that they embraced so completely.

Ironically the single-minded business executive, the spiritual seeker and the carer may look completely different, live very different lives and yet they are all making the same fundamental error – they live their lives largely in one dimension.

Our view is that in order for us to be a fully functioning human being, we need to bring 'all of us' to our daily lives not just 'fragments of us'. We need to be very capable in all three dimensions, 'I', 'WE' and 'IT'. But to actually reach our true potential requires us to go beyond capability in each dimension – we need to develop 'verticality' up all three of these dimensions. This vertical development is the crucial '4th dimension'. Developing our altitude in all three worlds enables us to become 4D leaders. And by developing a deep understanding of how each dimension affects and interacts with the others we can go still further to create a coherent 4D life.

Think of each of these dimensions as a stack or tower. As an accomplished 'doer' capable of making things happen the single-minded business leader may already demonstrate verticality in the world of 'IT'. But he is largely one-dimensional because his inner world of 'I' and his interconnected world of 'WE' are minimally developed. It often feels like many executives have built the Burj Khalifa tower in the world of 'doing', but in the world of 'being' there is a concrete car park and in the world of 'relating' there is a pop-up tent (see Figure 0.3a).

The spiritual seeker may possess breathtaking personal control and have cultivated a quiet, tranquil mind in the world of 'I'. They may be an accomplished 'guru' capable of piercing insight on the human condition. On that dimension the spiritual seeker may also be proficiently vertically developed, but their limited 'IT' and 'WE' dimensions make them seem peripheral to the modern world (see Figure 0.3b).

FIGURE 0.3   Variations of 1D living

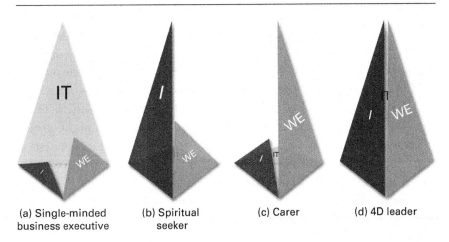

(a) Single-minded business executive

(b) Spiritual seeker

(c) Carer

(d) 4D leader

On the other hand, the carer may have significant verticality on 'WE'. They may be extremely empathetic, focused on others and enjoy successful and highly productive relationships, but if they only possess limited verticality on both 'IT' and 'I' then they will never fulfil their full potential as a compassionate individual (see Figure 0.3c).

Exceptional leaders understand and move between all three dimensions, developing verticality in each. They are mainly driven in the objective world of 'doing' ('IT'). They appreciate that the subjective world of 'being' ('I') influences how they show up in the objective world and have learned to manage and harness their interior power to become even more proficient in the external world of action. And they appreciate that nothing is done alone and therefore they are also effective in the interpersonal world of relationship ('WE'). 4D Leadership is achieved when we have developed significant verticality across the numerous lines of development that span each of these three dimensions of 'I', 'WE' and 'IT' (Figure 0.3d).

Vertical development across 'IT', 'I' and 'WE'

Most large businesses have Learning and Development (L&D) departments charged with designing and implementing people development initiatives. But there are actually two types of development – horizontal and vertical. Horizontal development is the acquisition of skills, knowledge and experience or 'learning'. Clearly learning is important because leaders need technical skills relevant to their role, they need to be knowledgeable about a variety of factors or business issues and they need to be skilful in a number of areas but learning is *not* development.

In nearly 20 years' working with multi-nationals we have noticed that very few L&D departments actually make this distinction clearly enough. Very few organizations separate learning processes from development programmes. This is not a slight on L&D departments or the hard working professionals within them, it's simply an observation of the way L&D departments have evolved within most businesses. Most companies' L&D departments have tended to focus on the more readily deliverable 'L' without much if any attention on the more challenging 'D'.

Horizontal learning is like moving from a side plate to a dinner plate while vertical development is like a whole stack of dinner plates. Obviously skills, knowledge and experience are very important to productivity and performance but they do not drive verticality across the three dimensions.

So in business we talk at length about executives needing to scale the 'learning curve' and acquire the skills they need to be effective in their new job. For example, when appointing a new CFO we may explore whether he or she has the requisite Investor Relations experience, or has sufficient international experience or media skills to be able to succeed. Is their knowledge of the market strong enough? All of these things are enormously important. But what we rarely assess is how mature or developed the leader is. We are more interested in *what* they know than *how* they know. Traditionally, their ability to convert learning into development is not part of the consideration. And this is primarily because it is much easier to measure knowledge, skill and experience. Determining a leader's values or level of maturity is much trickier.

However, in a rapidly changing VUCA world it is development not learning that will give us the true competitive advantage by allowing us to expand our capacity and increase our altitude or verticality across each of the three dimensions of 'I', 'WE' and 'IT'. Vertical development takes performance to a new level. It is profoundly different from learning and the two terms should not be used interchangeably. Learning may allow us to become more proficient but vertical development unlocks significantly higher levels of capability that can step change performance. Learning 'adds more apps', vertical development upgrades our operating system.

Perhaps the best way to think about the difference between the two is to consider the life of a six-year-old child. If you ask a six-year-old the question '$4X = 16$; what does X equal?' they don't even understand the question. This is because their frontal cortex is not fully developed and they are unable to think in an abstract way. However, if you ask a 12-year-old child he will probably be able to tell you that $X = 4$. The frontal cortex is much more fully developed at 12 and this development has massively increased cognitive capacity, brain processing speed and facilitated abstract thought. As a result the child's ability to understand algebra has come 'online'. The older child has a level of capability and sophistication that didn't exist at six. Vertical development offers that kind of quantum leap forward for leaders. There is no reason that the kind of development we see in children cannot continue into adulthood to enable us to thrive in today's complex world. Unfortunately very few leaders ever 'upgrade their own personal operating system' because (a) they are too busy, (b) they don't know they can, (c) they don't appreciate the relevance and the impact it can have and finally (d) even if they did they don't know how to.

If you have children of your own or have spent much time studying child development you will have noticed that most 14-year-olds can function pretty well in an adult world. Introduce them to your friends at a dinner party and they can network and hold their own in a conversation. After reaching this level of capability there is often little imperative for a 14-year-old to develop further which means that beyond 14 people definitely get older, they may learn new skills, acquire knowledge at University or in a job, have experiences with others, but they don't necessarily or automatically develop as adult human beings.

As a result many executives may be extremely knowledgeable about all manner of commercial activity. We may have experienced all sorts of market cycles, cultural challenges and geographic postings, we may know a great deal about a lot of things – but that is all learning, it is not development. As a result we may be 40- or 50-years-old but effectively we've remained a 14-year-old on the inside. This is why we see so many power battles at the top of companies, 'toys out of the pram' episodes, tantrums, bullying and all manner of activities that frankly are more common and certainly more expected in the school playground than a corporate boardroom. Sometimes this lack of development manifests as egocentric narcissism (Farbrot, 2014) or hubris (Garrard, 2013).

There is little doubt that vertical development of the leadership cadre is the single biggest determinant of future success and if ignored the single biggest obstacle to growth. It is this lack of development that is at the very heart of business success and failure. Recent research suggests that the more sophisticated a leader the greater their ability to drive organizational trans-formation (Rooke and Torbert, 2005).

There is also little doubt that what we readily define as 'talent' is actually development. In other words those individuals we assume to be different because of some innate talent or special ability are actually just more verti-cally developed – they are using a more sophisticated operating system. They are able to access more of who they are as human beings. Considering that high performers (the talented) deliver 48 per cent improved perfor-mance over average performers in highly complex jobs (Hunter, Schmidt and Judiesch, 1990) and good leaders create three times more economic value than poor leaders and extraordinary (talented) leaders create signi-ficantly more economic value than even the good leaders (Zenger and Folkman, 2009) then vertical development clearly holds the key to unlock-ing game changing talent and consistently elevated performance in any business.

When leaders develop vertically to become 4D leaders they unlock whole new levels of capability and can transform performance. They often have significantly increased energy levels, are much more resilient and less easily exhausted. Their leadership presence increases. Cognitively, they are significantly more sophisticated and are able to understand multiple layers of complexity and polarity. They are systems thinkers and can appreciate the interdependencies both inside and outside their organization. Their high degree of self-awareness means that they are often more receptive to input and understand that their views may be partial. As a result they are often inquisitive particularly in relation to their own further development.

Despite the complexity and ambiguity of the world today, we all have the potential to develop as leaders. It requires a focus on upgrading our operating system, not just adding on more 'apps' in the form of skills and experience. It requires vertical development. In this VUCA world the only way out is up.

As individuals, teams and businesses we need to evolve and progress horizontally and vertically. There are multiple ways we can do this and exactly how we do this depends on the type of business we are in. However, over the last 20 years we have identified probably the eight most commercially relevant *lines of development* for most businesses (see Figure 0.4). Drawing on a very rich scientific literature on adult 'development' these eight separate but interconnected and cumulative lines of development facilitate verticality across all three dimensions – 'I', 'WE' and 'IT' – and this book is a practical as well as theoretical guide to our journey toward 4D Leadership.

In Chapters 1 and 2 we will explore the most familiar dimension for most of us – 'IT'. This is the external observable world of 'doing'. Most senior

FIGURE 0.4   Lines of development

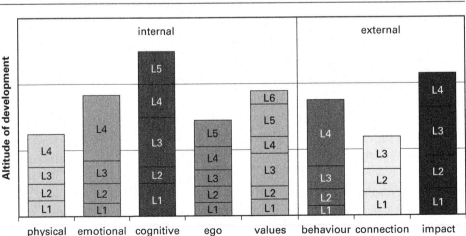

leaders spend the vast majority of their time in this dimension and Chapter 1 will explain why. Chapter 2 then unpacks the line of development that really matters in 'IT' – behaviour – so that we know what behaviours to focus on to become a more effective leader and pull away from the competition. Rigorous research has identified that, in complex dynamic businesses, there are only 11 behaviours that really matter when it comes to productivity and performance. Chapter 2 also explores holocratic governance as a way to drive performance and network analysis. Understanding the real functional, emotional and leadership networks that are operating in the business as opposed to the ones that are expected given the organizational chart can step change results.

Chapters 3 and 4 explore the dimension of 'I' or the internal subjective world of 'being'. In business this dimension is almost exclusively ignored and yet it is this dimension that holds huge potential to create disruptive competitive advantage and the ability to future proof any business. Specifically, Chapter 3 will explore three of the internal lines of development – physical, cognitive and emotional. There is so much confusion around performance, what causes it and what prevents it. Unpacking these lines will shine some much needed light on the subject from what may be a completely new perspective. You will learn simple, practical tools to help increase your energy levels (without changing your diet or going to the gym) and access your very best, most creative thinking when you need it most. You will also appreciate emotion for what it really is – rather than what we've been traditionally told it is – so you can harness your energy and amplify your emotional intelligence, resilience and perceptual awareness. These tools will also help you to increase engagement as you take others with you on the developmental journey. Chapter 4 takes a detailed look at ego maturity. Our traditional understanding of 'ego maturity' can often mean that leaders are confused and occasionally a little offended to find such a topic in leadership, but when fully understood in this context this line of development may offer the biggest potential for fast performance improvement and company-wide transformation.

In Chapters 5 and 6 we unpack the dimension of 'WE' or the interdependent world of 'relating'. A leader can only ever be a true leader if they develop followership. If no one is following the leader then they are a leader by title only. Our ability to develop strong, productive relationships is paramount to success in all areas of life. As a result Chapter 5 will unpack the values line of development. When we have a greater awareness of our own values and the values of those around us, disagreements and irritations melt away as we are better able to see the other person's point of view and alter our communication so as to resolve issues faster. And finally in Chapter 6 we'll look at the connection and impact lines of development. We will unpack the importance of 1st, 2nd and 3rd person perspective, taking in the creation of healthy, functional and productive relationships. And we will revisit network analysis as a way to capitalize on existing connections in the business and exerting much greater influence in all areas of your life.

From the end of Chapter 2 onwards there will also be 'Action Steps' so you are reminded of the action you need to take and exercises you need to practise in order to facilitate vertical development up each line across all three dimensions. If you only read and implement these action steps it will absolutely change the performance of the business.

It's important to realize that adult development is not linear, the lines are not always equal and they are not sequential. Everyone is different and the journey is different for each leader. But whether you are an experienced senior leader looking for a new perspective to give you an edge in a tightly squeezed market, a HR professional looking to transform the effectiveness of your L&D initiatives or you are new to leadership, collectively these eight key lines of development can facilitate 4D Leadership and will have a profound impact on your performance and results. But perhaps even more importantly they will have a profound impact on your health, happiness and fulfilment as a coherent 4D leader.

PART ONE
The objective world of 'doing' ('IT')

The escalating leadership challenges in the VUCA world

01

Late one Friday afternoon I received a call from a CEO who was desperately worried about his COO. 'I think he is on the point of some sort of breakdown'. The two leaders had been working incredibly hard and very closely to turn their company around under extremely difficult circumstances. They had been wading through numerous organizational, market and operational challenges whilst under considerable financial pressure and media noise. The COO was an extremely able leader, a real hard worker, genuine and really trying to do a great job for the company. He was putting in increasingly longer shifts and seemingly getting nowhere. He was becoming more and more frustrated by the lack of progress and was starting to feel as though he was letting others down and was annoyed by his own inability to single-handedly make a big enough difference. Thankfully, we were able to intervene quickly enough and initiate a plan to turn him around so he could then go on and turn the company around.

Unfortunately such stories of executive pressure are not isolated incidents. Keeping up with the relentless pace of change is part of the 'modern game' of business. It goes with the territory and is all part of the exhausting challenge that most executives buy into. Most leaders feel time poor, work long hours to try to keep on top of their huge workload, carry around an extensive, never ending 'to do' list. Executive teams wrestle endlessly with their organizational priorities, negotiating the various cross-functional trade-offs and trying to strike the balance between cost reduction, customer value and profit margin. The belief is that if they can keep their organizational 'to do' list down to a manageable size then there is a real chance they will be able to execute their strategy, deliver the promised returns to the shareholders, meet market expectations and make a pile of money via their L-TIP (long-term incentive package or bonus).

The kind of pressure that most C-suite executives are under is not for the faint-hearted. Working at this level of intensity in complex multi-national businesses takes its toll. The cost is normally paid by the senior leaders themselves in terms of their health or their family relationships, who may rarely see their father/mother/spouse/children. In 2014 Mohamed El-Erian stood down as CEO of finance company Pimco for this very reason. His wake up call arrived one evening when he was trying to get his daughter to brush her teeth and reminding her that in days gone by she would just do what he asked without having to be told multiple times. His daughter then produced a letter she had written which contained a list of 22 things that she had asked him to do which he had not. On the list were 22 important events he had missed in that year alone including a parent–teacher conference, a Halloween parade and her first day of school. The letter prompted El-Erian to reassess his priorities and he stood down to spend more time with his family (Thomas, 2014).

Alternatively the company itself pays the price in terms of failed strategies, poor decision making and loss of market share. Corporate history is littered with stand out examples from high street jewellery business Ratner's that was effectively destroyed by some ill-thought-out remarks by their then CEO Gerald Ratner to the most recent departure of Phil Clarke as CEO of Tesco. Clarke famously worked his way up from shelf stacker to CEO over almost 40 years but during his reign the company began to flag amidst stiff competition from discount retailers such as Aldi and Lidl. Under pressure to continue the success of his predecessor Clarke decided to cull most of the top talent and created a power vacuum but did little to improve the brand or the culture. He was forcibly removed from office after just three years at the helm.

And if the pressure doesn't get you then the job insecurity often will. The life expectancy in the job of an average CEO is not great. Plus all of this is now conducted in the public eye with the business pages of most newspapers awash with stories about executive failures, greed, hubris or other sorry narratives which often simply fuel excessive caution or excessive risk taking.

Many argue that the massive rewards available to the C-suite should be compensation enough for such pressure and cite that there is no shortage of people striving to make it to the top. But what kind of leaders make it to the top of corporate systems that reward aggressive action; that are often built around power hierarchies with hub and spoke leadership structures? Are such individuals adequately equipped to deal with the current rate of change and complexity? Why is leadership so difficult these days? Let's pull back for a moment to when the world was a little simpler. When running a company was a little more straightforward.

Business then compared to business now

Forty years ago business was much more straightforward. A company was owned by shareholders and there was an Annual General Meeting (AGM) to which the CEO had to report progress. Aside from this the Executive Board could pretty much do what they liked without a great deal of interference. If a poor year occurred they could create a story to explain to shareholders and press on with their plan in whatever way they wanted. If they needed to raise more money they would normally just issue a few more shares. A one-page organizational chart was often sufficient to describe the relationships, reporting lines and hierarchy leading up to the CEO at the top of the business. The CEO for his part, and it was almost always he, was the boss. The buck stopped with him and he made all or at least most of the major decisions. It was a busy role and it had its pressure but it was manageable and not overly complicated. Today the CEO's task is considerably more complicated. They have to lead and integrate a wider range of functions and operations, every one of which is significantly more complicated than it used to be. The same is true of the lives of the CEO's main Executive Board members.

In the 1970s the CFO or Financial Director performed an accounting function and was basically the person that balanced the books. They would have been responsible for issuing reports to the market and keeping shareholders happy but that was about it. Even in a large global company it really wasn't that complex. Now the funding of most big businesses is mind numbingly complex. For example we work with a leading retailer and they have 13 separate investing banks that back them. Investor Relations (IR) has become a huge function in its own right for most big businesses.

Today the CFO must go repeatedly to that community and keep them onside. In addition they must meet with analysts and constantly feed the media and the City stories of how well the business is doing and will do in the future. Most modern multi-nationals have whole teams of people engaged in tax avoidance accounting, off-shoring and other 'non-domiciliary' manoeuvres which most people would consider cheating the public purse. When these manoeuvres are uncovered by some enterprising journalist they often appear on the front pages of tabloid newspapers. For example a Starbucks store in London required police protection from protestors after it was discovered they hadn't paid corporation tax for four years! But they are not alone – Amazon, eBay, Facebook, Google and Ikea were all discovered to have paid little or no corporation tax despite having large UK operations (Neville and Malik, 2012). Comedian Jimmy Carr and singer Gary Barlow were also exposed for using 'aggressive' tax avoidance schemes (McLennan, 2014). And whilst people clearly feel outraged around such activity condemning it as 'morally wrong' it's usually perfectly legal.

Indeed maintaining the legality of such activity adds a further layer of complexity to financial management. And that's not to mention having to comply with increasingly tough corporate governance rules such as Sarbanes-Oxley. Finance departments must perpetually accrue large sums of money and set them aside in anticipation of future financial demands. Operating in multiple geographies can often mean some of the biggest swings on their balance sheet are fluctuations in currency prices. In fact some companies can make more money from playing the currency markets than they can from their own operational activity. If they want to raise funds for geographic expansion, mergers and acquisition or investment in product development their options are so varied they are almost bewildering. It is no wonder that most large companies' finance departments now lean pretty heavily on the big four accounting firms, paying them millions of pounds a year for tax advice and auditing support. So the CFO or Financial Director role is no longer straightforward. It's extremely complicated. We must also not forget that he or she doesn't just have one P&L (profit and loss) statement to worry about. Many multi-national companies incorporate multiple subsidiary brands or business entities. One of our clients, for example, is no longer one business but has upwards of 300 sub-owned separate companies under their group brand name.

Life is no less complex for the Marketing Director. In the 1970s Marketing Directors were charged with increasing sales and improving market share. To this end they would oversee marketing strategy and work with others in the marketing team to execute that strategy via the 4 Ps of marketing – product, price, place, promotion. The main channels for advertising were TV, print, radio, sales promotions, sponsorship and direct marketing. Again it wasn't necessarily easy to achieve consistent marketing success but if you had the budget it was pretty straightforward. Marketing is a *totally* different animal today. TV and print advertising are much more nuanced especially with the explosion in the number of available terrestrial, satellite and cable channels not to mention YouTube and the trend for much smaller viral channels to broadcast the views of single individuals with large followings. In addition, the evolution of Sky Plus and Tivo now make it very easy for viewers to fast forward past a brand's well-crafted adverts. Similarly the printed advertising market has changed dramatically with significantly more general and niche publications available in which to try to connect to the customer base. But the job of the Marketing Director has not only been made more difficult by the changes to TV and printed media options, it has been massively disrupted by the growth of the internet and the arrival of social media platforms. Large companies such as Gatorade, Dell and Unilever now operate social media control centres that monitor what's being said about their business and brands on a constant basis.

For example, Gatorade measures everything from blog conversations to tweets and Facebook posts and runs complex sentiment analysis to ascertain how their market really feels about their products and brand. Gatorade knows what customers say about them almost as fast as they've said it and it's changing their business from the inside. While monitoring their 'Gatorade has evolved' campaign which featured a song by rap artist David Banner, their mission control centre noticed that the song was getting a lot of attention on social media. Within 24 hours, they had collaborated with Banner to put out a full-length version of the song and distribute it to Gatorade followers and fans on Twitter and Facebook. Gatorade also uses the insight they glean from social media and various analytic tools to optimize landing pages and ensure followers are being sent to the top per-forming pages. As a result the company has increased engagement with its product education videos by 250 per cent and reduced its exit rate from 25 per cent to 9 per cent (Ostrow, 2010).

In Dell's social media centre 70 employees monitor roughly 25,000 Dell related messages via Twitter, Facebook, blogs and other social media every day – in 11 different languages responding to most queries or complaints within 24 hours (Holmes, 2012). Forget about 4 Ps – marketing is a moving feast that requires creativity and ongoing innovative brilliance just to break through the noise.

What we used to describe as 'marketing' is now spilling over into other areas like recruitment blurring departmental lines and amplifying inter-departmental connectivity (and complexity). Take Heineken, the Dutch beer company for example. They created a marketing campaign wrapped around their internship selection process that sought to demonstrate to potential recruits, current employees and therefore by default, customers, that even business activities like recruitment can be turned into an amazing opportu-nity. The message was clear – If Heineken did interviews they would prob-ably be the best interviews in the world! The video – called 'The Candidate' – showed secretly filmed clips from various candidates and how they dealt with a number of surprise scenarios that they thought were real – an over familiar interviewer, a suspected heart attack and a fire drill. The video culminated in the winning candidate – Guy Luchtig – being told he'd got the job in front of 41,000 football fans (potential customers) at a Champions League Final in Juventus Stadium, Turin. So far the YouTube video has been viewed over 5.6 million times, 91 per cent of Heineken employees have watched it and found it stimulating for their job, 'The Candidate' gained 422 million earned media impressions, it increased traffic to Heineken's HR site by 279 per cent and following the campaign, CVs submitted to the company increased by 317 per cent. Not only did the campaign showcase Heineken's culture and ethos brilliantly it positioned the company as an employer of choice – thus attracting more talent. And it probably didn't hurt sales either.

Today's HR Director (HRD) is also finding that their world has changed beyond all recognition. In the 1970s the HRD's role was largely focused on pay, rations and recruitment. They were tasked with finding and recruiting the best people, working out what those people should be paid and making sure they were trained properly. They also helped deal with disputes while keeping the lights on and the workforce happy. Again, not always easy but the role was relatively straightforward. Not now. The HR Director is generally expected to deliver a near impossible task on top of all their previous responsibilities. Perhaps the most challenging is the expectation that they will win the 'war on talent' even though doing so effectively is not always an HR role as evidenced by Heineken. They are expected to ensure employees are fully engaged, optimally motivated and can help the business develop their social licence to operate. As executives of each individual department or division become increasingly overwhelmed by the complexity of their own roles and escalating expectations, the line of responsibility for the 'people issues' has often been abdicated to HR. Consequently HR is often struggling to close the gap between their old role and the increasing demands of the new one. To add to their pressures they are often the division that gets the brunt of the blame when the business can't find, recruit or keep the right talent that will somehow, miraculously save the day.

So as the CEO looks around their top team they see a CFO under intense pressure, a Marketing Director with an extremely complex agenda and an HRD with a near impossible task. And they haven't even begun to wonder about the Chief Information Officer's (CIO) struggles, lack of quality resources, increased customer and employee IT demands and a series of obsolete systems that are no longer fit for purpose. They haven't started to wonder about how the Strategy Director will pull some innovative and disruptive rabbit out of the hat or convert the strategy advisory firm's

100 page deck of market analysis into something that will provide competitive differentiation. They have yet to even debate how the Operations Director can cut the cost base so radically that they can still deliver great service without compromising safety and still ensure profitability. Nor have they thought about how to find time for a conversation with the Commercial or Sales Director on how they can build the top line when the trading conditions are near impossible in many of the geographies where they operate. All in all straightforward is gone; today we live in a very different world from the one our 1970s counterparts lived in. The world of 'doing' ('IT' dimension) that we are completely consumed by in our daily lives is fundamentally more complex than it's ever been in history.

So how did business become so incredibly difficult?

The swing to shareholder value

In 1970 economist Milton Friedman wrote an article in the *New York Times* stating that the sole purpose of business was to make money for its shareholders. At the time Friedman was the leader of the Chicago School of Economics; he would later win a Nobel Prize in Economics and was described by *The Economist* as 'the most influential economist of the second half of the 20th century ... possibly of all of it' (2006). Friedman suggested any business executives who pursued a goal other than making money were, in his words, 'unwitting puppets of the intellectual forces that have been undermining the basis of a free society these past decades'. They were guilty of 'analytical looseness and lack of rigor'. They had even turned themselves into 'unelected government officials' who were illegally taxing employers and customers (Denning, 2013). The business community took note.

Several years later in 1976 this idea was given an 'action plan' when finance Professor Michael Jensen and Dean William Meckling of the Simon School of Business at the University of Rochester published a paper that would begin a seismic corporate shift toward shareholder value maximization.

Jensen and Meckling identified the 'principal–agent problem' and created 'agency theory' to explain and propose a solution to this problem. The authors believed that the shareholder (principal) was often disadvantaged by the firm's senior executives (agents) because there is an incentive to optimize their own self-interest and not necessarily the interests of the shareholders. Although logical the authors provided no evidence to support their argument and yet they suggested that a CEO for example may believe that his time and comfort is so important that he insists on first class business travel thus creating an 'agency cost' that diminishes the return to investors. The solution was to give senior executives a compelling reason to align with the shareholder and maximize shareholder value and what better way to do that than to make them shareholders themselves.

If the agents became principals then voilà – no principal–agent problem! What Jensen and Meckling stated had merit but the subsequent interpretation of their paper by business did not. It would go on to be the single most frequently cited article in business academia and proved to be a watershed moment in business history that completely changed the game. It provided senior executives and shareholders with a way to turn Freidman's earlier vision of what business should be all about into a commercial reality. In the 1970s stock-based compensation packages accounted for less than 1 per cent of CEO remuneration. From 1976 onwards executive compensation became increasingly stock-based. Most executives are still largely focused on driving the business forward in the interest of shareholder return. However, the pay packages of most are also now massively inflated by the addition of shares and share options. As a result 'shareholder return' has often become a major concern and focus for many executives. For the more money-motivated 'shareholder return' has become a thinly veiled euphemism for 'cash in my pocket'.

Of course shareholder return is a very laudable goal of business not least because it supports most of our pension funds but paying executives in shares has also resulted in a significant distortion of focus and executive behaviour. Some executives now put considerable effort into squeezing every last drop of profitability out of a company in the short term because it maximizes the return to shareholders, and significantly inflates their own personal bonuses. No wonder the business community embraced Jensen and Meckling's paper – it gave them a mechanism for significantly increasing their own pay under the legitimate guise of working on behalf of the shareholders. By 2009 stock-based remuneration accounted for up to 97 per cent of leadership remuneration (Martin, 2011).

Ironically the inference of the original paper was that executives were feathering their own nest with corporate resources that diminished shareholder return. And whilst this may have been true in the odd instance there was no widespread evidence for such behaviour. Since the inclusion of share options in senior executive pay arrangements there is a great deal of evidence of everything from obscene salaries to corporate corruption to the backdated options scandal and outright fraud. Rather than solve the hypothetical principal–agent problem it actually created the principal–agent problem and ramped it up considerably.

And what's worse it didn't even work. If you look at the shareholder returns on the S&P500 between the end of the Great Depression in 1933 to the end of 1976 when agency theory and shareholder value really took hold in the corporate world the total return to shareholders was 7.5 per cent compounded annually. From 1977 to 2010 total shareholder returns were just 6.5 per cent (Martin, 2011).

Disastrous shift from real market return to expected future return

Agency theory also created several new problems along the way. Executive share ownership destroyed long-term shareholder value by inadvertently shifting focus from real market returns to predictions of expected future income, thus resulting in shorter and shorter time horizons. In the real market people are employed to create and deliver products and services to customers. Senior leaders are able to exert a lot of control over this real market through their strategy planning and decision making.

The 'futures market' is not based on real products or real returns; it is conjecture – a best guess about what will happen. Nothing is actually created. All that happens is that shares in companies (and other financial instruments) are traded based on how well or otherwise the investor *expects* the company to perform. So how the company is perceived and how well they are expected to do in the future can make the difference between a leader receiving a basic payout or a bumper bonus that could set them up for life. This can have an extremely distorting effect on executive behaviour. And this is not a derogatory statement about senior business executives – it's an observation of human nature. The reality of modern business is that when presented with an opportunity to facilitate a life-changing bonus payout most human beings will take that opportunity. And this fact alone is why we desperately need vertical development in the 'I' and 'WE' dimensions.

The situation at the moment is that if the Executive Board delivers healthy profits one year they may experience a nice bonus but if they can deliver healthy profits and a relevant *story* that allows the market to expect market busting returns over the next three years then the share price will almost certainly rise because of those expectations. Such share price inflation can often be sufficient to increase the executives' L-TIP payout and trigger mass retirements before the growth is actually delivered. So if the company had a good year the incentive is to cash in as quickly as possible before the share price drops and their share portfolio becomes worth a lot less. It may motivate executives to become hyper-mobile, moving from job to job before the consequences of any tough measures they may have instituted or avoided to drive profits in the short term actually bite and cause commercial performance to drop. So by linking executive compensation to share price there is a direct and very tangible connection between compensation and expectations rather than compensation and results.

Executives are essentially incentivized to be overly optimistic about the future because their pay depends on it. They have to tell a story of unrelenting growth. They are incentivized to hide bad news and 'big up' any actual improvements. But nothing grows unchecked for ever so eventually even the great companies and great leaders have to face periods of low or negative growth.

If executives are being primarily incentivized by the futures market then quarterly reports can readily morph into fairytales where the real picture of genuine decline is 'managed' so as not to spook the investors and cause the share price to tank. 'Green shoots of recovery' are trumpeted to improve the share price and create 'headroom' to operate. How much each Executive Board gets embroiled in this game of managing market expectations varies widely.

Occasionally a courageous leader like Unilever's CEO, Paul Poleman will step forward and refuse to report quarterly. Poleman believed the obsession was distorting behaviour in the company and that he and his senior team were spending too much time producing documents to satisfy the City instead of developing the business to satisfy the customers. Unfortunately not enough leaders followed suit and so business is still engaged in the quarter by quarter battle.

Between Freidman's landmark article, considered by leadership commentator Steve Denning to be 'the world's dumbest idea', Jensen and Meckling's paper was effectively hijacked by business leaders as justification for doing the very thing the authors warned against and today the world of business is unrecognizable. Leaders have become increasingly consumed by short-term, quarterly results. Bonuses and incentive packages are widely used to drive short-term performance even though the long-term damage caused by offering short-term rewards is one of the most robustly proven findings in social science (Kohn, 1993). And even though the vast majority of shares bought and sold in the US and the UK are executed automatically via high frequency trading (HFT). In other words we are running businesses to keep the share market happy and placate investors even though most of the movement in the share price is created as a result of short-term fluctuations that no business can effectively manage (Steiner, 2014). Shares are not being bought and sold by a human being who is assessing the stability and value of your company in the way Benjamin Graham or Warren Buffett would buy and sell shares, a machine is buying or selling your shares based on micro movements in the market as a whole or a particular sector or stock. HFT causes 'flash-crashes' when the price of a stock or several stocks take a brief but violent nose dive only to recover quickly afterwards. And frankly not even the company narrative can manage that.

But of course the change in the way that leaders are paid and the impact of that on leadership behaviour and the way organizations are run is not the only change that has occurred in the last 30 years. There have been numerous other large- and small-scale changes that have made the job of a senior executive incredibly difficult in the 'IT' dimension or the world of 'doing'.

For example much has been written about globalization as an accelerant of change. The acronym PESTLE is often used to denote other types of large-scale change in addition to globalization. PESTLE stands for 'political, economic, social, technological, legal and environmental'. Of these, technological change seems to attract the most attention and is certainly the fastest paced with arguably the potential to have the greatest impact on business over the next decade. At the very least it will significantly add to the increased complexity business is facing and how a business operates.

Technological acceleration

In 1981 futurist, author and inventor R. Buckminster Fuller proposed something called 'the knowledge doubling curve'. Fuller noticed that the more knowledge we accumulated the faster we created more knowledge. For example until 1900 human knowledge doubled every one hundred years or so. By 1945 the complete knowledge of mankind doubled every 25 years. Today on average knowledge doubles every 13 months (Schilling, 2013). IBM predicted that knowledge would double every 11 hours (IBM, 2006).

Whatever the rate right now we are talking about a very rapid, very large expansion of knowledge that is changing the world. When Fuller first hypothesized about knowledge doubling it was a remarkable notion and yet at the time there was no internet, no worldwide web, no smart phones, no PCs or laptop computers, no satellite TV, no digital technology, no smart sensors, limited artificial intelligence and no social media. Considering the technological innovations of the last decade alone it's easy to see how this trend is so transformational and it's not slowing down.

Take data for example. Today companies are drowning in data. Everything creates or can yield data in a constant 'datafication' of our world. Data is no longer just held as words, numbers or images and archived. It is being digitized and datafied for ongoing collection and analysis.

Say you are reading this book on a Kindle, iPad or smart phone. It's been estimated that 130 million books (Nosowitz, 2010) have been published since the invention of the Gutenberg printing press in 1450 and about 15 per cent of that has so far been scanned by the Google Book Project (Mayer-Schönberger and Cukier, 2013). Amazon also gives us extensive access to old books in digital form. But the text you read on the screen is not just digitized, it's datafied. That means you can change font size, add notes, highlight text or search the book for a particular word or phrase. This datafication also means that data is gathered about what you read, when you read, how fast you read, how long you read for, whether you skip pages or highlight text and if you do, what text you highlight or skip. Although not currently used in this way that information could be extremely useful to authors and publishers. As an author I could see what pages readers skip past so I can revise a new edition accordingly. The publisher could use highlighted information to ascertain trends or areas of specific interest that could indicate topics on which to commission new books.

Everything is creating data. There are new types and forms of data that are quickening this knowledge doubling. For example sensors that collect data are now fitted to car and aircraft engines. Engine manufacturer Rolls-Royce has transformed itself from a loss-making British firm into the world's second-biggest maker of large jet engines by pursuing sensor technology (*The Economist*, 2009). Today Rolls-Royce monitors the performance of more than 3,700 jet engines they manufactured via thousands of built-in sensors. The data allows the airlines to operate more efficiently and makes the skies safer. For example, lightning strikes are a common occurrence in air travel and they used to cause delays because they would automatically trigger a full engine inspection once the plane landed. This would slow down turnaround time, irritate customers and affect 'On-Time Performance' (OTP) – a key performance indicator of air travel. The built-in sensors have stopped all that because if an engine so much as murmurs unexpectedly a torrent of data is automatically sent back to Rolls-Royce HQ where screens jump into life, graphs are created and technicians assess the real-time impact of the data. In fact very often the pilots will know if there is a problem to be fixed before they've even landed.

It's also now possible to monitor your own health using a variety of wearable devices and smart phone apps that collect information such as heart rate, activity level, sleep patterns and calorie intake. US computer scientist

Professor Larry Smarr states, 'In a world in which you can see what you are doing to yourself as you go along the hope is that people will take more personal responsibility for themselves in keeping themselves healthy. We are at day zero of a whole new world in medicine and what will come out the other end is a far healthier society that is focused on wellness rather than fixing sickness when it's way too late.' And he should know; he used his own data to self-diagnose Crohn's disease long before any physical symptoms emerged giving him the time and information to manage the condition appropriately. Access to knowledge we simply didn't have before gives us the ability to monitor our own health and heralds a new and exciting frontier of preventative medicine based on data (BBC Two, *Horizon*, 2013).

This knowledge doubling has also been coupled with increased techno-logical capability and storage to create the latest business trend – 'Big Data'. The premise behind Big Data is that everything we do, say, write, visit or buy is leaving a digital footprint or soon will be. And that data can then be analysed to extract mission critical business insights. We are entering a brave (or crazy) new world where hypothesis will give way to probability. If you buy certain products from certain stores those stores will make assumptions about you and target you for particular deals or offers. US retailer Target famously got into trouble over big data algorithms that resulted in a school age girl receiving money off vouchers for baby products. The girl's father, disgusted at this inappropriate advertising complained about the promotion only to discover a few days later that his daughter was actually pregnant. Target knew about it before her father based on her buying behaviour and issued the coupons based on probability (Duhigg, 2012).

There are now more objects and appliances collecting more types of data than people on the planet and they are increasingly being connected to-gether by the Internet of Things (IoT). The IoT is essentially a vast network connecting wired or wireless devices that exchange data and will usher in a new level of automation, monitoring and management that will change the way we live.

This explosion in technological capability is described by Moore's Law. In the 1970s Gordon Moore, one of the inventors of integrated circuits, noticed that it was possible to squeeze twice as many transistors onto an integrated circuit every 24 months. Moore's Law therefore explains this exponential growth rate in the advance in technology. And it is this expo-nential growth that has changed just about every business in every sector in every economy and it has made the Internet of Things possible. US inventor and futurist Ray Kurzweil points out that there will be 1,000 times more technological changes in the 21st century than there were in the 20th cen-tury (2013). According to Kurzweil even Moore's Law will be obsolete by

2019 because the rate of advancement will be even more rapid than the exponential growth it currently describes.

In his seminal essay 'The Law of Accelerating Returns' (2001), Kurzweil states, 'There's even exponential growth in the rate of exponential growth. Within a few decades, machine intelligence will surpass human intelligence, leading to The Singularity – technological change so rapid and profound it represents a rupture in the fabric of human history.' Kurzweil also predicts, based on very detailed calculations, that supercomputers would have the processing power of one human brain by 2010, and personal computers would have the processing power of one hundred human brains by around 2020. By 2030, it will take around 1,000 human brains to match $1,000 of computing power. And such is the speed of development brought on by knowledge doubling that by 2050, $1,000 of computing power will equal the processing power of all the human brains on Earth (Kurzweil, 2001).

Of course this rapid change has far reaching implications for how we operate and what we 'do' in the external observable world of 'IT'. It will impact every business on the planet. Nothing is static. Everything is fluid and dynamic. The speed, size and scope of change is literally creating, collapsing and re-creating the playing field faster than ever before. And that means that doing more and working harder and longer on your never ending 'to do' list is simply not enough. This strategy will simply not deliver the competitive advantage we need to survive and thrive in the 21st century.

The risk and the opportunity in the VUCA environment

If your business currently enjoys some sort of competitive advantage *beware*, it may be lost in a few short years, maybe even months.

Think of some of the 'Blue Chip' corporate giants that have either disappeared or been dealt a severe blow in recent times. Kodak invented the digital camera but chose not to market it because they felt it would cannibalize their film sales business – now the brand is dead. Microsoft – one of the most successful companies in history has been significantly hampered in the new technology world because they completely underestimated the impact of cloud computing. Dell is also another big name that is struggling with the shift away from hardware to cloud services and smart technology. More and more people are replacing their need for a computer with their smart phone or tablet. In 2004 Blackberry released the Blackberry 6200 series – effectively the first real smart phone and Blackberry cornered the business mobile phone market. It was a market leader in every sense of the word.

Today Blackberry are hanging on by a thread because they underestimated the appetite for apps and touchscreen technology amongst other things.

All the while other companies like Facebook, Amazon and Google have emerged from the chaos or companies like Apple have risen up from the ashes of their past mistakes to become the new brand Gods. Many of the new global powerhouses didn't even exist a decade ago.

So if your business is currently struggling to compete in this VUCA environment – take heart, you could leapfrog the competition within a year if you know how. No business is immune from either the opportunity or the threat this new corporate norm presents. The shift is forcing changes to strategy, business models and operational efficiency in even the biggest companies. Take Tesco for example, one of the UK's largest publicly owned companies. It became the dominant retailer in the UK with £1 for every £7 spent in British shops being spent in Tesco (Wallop, 2007). This was achieved partly because it won the 'space race' and hoovered up all the best retail sites in the UK enabling it to build more and bigger stores and drive sales. However, with the advent of internet shopping they have had to dramatically shift their strategy away from increasing their 'footprint' and longer store opening to a more digital 'click and collect' model. This shift in buying behaviour means that not only are Tesco competing with other mainstream retailers such as Morrisons and Sainsbury's but their market share is being eroded by retail discounters such as Aldi and Lidl whose business model is so different from their own that it makes it extremely difficult to defend against. Plus big players like Amazon and eBay who having largely cracked home delivery difficulties, are now experimenting with food delivery. In less than a decade a company that once thoroughly dominated the food sector in the UK is now vulnerable.

Companies that embrace change in a smart and effective way, like Rolls-Royce, are seeing their businesses transformed. In recognition of the implications of data collection and analysis Rolls-Royce now offer to monitor the engines they manufacture. Customers are now charged based on engine usage time and repairs. Effectively they offer an ongoing assessment and dynamic servicing value add where each engine is assessed individually, parts are replaced on a case by case basis not on a time based servicing schedule and this servicing now accounts for 70 per cent of the civil-aircraft engine division's annual revenue (Mayer-Schönberger and Cukier, 2013).

New products, services, sectors and industries will emerge such as the (almost) waterless washing machine. The technology, developed by a company called Xeros uses a cup of water, millions of tiny plastic beads and a couple of drops of special detergent which together remove stains and odours from garments. The company estimates that if all UK households converted to this new washing machine, they would save approximately seven million tonnes of water every week and use 50 per cent less energy (Zolfagharifard, 2014). The energy and water savings alone are incredibly exciting considering the cost and growing scarcity of these resources. That said, it's unlikely that the washing machine manufacturers and associated product manufacturers share that excitement. It heralds the end of their business – unless they too innovate and adapt. All business must adapt or die. Unfortunately few businesses are currently equipped to do so because they are so consumed by the delivery of short-term results.

Consequences of 1D emphasis on 'IT' dimension

The unrelenting burden to deliver short-term returns to shareholders; the pressure to sustain a share price and to maintain share-based salary packages; the knowledge doubling technology revolution with all the other PESTLE advances; the turbulence of a VUCA world; the increased complexity of every role around the Board table; globalization moving at a relentless pace; the short life expectancy of the Executive Board suggest that leaders may now indeed be 'in over their heads' (Kegan and Lahey, 2009). Leaders are at imminent risk of exhausted collapse or commercial failure.

In 1994 former Barclays chief executive John Varley left Barclays for one year because he was 'feeling quite worn out' and 'needed to do something different', and Jeff Kindler, of Pfizer, resigned as chief executive of the US pharmaceutical giant to 'recharge [his] batteries'. In 2003 Tim Martin, CEO and founder of JD Wetherspoons, took a sudden six-month sabbatical before returning to the pub chain in April 2004 as non-executive chairman, working three days a week (Treanor, 2011). In 2013 Sir Hector Sants announced he would be temporarily stepping down from his senior role in Barclays due to extreme exhaustion and stress. Before joining Barclays Sants was head of the Financial Services Authority (FSA) from 2007 to 2012 which can't have been much fun during the global financial crisis. While on three months' sick leave Sants tendered his resignation and did not return to Barclays (BBC News, 2013).

Such intense pressure is exacerbated by the fact that this escalating pressure and VUCA environment tends to attract the heroic figures who may often believe in their own invincibility. Indeed the Daedalus Trust (daedalustrust.org.uk) was founded to raise awareness and understanding of the changes in individuals, groups and whole organizations that can come with the accumulation and exercise of power. Such changes are often described by the Greek term 'hubris'. And as Mathew Hayward, associate professor of management at the University of Colorado reminds us, 'A good case could be made for the argument that hubris is at the root of the ills that have plagued businesses in recent years' (Hayward, 2007).

The 1.0 version of the corporate system we've constructed over the last 30 years has baked in a set of conditions that spawns and then promotes charismatic, powerful leaders who can rise to the challenges outlined above. In fact many of our most successful companies are run by such autocratic individuals often operating a 'hub and spoke' leadership model. They are not big advocates of a 'collective' approach; they under invest in team development and tend to make most if not all of the big decisions themselves.

The responsibility virus

But how long can such an individualistic approach to leadership really be sustained? One of the greatest risks in a fast paced world of autocratic leadership lies in what Roger Martin refers to as the 'responsibility virus' (2003). Shareholders, or at least the share market, expect Herculean results every quarter, year after year after year. In an effort to deliver, Boards continue to seek the heroic charismatic autocrat who can single-handedly deliver incredible performance and make everyone happy.

Imagine the scene – the Board is distressed the numbers are not adding up and the market is nervous. The incumbent CEO has not delivered on his grand promises. He's got to go. The fact that he wouldn't have been chosen in the first place had he not made those excessive promises is conveniently forgotten. So the Board seeks out a new autocratic hero to 'save the day'. He arrives, all guns blazing to whip the business into shape. It often starts with a profit warning of some sort to 'reset' expectations. Such a reset often involves details of how bad things have been left by the predecessor. Such declarations help to significantly reduce the share price and provide some time and 'headroom' for the turnaround to occur. It normally starts with a 'strategic review' of all critical decisions and plans plus a 'tour of the estate' including meeting the key executives. In an emergency such a direct and robust style can be comforting as everyone breathes a collective sigh of relief as the new person takes the helm. The hero may 'take charge', but the problem with 'I'm in charge' is that there is almost always an unspoken addendum of 'and you're not'. This usually prompts the other executives in the team to send the corresponding, although also silent message of, 'OK, fine you're in charge – knock yourself out!' This initial exchange creates the perfect breeding ground for the responsibility virus to flourish which often leads to eventual failure (Martin, 2003).

The new leader is obviously keen to succeed and needs to do it quickly to demonstrate to the City and the Board that it was a wise appointment. There is a lot of expectation on their shoulders. They are often authoritative and the hype that surrounds the appointment can be both reassuring *and* put the other executives on the back foot. The inference is 'wow this person knows what they're doing (we'd better defer to their judgement)'. The new leader will invariably draw up a 'battle plan' for the 'first 90 days' and muscular action begins to get the business back on track. With such urgent action and an atmosphere of change a culture of fear can develop as senior executives naturally start to wonder whether they will be surplus to requirements and escorted out of the building. Such a climate can inadvertently amplify the developing autocracy as people are inhibited from speaking up, concerned that any declarations, positive or negative, may count against them. Everyone gets nervous about who may be held accountable for earlier mistakes, few executives step forward to take ownership of the past or the future and the 'responsibility virus' spreads like wild fire.

The leader may for example look at sales – they are not as good as they should be. This is then discussed with the sales director. The sales director is a bit flat – he's lost a few accounts recently and he's got an important pitch coming up. They suggest that the pitch might go better if the leader is involved – a demonstration of how serious the company and the new leader takes the business. The leader, desperate to make a positive early impression, agrees and they work up the presentation together. Keen to ensure success the leader suggests they take the lead in the pitch otherwise it might look a bit odd. The sales director agrees and takes a more passive position – even though sales are their domain and responsibility. The sales director feels a little aggrieved but also relieved because they're off the hook and the leader's heroic style is sure to preserve the client.

The leader is surprised to witness the sales director on the back foot and not being sufficiently robust. He starts to wonder whether the noise around the sales director being 'in over their head' is correct. As a result the leader slips into 'over-responsibility' for the outcome rather than supporting or coaching the sales director to deliver the required result. The leader may initially reconcile their decision as a temporary measure to help the sales director just this once so they get their mojo back and everything will be fine. Not wanting to challenge the new leader explicitly the sales director may become much more compliant than they really want to be. They wouldn't have let the previous CEO lead a big pitch but maybe it would help this once. So they step back into 'under-responsibility'.

Only it's not 'just this once'. It becomes a regular situation. The leader steps into over-responsibility again and again, heroically driven to turn things around fast. And the more the leader steps in the more the sales director steps out because rather than boosting confidence it diminishes it. Plus before long it's not just sales, but operations, HR and marketing have also stepped out as the leader has stepped in.

Sometimes this move into over-responsibility can also be the deliberate action of a leader who actually wants to have complete control. If the other executives don't respond as quickly or decisively as the leader wants them to, the leader may step into over-responsibility again and again until he has wrestled the bulk of the responsibility from the executive team. Hesitation on the part of executives, outright disagreement (sometimes deliberately provoked by the leader) or an over-riding self-belief by the leader that 'it would be quicker, or better if I just did it myself' result in the leader ending up with the bulk of the responsibility. Usually however excessive responsibility resting with the leader is just the unintended by-product of high expectations and fear. The new leader didn't intend to get so involved in so many of the business areas, they certainly didn't expect to or want to but circumstances and the responsibility virus conspired to create that end result.

For the autocratic 'my way or the highway' leader advances in technology and constant connectivity have amplified the issue because it's easy for the leader to be 'kept in the loop' or they may simply expect to have things 'run past' them before any decisions are made.

In their drive to make an impact quickly the new leader may deliberately kill off capability especially if it threatens their ability to get things done quickly. More commonly, in their drive to control the narrative and deliver results, the 'heroic' charismatic leader inadvertently impairs the capability of the executive team. Although the leader's decisive action may have been the primary cause of the passivity of the executives the leader starts to think that their passivity was the cause of the previous poor performance. A vicious cycle develops with increased passivity and increased over-responsibility. More and more power accumulates around the new leader, morale can start to suffer and the pressure to make all the decisions and get them all correct mounts on the new leader.

For a while the leader may be able to cope with the upsurge in workload and responsibility. It doesn't help the business though because they are even more tangled in the weeds of short-term business activity in the 'IT' dimension of 'doing' and don't have a second to consider the bigger picture. It may even work for a little while and the leader may get those early runs on the Board. Of course the volume, pace and complexity of what needs to get done in a modern business is impossible for one person to manage – even for a heroic leader. The leader becomes a bottleneck, cracks appear or the results don't materialize fast enough. Human nature is such that we will always seek to take the credit when things go well and avoid blame when things go badly (Langer, 1975). And that is true for the leader and the rest of the C-suite.

As the leader approaches the point of failure, they will do a complete reversal into under-responsibility and buckaroo management.

'Buckeroo management'

Remember that game called 'Buckeroo' that kids played before Xbox? There was a plastic donkey and each player had to put an object on the donkey like a spade, bucket, rope or cowboy hat. Each player would add a new object until Buckeroo became overloaded and bucked everything off and the game would start again. When a business is infected with the responsibility virus the leader becomes the donkey. All the responsibility gets piled on to the leader until finally they can't function and buck it all off expecting other senior leaders to pick up the slack.

In an attempt to avoid exhausted collapse and impending failure or in a desperate attempt to get the senior executives to 'step up' the leader may 'go ballistic' at the executive team. As their own survival may now be on the line some leaders will literally yell at their colleagues or become extremely direct and threatening. They may berate their marketing director for needing too much input and tell their operations director to 'man-up'. The leader is angry because the team have not stepped forward to ease the burden. The leader often feels as though they were set up and that the rest of the team didn't pull their weight – almost urging the leader to fail. They don't appreciate that their approach from the outset made it impossible, unwise or just extremely difficult for the team to step forward.

This situation is a real challenge for the executive team as well. Not only do they experience the failure along with the leader but they also experience the reversal of the heroic leader. They may blame the leader because after all, the leader, 'was in charge' and therefore brought it on himself, but such abdication doesn't help that much. The reality however is that they were both complicit in the spread of the responsibility virus and it's a slippery slope to individual and collective failure.

Overwhelmed by the amount of responsibility the leader has either deliberately or inadvertently taken on they abruptly step back and demand that the other executives step up to bridge the gap. They of course can't bridge the gap quickly enough because the leader either hasn't allowed them to mature and develop as leaders in their own right or their ability and confidence has been eroded during the leader's over-responsibility.

This, of course, adds fuel to the fire for the leader who assumes his team are useless – thus providing someone to blame. His executive team are not useless, it's just they have created a dysfunctional 'all or nothing' system that doesn't work. Either the leader wrestles 80 per cent of the responsibility leaving the remaining executives with 20 per cent which doesn't work because the leader then gets overwhelmed and the executive team don't develop as leaders. So the leader gets upset at his team, bucks off most of the responsibility by dramatically stepping back to 20 per cent responsibility, expecting the team to pick up the extra 60 per cent, but that doesn't work either because the gap from 20 per cent to 80 per cent is too wide for them to bridge in such a short time.

Not only that but the pain of the experience often flips the maligned executives into over-responsibility as they decide to never again put themselves in a position where they rely on a leader who lets them down. So they step into over-responsibility with their own team or in their next position – effectively turning into the very heroic leader they are protecting themselves from! This flip flopping between too much responsibility and too little perpetuates the responsibility virus and keeps business in the endless cycle of buckaroo management and hiring and firing.

What's needed is balanced accountability where the whole executive matures as a team and collectively shares the weight of responsibility appropriately. Something that is only possible with the vertical development of the 'IT', 'I' and 'WE' dimensions and 4D Leadership.

Although most senior leaders are already proficient in the 'IT' dimension and therefore exhibit some verticality in the external objective world of 'doing' it's worth noting that being vertically developed in the right areas is still critical. Chapter 2 will therefore unpack the leadership behaviours that matter so we can all focus on the behaviour that is going to deliver the results.

Vertical development in the 'IT' dimension

02

Ultimately most executives are judged by what they 'do' in the external, observable dimension of 'IT'. Clearly we need to get things done but the overwhelming pressure of modern business, outlined in Chapter 1, makes high quality, consistent productivity almost impossible. There are only so many hours in the day and being brilliant at prioritization and ensuring our time is spent efficiently and effectively has become absolutely vital. So what behaviours should we focus on in order to make real progress? This chapter answers that question. If we want to succeed in the objective world we need to know what behaviours are going to have the biggest impact on results and how we can more effectively prioritize our 'to do' list. This will ensure that we focus on the right things for maximum benefit and the right people are doing the right things in the right way.

But before we get to the solutions it's important to appreciate what is causing performance problems in the 'IT' dimension and how many of our current 'solutions' are often making matters worse.

The performance curve

Initially it can be beneficial to increase the pressure in any system. After all, if there is no pressure or urgency to achieve then nothing much gets done or the output is poor. Unfortunately given the modern business environment there is often far too much pressure in the system and this excess is often the source of underperformance. Unfortunately most leaders don't appreciate the balance between pressure and performance. As a result the organizational response to poor performance is almost always – 'Flog it harder'. If performance isn't as high as required a team, individual or system is simply pushed even harder but this just exacerbates the problem.

The relationship between pressure and performance has been understood for over 100 years (Yerkes and Dodson, 1908). We all need *some* pressure or 'stress' in order to perform well in the doing dimension of 'IT'. Thus it's difficult, if not impossible to break the world 100 metre sprint record when you're jogging down to the shops for milk and no one is watching. A certain amount of pressure is necessary to deliver our best effort whether at work or in sport. This positive impact represents the healthy 'upslope' of the performance curve and it is often referred to as 'good stress'. If we keep turning up the heat we will eventually reach our 'peak performance'. But, if we continue to load pressure beyond that point we start to impair our performance until we eventually reach the point of crisis and performance plummets (see Figure 2.1).

When we have too much on our plate, or we put excessive pressure on others, performance can drop very quickly and very dramatically. A leader infected with the responsibility virus might think their performance is tracking upward along the lower dotted line in Figure 2.1 but it's not. They have crossed a threshold and entered the 'down slope'. The resulting dip in performance may not even be noticed in the early days because the gap between what they intend to do and what they are actually doing may initially be small. As a result most people don't even realize there is a problem until they are well down the down slope. Once they realize they are not

FIGURE 2.1 Pressure performance curve

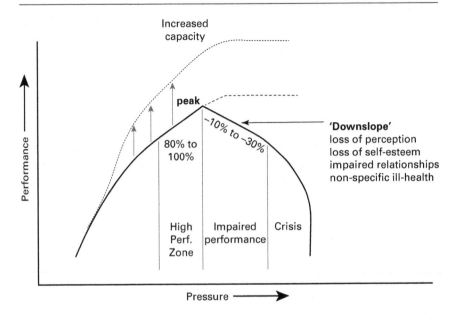

delivering against expectation this then increases the pressure, which accelerates the decline still further.

Too much pressure results in impaired performance and too little pressure results in sub-optimal performance. Most people in organizations live their life on the down slope because there is *too much* pressure in the system. And that can't be rectified by working longer hours or harder.

Learning to judge the degree of pressure your requests are putting on those around you is vital if you want to achieve peak performance. The simplest request could result in a 'Buckaroo'. So leaders need to understand the tell-tale signs that reveal whether they and their teams are operating at peak performance or on the down slope.

Downslope symptoms therefore include:

- loss of perception;
- irritability;
- impaired relationships;
- non-specific ill-health;
- delayed project completion for no apparent reason;
- increased passive resistance;
- increased number of errors;
- normally competent people dropping the ball or forgetting to follow through.

Noticing such signs requires a degree of sensitivity from the leader and the ability to solicit the correct data from the team about their energy levels (assuming they will tell the truth without fear of retribution or being branded as 'weak' or 'inadequate').

Performance management is hampered by the mis-measurement of talent

One of the inevitable consequences of underperformance is that leaders can start to believe that their people are just 'not up to the job'. So many leaders turn to their HR department asking if they can find some better performers. In fact there are so many organizations making such demands this is called the 'war on talent'. The recruitment and retention of better people has now become one of the most important areas of focus for any HR Director.

Unfortunately knowing whether you are hiring, or promoting, the right person who can perform to the right standard is a particularly tricky problem. Candidates can deliberately 'pad' their CVs with experience or qualifications they don't actually have. It's never clear if glowing references from previous employers are genuine because the individual is talented or the company simply wants to get rid of that person. Plus even if we do manage to recruit a highly skilled individual, whether they perform to the best of their ability will very often depend on how they fit in with the rest of the team and whether they thrive in the corporate culture.

Trying to build a team that can perform is significantly hampered by the widespread mis-measurement of talent. When it comes to talent assessment there are basically two different approaches – descriptive or developmental. Virtually all organizations and most of the assessment industry are still stuck on descriptive approaches even though they have failed to deliver on their promise.

The descriptive approach is either applied to observable behaviour or to some internal quality or aspect of personality. The focus on behaviour comes from the realization that the final common denominator in driving results is behaviour. So organizations often create a list of desired behaviours in which they want their leaders to be competent. Such behavioural 'competency frameworks' try to measure a defined set of behaviours in the belief that if these behaviours were present the results would improve. When this approach doesn't really deliver the expected benefits companies often switch to assessments that measure the internal qualities that are allegedly shared by successful leaders.

All such descriptive methodologies are based on the mistaken belief that our ability to lead and deliver results in competitive markets is down to some quirk of personality, personal style, specific strengths, behaviour, preference or a certain 'type' of person. Furthermore descriptive approaches assume that there are only a limited number of such qualities for all situations and that these qualities do not change over time.

Each personality assessment measures their own unique version of the 'big five' personality traits. Thus they focus on the key characteristics of openness, conscientiousness, extraversion, agreeableness, and neuroticism (often referred to with the acronym OCEAN), or some variant of these. The belief is that different personality characteristics may be important for different job roles. This descriptive approach assumes that human nature is fixed and that characterizing people as possessing a set of static qualities is helpful.

If the organization's preferred personality test fails to deliver, many businesses then turn to one of the many 'typology' instruments such as Myers-Briggs Type Indicator (MBTI), Belbin Team Roles or Enneagram to help find the talent that will transform performance. MBTI is based on

Carl Jung's original work in the 1920s looking at how people take in and organize information (he called this perceiving and judging). Still widely used particularly in career counselling, MBTI is popular because it's simple and reduces the complexity of human behaviour, decision making, motivation and management style into four basic types. There is quite a bit of data suggesting that different MBTI types tend to be more or less represented in certain professions. At best the MBTI helps people start to understand differences and at worst it distracts leaders and focuses them on narrow specifics rather than development and potential. Belbin team profiles seek to identify behavioural strengths and weaknesses of individuals within a team and were very popular in the 1990s but have largely lapsed into disuse. The Enneagram typology is the latest instrument being advocated, particularly in the USA (less so in Europe), which is ironic because the origins of the Enneagram go back hundreds of years. The Enneagram categorizes people based on nine basic personality types and their complex interrelationships. As a tool for self-understanding it may illuminate some novel and interesting dimensions but it doesn't necessarily guide development. There are literally hundreds of typologies to choose from but like all descriptive methodologies they can distract the organization from addressing the real performance and development needs.

Once an organization has realized that the predictive power of typology assessments is low, they may then turn to 'strength assessments' of which there are many such as the Clifton StrengthsFinder (Rath, 2007). The identification of 'strengths' seems to make a lot of sense. However, most of these instruments cherry pick their own muddled up collection of personality traits, behaviours and emotional intelligence skills and test against this arbitrary list. They generally use a self-report methodology. This is despite the fact that the research suggests that while people can often identify aspects of their inner personality their ability to correctly diagnose their own behavioural strengths or emotional intelligence has very little correlation to their actual observed behaviour. Many of these instruments create a 'definitive' report based on self-evaluation. In addition these instruments presuppose that there are a limited number of 'strengths' that are necessary to drive results and these strengths will consistently deliver results in very different types of businesses and markets in a VUCA world. All in all the output of these types of instruments is often a work of fiction that doesn't help the individual to perform or develop.

Those that have rejected personality profiling, typology and strength finders may then succumb to other variants that talk about 'styles', 'preferences' or 'competencies' as the way to approach talent assessment. These constructs are usually variations of the other approaches outlined above and make the same basic errors. Yet millions of people are using these descriptive tools in the hope that they will provide the magic bullet insight into talent recruitment and performance management.

The real issue is that people are much more complex than we give them credit for and there are so many ways that they can be brilliant that trying to 'describe' their brilliance with just a limited number of types, personalities, strengths, styles, preferences or competencies does not adequately take account of how people actually function. Also descriptive methodologies can't predict whether an individual has the potential to succeed if promoted. And they don't really tell us anything about how we need to develop.

There is no doubt that such 'descriptive' methodologies do generate a lot of really fascinating information about the person being profiled. People often become totally engrossed in their 'reports'. Such profiling can, in fairness, significantly raise awareness but they do little to guide development. But perhaps the most dangerous thing about descriptive approaches is they can lock individuals into what Carol Dweck called a 'Fixed Mindset' (2007). Following decades of research into achievement Dweck, a world-renowned Stanford psychologist, proved what many of us have suspected for some time – achievement and success is not down to talent and abilities but mindset. Dweck proposes that there are just two – fixed and growth. Those with a fixed mindset take the view that they are born at the 'finish line'. In other words they believe they are born with a specific set of skills, preferences and abilities dished out via the great genetic lottery. And because these traits are genetically determined they are fixed in stone (even though we now know that genes don't work this way, and are far from 'fixed'). The view is that if their mother was great at maths or their father was a brilliant musician then chances are they will be too and if not – tough! The growth mindset on the other hand believes that whatever abilities people are born with is just the starting point. The growth view is that human nature is not fixed and people can learn, adapt and develop as much as they want.

Dweck states, 'For twenty years, my research has shown that the view you adopt for yourself profoundly affects the way you lead your life.' Hence the danger with descriptive personality profiling tools – they help to cement an individual into a particular belief about who they are and what they are capable of. 'Oh well I'm just introverted – it's just the way I am', or 'There is nothing I can do about that I'm just not good with numbers.' Descriptive profiling tools lock people into a fixed mindset rather than fostering a growth mindset which allows them to see that wherever they are right now is actually just a developmental level that can be vertically developed.

All the evidence suggests that brilliant leadership cannot be reduced to a set of strengths, preferences or types. Leaders come in all shapes and sizes and successful leadership is much more about the individual's developmental level than some divine spark or quirk of personality.

There is a dawning realization in the academic and assessment community that the whole approach to talent assessment needs to change. A developmental methodology can generate significantly better results not least because it can predict performance – something the most descriptive approaches can't. The cutting edge thinking about talent assessment has completely shifted away from description to identifying which specific lines of development are most relevant in each business and how to effectively differentiate those lines and measure them effectively.

Artificially inventing a set of behaviours a company believes are important and trying to get the leaders to adhere to them, doesn't work. But the developmental approach allows us to avoid the biggest traps most companies fall into when seeking to address leadership behaviour.

Common pitfalls in assessing leadership behaviour

The mistakes organizations make when looking at leadership behaviour are so widespread that we felt it worthwhile to clarify them so they can be avoided.

Using career advancement as a surrogate for organizational performance

One common mistake organizations make in designing a 'behavioural competency framework' is to identify those leaders who have advanced effectively in their careers at the firm and then ask them to describe their 'wish list' for desirable leadership behaviours. This may result in a list of behaviours that are associated with rapid career advancement but are not necessarily what deliver organizational performance. The corollary is that the frameworks simply describe behaviours used by leaders regardless of the relationship between these behaviours and performance. As a result the frameworks can be quite overwhelming, causing enormous confusion and again they do not clarify to what degree the behaviours need to be present.

Looking too narrowly within

Organizational blindspots can occur when frameworks are developed internally by an organization without enough external reference. Invariably this means important behavioural groups are missing, simply because they don't form part of the way leaders currently operate in that organization. A common example is cross-boundary team collaboration which is seldom found in organizations where individuals and functions tend to work in silos. So this behaviour is frequently missing from their frameworks. Even if the organization is reasonably effective despite their lack of cross-boundary collaboration they are oblivious to just how much better they could operate if they included and improved that behaviour.

Failing to understand the relationship between environment and behaviour

As a result of some of these problems, a different approach has become popular more recently. This one recognizes that the VUCA environment makes quite different demands on leaders. Typically, a group will attempt to predict what the organization will be like in the future and then define what leadership behaviours will be needed in that future setting. Unfortunately, in an inherently uncertain environment, it is hard to know what is going to happen even one year ahead, let alone over a 5–10 year time frame. So this approach is doomed and tends to produce a list of fictional competencies that have no empirical link to performance. Linked to this is the practice of periodically scrapping outdated models only to replace them with another similarly flawed model that will, in time, suffer the same fate.

Trying to make the framework do too much

Sometimes through poor design or sometimes as a deliberate response to the criticism that competencies are too one-dimensional we often see 'meta-competencies' that don't just include behaviours but a whole bunch of other characteristics such as knowledge, experience, preference, values, emotional maturity, technical skill etc. Because these sets of characteristics need to be measured quite differently, muddling them together creates serious problems in practical application. Linked to this, and also due to poor design, we see dimensions that do not consist of discrete behaviours that belong together. Instead they are fuzzy, overlapping and contain more than one independent dimension, which makes accurate measurement very difficult.

Lack of understanding of 'verticality' in behavioural assessment

Each behaviour should be defined as showing up to different degrees, present to different levels of sophistication and follow a clear conceptual model. The levels should represent a qualitatively more powerful way of using the competency, not just 'doing' more of the same. If this is not done explicitly, the model is of limited use for personal development.

So many well-intentioned organizational attempts to quantify leadership behaviour end up mired in guesswork and faulty methodology. As a result their 'competency framework' invariably fails to deliver the desired transformation. The good news is that if the organization doesn't have the time, inclination or ability to conduct their own research and get their methodology right they don't need to guess anymore. There is a rich vein of literature on leadership behaviour and specifically which behaviours have been shown to change the outcome in dynamic variable environments. Furthermore, the levels of development of the key behaviours that have been shown to drive transformation in the VUCA world have also been identified. This last point is absolutely crucial because it's not enough to know what the key behaviours are – we need to be able to measure our level of ability in that behaviour so we can improve it if necessary.

Vertical development of the behaviour line of development

Businesses' over reliance on leadership competency frameworks has been questioned for years and such an approach has been described as deeply flawed (Cockerill, Schroder and Hunt, 1993). Nevertheless, in a quest to find and develop better leaders many organizations have invested a great deal of time and money in leadership competency models or behavioural frameworks. In fact, many businesses have developed their own behavioural framework. Building their own competency framework certainly makes logical sense given the impact what we do in the 'IT' dimension has on results. But despite all this effort competency frameworks have not really helped to improve performance. We will explain why this is later in this chapter but the even better news is that most organizations have yet to tap into the potential of the cutting-edge thinking in this area by Professor Harry Schroder, originally from Princeton and the University of South Florida, and Dr Tony Cockerill, originally from the London Business School.

The 11 performance-driving behaviours

What makes Schroder and Cockerill's model so powerful is that they started by asking the right question – 'What behaviours differentiate those leaders who produce superior organizational performance in a complex, dynamic and challenging environment?'

Not only is that question as relevant today as it was the day it was asked, thereby future-proofing the results but it encapsulates observable phenomena of behaviours while also differentiating leaders who create high performance from those who create average or low performance and it is also environmentally specific. Needless to say the resulting research into the answers to that question took many years and required considerable resources that most of the other approaches simply did not commit to. And what that research found was that when they studied people from initial idea through to successful implementation there were just 11 leadership behaviours that determine organizational success (Schroder, 1989; Cockerill, 1989a; Cockerill 1989b).

So, far from there being an endless list of performance driving behaviours that organizations need to discover that determine results in their particular business the research reveals that there is a very limited list of behaviours that really count. And these behaviours can be organized into four key behavioural clusters (see Figure 2.2).

First behavioural cluster: Imagine

The 'Imagine' cluster describes all the behaviours we need to do in order to gather together all the information we will need to build and progress an idea or design a solution successfully. There are three behaviours that are critical in the 'Imagine' phase:

- Seeking Information – how well do we seek out the information we need to move the task, idea or design forward?

- Forming Concepts – how well are we able to marshal the ideas and information gathered into a workable commercial concept?

- Conceptual Flexing – how well are we able to develop multiple ideas simultaneously and not become overly stuck on one?

FIGURE 2.2   The four performance-enhancing behavioural clusters

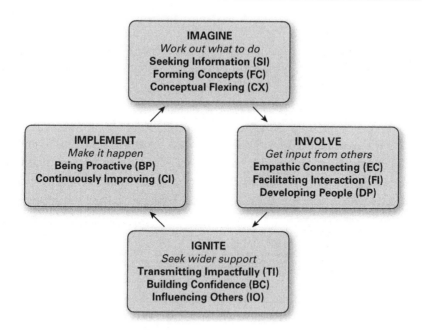

Second behavioural cluster: Involve

Once we have completed the 'Imagine' phase and developed some workable concepts we must 'Involve' others and engage them in the process or task. There are three behaviours that are critical in the 'Involve' phase:

- Empathetic Connecting – how well do we listen to other people's perspectives and play back their understanding of what was meant to create connection and engagement?

- Facilitating Interaction – how well do we support and facilitate genuine interaction and build a coherent shared team output?

- Developing People – how able are we to support and play a part in the development of others to ensure success?

Third behavioural cluster: Ignite

Once the concept has been developed and people are engaged and able to deliver it we need to be inspired to get into action mode. There are three behaviours that are critical in the 'Ignite' phase:

- Transmitting Impactfully – how clearly and compellingly do we transmit our plan to others involved in the idea or task?

- Building Confidence – how well do we inspire and build confidence in the idea or task, ourselves and others?

- Influencing Others – how well do we influence and build partnerships with the people necessary for success?

Fourth behavioural cluster: Implement

Once everyone is on board with the idea or task, clear about what is required and confident they can deliver, the final stage is driving implementation. There are just two behaviours that are critical in the 'Implement' phase:

- Being Proactive – how proactive are we in making things happen and removing barriers to action?

- Continuously Improving – how focused are we on measuring results or taking action to continually improve business performance?

The model, often known as the High Performance Managerial Competencies framework (HPMC), is the most widely used basis for leadership behavioural assessment globally. And it's also worth pointing out that Schroder and Cockerill's original research was validated in simulated and real world VUCA environments. Highly trained observers were used to identify behaviours and a broad set of organizational performance measures to validate these behaviours. In addition, the model drew on the very best available research such as Princeton Strategy Research, Professor Richard Boyatzis' Study for the American Management Association (1982), Florida Council on Education Management (FCEM) Competency Research (Croghan and Lake, 1984), the Transformational Leadership Study (Bass, 1999), as well as the Harvard, Michigan (Katz, MacCoby and Morse, 1950) and Ohio State Leadership Studies (Stogdill and Coons, 1957). It is therefore easy to see why so many shortcuts are taken in most other approaches – the time and resource required to do this kind of research are considerable and yet the shortcuts always result in the organizational framework problems highlighted above.

The main value of this research is that it allows us to keep our focus on just these 11 behaviours because these are the 'doing' activities that really make a commercial difference and have the capacity to transform results in the 'IT' dimension. That said, simply concentrating on the surface phenomena of these behaviours will not necessarily lead to 'inner' development. What we see by way of behaviour in the exterior dimension of 'doing' is also the product of an individual's development across several other inner lines of development – especially emotion and ego. Plus these behaviours are learnt not innate. They emerge given certain environmental demands and proper coaching and development which means massively improved performance is accessible and possible for most leaders not just the chosen few.

Level of competency within the 11 behaviours

Having identified these behaviours the only difference between success and failure was the levels of development or sophistication each leader used across each of the 11 behaviours. Six levels of development were identified for each behaviour (Table 2.1).

TABLE 2.1 Level of development for each behaviour

Level	Description
6. Strategic Strength (SS)	Leader bakes the behaviour into systems or culture to create a legacy so that the organization does not need to rely on them for impact.
5. Strength (S)	Leader uses the behaviour with an impact on the wider team or business unit and does this consistently across a range of scenarios.
4. Developing Strength (DS)	Leader consistently adds value to the specific task and occasionally has a wider team or business unit impact.
3. Adding Value (AV)	Leader adds value to a specific task and does this frequently across a range of scenarios.
2. Undeveloped (UD)	Leader understands the behaviour, but has not yet developed the ability to apply it to any consistent degree, so it does not add value.
1. Limitation	Leader negatively uses the behaviour to block or impair their own or others' performance creating a damaging impact.

The more successful and influential a leader is the more behaviours they exhibit as a 'Strength' or 'Strategic Strength'. Therefore when a leader knows their level of development across all of these 11 critical behaviours as well as how developed these behaviours are for each member of their senior team then these insights can massively improve overall performance. It is however worth pointing out that these levels of sophistication within each of the 11 behaviours don't represent incremental improvement – they represent qualitatively different behaviours that profoundly impact performance positively or negatively. And the model works at individual, team and organization level, largely due to the six levels. Consequently this takes it way beyond a simple functional competency model into a blueprint for developing high performing organizations.

By profiling the senior team using Complete Coherence's Leadership Behaviour Profile (LBP) leaders can gain a highly accurate understanding of individual and team behavioural capability. Understanding, with precision, what behaviour and what level of behavioural capability each leader operates at can help to direct task and responsibility allocation for maximum results. It also provides a very specific leadership developmental road map so that individuals and teams can receive individually tailored developmental coaching to escalate capability which will in turn further improve efficiency and productivity.

The data required to build an individual or team LBP can be collected in several ways. The most widely used methodology is a 360-degree feedback online questionnaire which collects views about an individual's behaviours from themselves, their boss, some peers and their direct reports. This builds a composite picture of a leader's behavioural strengths and development areas from the different perspectives of the various 'reporters'. However, its major drawback is the accuracy of the data as it relies on subjective opinions from people who are unfamiliar with the behaviours and their developmental levels.

A more objective assessment can be made by a trained consultant conducting a structured interview with a leader about their behavioural choices in different scenarios. This builds a more accurate profile, but relies on the leader interviewing well and the assessor being sufficiently well trained to capture a good sample of behaviour. The most reliable assessment of a leader's behaviours can be made by a trained practitioner observing them in a business simulation or shadowing them in the workplace. The accuracy of each data collection method is illustrated in Figure 2.3 (Cockerill, Hunt and Schroder, 1995; Chorvat, 1994; Sackett and Dreher, 1982).

FIGURE 2.3 Accuracy of behaviour data from various sources

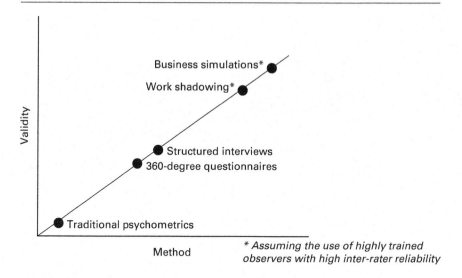

* Assuming the use of highly trained observers with high inter-rater reliability

If a behaviour is identified as a 'Limitation' then the leader inhibits the behaviour in a way that is eroding business performance. If a behaviour is identified as 'Undeveloped' the leader either doesn't currently use the behaviour or uses it very rarely. Most leaders will have one or two 'Undeveloped' behaviours. If a behaviour is identified as 'Adding Value' then the leader is already using that behaviour at a basic level to add value to the business. Most leaders have three or four behaviours that are 'Adding Value'. If a behaviour is identified as a 'Developing Strength' then that leader is using the behaviour consistently to add value but is not yet using it consistently to create a significant impact in the business. If a behaviour is identified as a 'Strength' then the leader is consistently using that behaviour and making a considerable impact on the long-term outcome of the business through that behaviour. Most leaders have four or five 'Strengths' or 'Developing Strengths'. Finally a behaviour is identified as a 'Strategic Strength' if the leader is consistently using the behaviour with high impact *and* is baking that behavioural strength into the business by implementing a systems or cultural change.

It is possible, by comparing a leader's behavioural profile to a global benchmark, based on data from 55,000 executives, to separate Directors from CEOs and Global CEOs by the number of 'Strategic Strengths' that a leader exhibits in their business (see Figure 2.4).

The shading in Figure 2.4 corresponds to the shading in Table 2.1. The individual leader, CEO Joe Bloggs, has been profiled and has one 'Strategic

FIGURE 2.4   The leadership behaviour global benchmark

Joe Bloggs Leader	Individual Contributor	Team Leader	Manager of managers	Director	Chief Executive	Global Chief Executive

Strength', one 'Strength', a 'Developing Strength' and four behaviours at the 'Adding Value' level. He also has four behaviours that are 'Under Developed'. He is compared to the CEO profile. This reveals that he has significantly fewer behavioural 'Strengths' than would be expected for someone at his level. This doesn't mean he can't perform at the CEO level but it does mean he will probably have significant developmental needs if he is to succeed.

So looking at Figure 2.4 this means that according to the global benchmark an effective Chief Executive will demonstrate:

- Two of the 11 behaviours as 'Limitation' or 'Undeveloped' skills;
- Two of the 11 behaviours as 'Adding Value';
- Three of the 11 behaviours as 'Developing Strength';
- One of the 11 behaviours as 'Strength';
- Three of the 11 behaviours as 'Strategic Strength'.

By identifying the current level of development of these 11 key behaviours, this of course means that a leader and their executive team are able to hone in, individually and collectively, on specific areas for development. Instead of wasting valuable time and money on blanket 'leadership training' or 'professional development' programmes these insights effectively provide a very tight brief for leadership coaching with the aim of elevating behaviours that are currently 'Adding Value' or 'Developing Strengths' to consistent

'Strengths' and where appropriate maturing 'Strengths' into 'Strategic Strengths'.

When fully present at the 'Strength' or 'Strategic Strength' level these behaviours will provide a competitive advantage because they enable leaders, teams and organizations to perform at outstanding levels in a VUCA world (see Table 2.2). Knowing where you and your people are in terms of these 11 performance driving behaviours can transform results and direct learning and development within the entire business resulting in massive improvements in individual and team performance with more targeted effort.

TABLE 2.2   Creating competitive advantage from behavioural strengths (Level 6)

Behaviour	Competitive Advantages
SEEKING INFORMATION (SI6)	• Ahead of the curve • Rarely caught out unexpectedly
FORMING CONCEPTS (FC6)	• Systemic thinking gets to the root of organizational problems • Powerful, creative strategies
CONCEPTUAL FLEXING (CX6)	• Able to respond fast to environmental change • Ready for any contingency
EMPATHIC CONNECTING (EC6)	• High employee engagement where people feel understood and valued • Competitive advantage through diversity and inclusion
FACILITATING INTERACTION (FI6)	• Valuable innovation through cross functional learning and collaboration • Teams able to form and perform to very high levels quickly
DEVELOPING PEOPLE (DP6)	• Able to attract and retain high potential people • Rich talent pool positions the organizations for sustainable growth
TRANSMITTING IMPACTFULLY (TI6)	• Strong identity and brand • Organizational alignment around the core messages
BUILDING CONFIDENCE (BC6)	• High employee engagement through the creation of a motivational and energized workplace • Market confidence
INFLUENCING OTHERS (IO6)	• Able to benefit from mutually rewarding partnerships • Strong stakeholder support
BEING PROACTIVE (BP6)	• Agile organizations able to effectively translate ideas into action • Empowered staff focused externally on customer delivery
CONTINUOUSLY IMPROVING (CI6)	• Reputation for quality and reliability • Able to learn from mistakes

TABLE 2.3   Negative consequences of behavioural limitations (Level 1)

Behaviour	Negative Consequences
SEEKING INFORMATION (SI1)	● Denial of reality ● Vulnerable strategies
FORMING CONCEPTS (FC1)	● Firefighting ● Symptom thinking
CONCEPTUAL FLEXING (CXI)	● Brittle and rigid culture ● Resistant to change
EMPATHIC CONNECTING (EC1)	● Alienated workforce ● Deep mistrust
FACILITATING INTERACTION (FI1)	● Silo syndrome ● Internal competition and conflict
DEVELOPING PEOPLE (DPI)	● Risk averse staff ● Hire and fire/revolving doors
TRANSMITTING IMPACTFULLY (TI1)	● Confusion about strategy ● Mixed messages sent externally
BUILDING CONFIDENCE (BC1)	● Low morale ● Victim mentality
INFLUENCING OTHERS (I01)	● Failed initiatives ● Win-lose mindset
BEING PROACTIVE (BP1)	● Bureaucracy ● Stuck in the past
CONTINUOUSLY IMPROVING (CI1)	● Multiple unconnected initiatives ● Reinventing the wheel

Conversely, where significant degrees of level 1 behaviour are being used by senior leaders, we see devastating consequences (see Table 2.3).

This developmental approach to leadership behaviour is not about turning weaknesses into strengths, it's about highlighting the behaviours where we are already 'Adding Value' or operating at the 'Strength' level and taking active steps to develop those behaviours further so more of them become 'Strategic Strengths'. Operating at the 'Strategic Strength' level means that we bake the very best of our leadership into the business, thereby creating a leadership legacy.

Understanding the 11 behaviours also enables us to identify our weaker behaviours or any behaviour that is being exhibited in an unhelpful way. For example if we identify a 'Limitation', that behaviour is almost certainly holding us back in our career. Whilst it is difficult to turn a behavioural weakness into a behavioural strength we can all elevate our limitations just enough so that they stop being a hindrance to our personal and collective performance.

Developing performance-driving behaviours and behavioural constructs

Leaders are not 'born' and they do not generally enter the workplace with these behaviours already present. Often they take time and exposure to a VUCA environment to cultivate. There may be characteristics that pre-dispose some of us towards the discipline of leadership but this is not a substitute for hard work on our own development. It is possible to fast track some of the development with good feedback, coaching and practice.

Some of the rarer behaviours in the 'Imagine' and 'Involve' areas will not be mastered without addressing some more fundamental development areas 'beneath the water-line'. A holistic approach to adult development is a necessary precursor to fully cultivate these behaviours and the even more complex performance-driving behaviours.

Although all of these 11 behaviours can be developed, we've never met a leader who has 'Strengths' or 'Strategic Strengths' in all 11 behaviours. At team or organizational level, all the behaviours need to be present and any gaps will have predictable performance implications in certain situations. So by profiling leaders within a unit, function or organization we can start to see what kind of Organizational Development (OD) challenge that business faces. At the individual level the best strategy for the development of leadership behaviours is:

- develop a core of behavioural strengths and then really excel at them;

- learn what behaviours are particularly valuable in your specific context and make sure that if these are not current 'Strengths' then you either focus on developing those yourself or work with others who already have those 'Strengths';

- be fully aware of any behavioural limitations and actively work to elevate that behaviour to 'Undeveloped' so as to eliminate their negative impact.

Each of the 11 performance driving behaviours are independent constructs and can appear in combination with any other behaviour. In fact any behaviour at any level can be combined to create more complex behavioural constructs (see Table 2.4). When we understand how the 11 behaviours can show up at six different levels and which ones are rarer and which ones are more toxic then there is immense potential for building our understanding of exactly what people do to create high performing or underperforming organizations. Below are some examples of how different behaviours can combine to form complex behavioural constructs. Refer back to Figure 2.2 for acronyms and Table 2.2 for level of competency.

Increasing effectiveness in the exterior world of 'IT'

For many leaders the 'IT' dimension is their most familiar habitat and many consider their commercial success as an entirely 'IT' phenomena. When we talk about business and business reporting we will largely look at the EBITDA (Earnings Before Interest, Tax, Depreciation and Amortization) or some measure of profitability to determine whether the company is doing well. In Jim Collins' influential book *Good to Great* (2001) he identified just 11 'Great' companies, in the 1,435 he studied, and his definition of 'Greatness' was outperforming the market by 3–17 times over 15 years. A company's social contribution in the 'WE' dimension or its ability to develop enlightened leaders is deemed largely irrelevant. Such a singular definition of 'Greatness' has been questioned since two of the 11 companies identified as 'Great' by Collins have since disappeared, one other has been acquired, one has halved in size, five others have become pretty mediocre performers and only two could still be considered successful. Nevertheless businesses' one-dimensional obsession with the world of 'IT' means most leaders and companies continue to invest most of their time and money into developing their prowess in the objective world of 'doing'. As a result most demonstrate significant verticality in this dimension.

This 'doing' dimension has the most tools to improve outcome and receives the most focus. There are literally thousands of books that cover strategies and manoeuvres to help improve performance in this dimension including a plethora of processes such as business process re-engineering, organizational design, Six Sigma and Lean methodologies. We don't intend to add to that particular literature. Despite this obsessive focus there is still even more

TABLE 2.4 Combination behaviours and complex behavioural constructs

Positive Behavioural Constructs		Negative Behavioural Constructs	
BP5 + DP4	EMPOWERMENT	BP4 + CX1	DRIVING OFF A CLIFF
BC4 + DP4	NURTURING TALENT	SI4 + FC4 + BP2	ANALYSIS PARALYSIS
EC5 + FI4	BUILDING TRUST IN A TEAM	EC1 + BC4	PRESSURE COOKER
FI5 + IN5	COLLABORATION	BC1 + PO2	WE'RE ALL DOOMED
IN5 + TI4	STAKEHOLDER MANAGEMENT	EC2 + TI3 + BC3 + PO2	STAMPEDE
CX5 + FC5 + FI5	INNOVATION CULTURE	PO4+ DP1	BLAME CULTURE
CI5 + DP5	LEARNING ORGANIZATION	SI2 + CF2 + PO4	SHOOTING FROM THE HIP

value to be mined in the 'IT' dimension, maybe not so much with the above overused methodologies but with new entrant approaches and extremely potent albeit lesser known techniques such as:

- Active pressure and polarity management;
- Holacratic governance;
- Network analysis.

Active pressure and polarity management

Turning up the heat, flogging yourself and your people harder does not yield results. We all know this from first-hand experience and yet when the chips are down that's exactly what we do. Usually it's because we simply don't know what else to do.

Leaders can however help improve performance significantly simply by turning down the heat, taking their foot *off* the accelerator so as to consciously reduce the amount of pressure in the system. This can feel counter-intuitive but it's absolutely necessary if the leader or their executive team is already on the down slope of the performance curve.

Two of the most effective manoeuvres to reduce pressure are clarification and simplification. A leader who invests time in making everything absolutely clear can enhance team performance dramatically. The ability to articulate your corporate strategy, ambition, purpose and vision in a way that makes sense to everyone in the business is a vital piece of work that can be truly transformative.

This may seem obvious but we are constantly amazed at how many people in senior teams are unclear about these guiding concepts. While everyone in business 'knows' what these concepts are and uses the words frequently when pressed it quickly becomes obvious that everyone in those discussions actually has a different interpretation of both the concept and how the concept relates to their business. It is impossible to have an educated and productive conversation about anything unless everyone involved in that discussion is clear that they are actually talking about the same thing.

Likewise the leader who perpetually looks to simplify the complexity of the task will reduce the pressure in the system and enhance the team's performance often without any other changes in workload. Relentlessly reviewing and driving for increased clarity is a great way to actively manage the pressure in business. One of the most critical areas that we need to drive greater clarity in is around the definition of the problems we are addressing, specifically since some of the issues are not even problems at all, they are polarities.

Polarity management

As leaders we often believe that our role is to generate answers and while clarification and simplification are critical ways to reduce pressure sometimes we can over simplify issues. For example, it is not unusual to hear executives say things like 'just focus on sales', 'cut costs', 'remove defects from the production process', 'improve customer service'. But many of the challenges we face in business are not amenable to such simple 'trade-offs' between one option and another. The various possible answers are often interrelated and dependent on each other in the same way the dimensions of 'I', 'WE' and 'IT' are interrelated and interdependent. It is, for example, pretty hard to cut costs and increase customer service at the same time.

The challenges we face and the options we consider as solutions are often not distinct and separate entities that fall neatly into set parameters or boxes. The issues are often not problems that can be solved at all. Rather they are polarities that need to be managed (Johnson, 1996). This may sound like semantics but it is a profound distinction and when properly appreciated it can make a massive difference to any leader or team's ability to get things done. Many teams waste an extraordinary amount of time debating and trying to 'solve' the 'problem' when it's not even a problem – it's a polarity. And polarities need to be managed not solved. Understanding this simple truth can free up a massive amount of leadership time and energy. Examples of polarities are the interplay between:

- Individual autonomy and team cohesion;
- Centralized co-ordination and localized ownership;
- Low price and value add;
- Customer care and operational efficiency;
- Internal competition and cross-functional collaboration;
- Adherence to process and commercial adaptability;
- Autocratic decision making and participatory management (Johnson, 1996).

In order to bring the idea of polarities to life let's explore the perennial tension between individual and team performance. Most organizations consider the individual to be the primary driver of performance rather than the team. As a consequence individual leaders 'own the sales targets', individuals have clear accountabilities and individuals largely report on progress. Whilst this may make managing results easier it fails to unlock the potential of the collective – hence the urgent need for vertical development in the 'WE' dimensions so we can harness that collective power.

For example an executive may complain that there isn't enough team work in his division. Individuals are working in their silos, there is no collaboration, trust or consultation, mistakes are being made and morale is poor. So he puts everyone through a team building process. Even if the programme worked, which is rare, and the individuals started behaving more collectively the new team focus creates a new set of challenges – work rate and the speed of decision making may slow because all the decisions are made collectively and individual innovation can all but disappear.

The reality is that team performance is dependent on both individual contribution and collective effort. Individual output is enhanced by the support of the team and collective performance is enhanced by the brilliance of the individual. Each of these 'poles' is dependent on each other. There are also positive (and negative) dimensions to focusing on both the individual and team effort. Getting the best of both requires us to understand how these poles affect each other. In the absence of such an understanding we simply get stuck into a constant flip flopping between the upside and downside symptoms of each polarity in an endless dance called the 'polarity two-step' (see Figure 2.5).

By seeing team and individual performance as two separate problems when we 'solve' individual performance we can inadvertently impair team performance and vice versa. Thus if we decide to improve overall organizational performance by investing in personal leadership development we may end up emboldening the individuals at the expense of the team's capability. Excessive focus on individual performance to drive greater individual

FIGURE 2.5   The polarity two-step

positives
of individual focus

positives
of team focus

Individual

Team

negatives
of individual focus

negatives
of team focus

initiative, creativity, fewer and shorter meetings may simultaneously create the downside of individual performance – isolation, no shared goals or synergy. Conversely if corrective action is taken to improve team work then the group may work as a cohesive unit, engage in mutual appreciation and increase energy but better team work is also often accompanied by too much conformity, no innovation and long, arduous meetings. So investing in one pole at the expense of the other can create an endless loop – hence the infinity symbol depicting the polarity two-step.

What's actually required is the right balance between investing in individual and team performance so we get the best of both worlds without activating the worst of either. If we get the balance wrong we get the opposite – the worst traits of both individual and team performance and none of the benefits!

This kind of polarity two-step is very common in business – whether it's the polarity between central control and local autonomy; quality and cost or the dance between team and individual. When we understand that many business problems are not problems at all but polarities that need to be managed we can start to make real progress. When we appreciate both the upside and downside of any argument we can be alert to the warning signs so we can rebalance before dropping into the downside of either polarity. And we can still maintain a focus on simplification when needed without entering into the polarity two-step inadvertently.

Holacratic or effective governance

A colleague of mine, Brian Robertson, in the US coined the term Holacracy™, meaning a 'comprehensive practice for structuring, governing, and running an organization' (2015). It replaces today's top-down predict-and-control paradigm with a new way of distributing power and achieving control. It is a new operating system which instils rapid evolution in the core processes of an organization.

The word itself arises from the term 'Holon' which describes something that is itself a *whole* and simultaneously a *part* of some other whole. For example a quark is whole but it's also simultaneously a part of an atom which is also whole but simultaneously part of a molecule which is whole but also simultaneously part of a cell. You are whole but also part of a family which is also whole but part of community which is whole but also part of a nation.

This whole/part relationship holds true for most things in life and business is no exception. A business unit or department is a whole entity in itself but also simultaneously part of the larger business which in turn is part of an industry. Holacratic or effective governance therefore offers a complete and practical governance approach that simultaneously honours the whole and the part.

Over the last 20 years working with organizations around the world, I have heard them universally lay claim to strong and robust governance. However, when we really dig into what is actually happening it turns out that most of what is claimed to be 'governance' is actually little more than legal 'compliance' or 'operational oversight'. Genuine, high quality, effective governance is much rarer in multi-national organizations than most of us would imagine. When I challenge organizations about the quality of their governance I inevitably get asked what I mean by governance. The simple definition is 'who decides who decides'. Who decided that certain decisions should be made by the CEO alone, others by the CEO with the CFO, while different calls actually get made by the Executive Board? Where was it decided that the decision gets made by one person or group and not another person or another group? And if we change the decision making forums who decides to change them? There is so much going on in the VUCA environment and so many decisions that need to be made that leaders often just get on and make them whether they were meant to, empowered to do so or were the best people to make the call or not. Very rarely do executive teams sit down and debate which decisions should be made by which forums and why. And it is extremely rare to find a review process for continually testing the remit or limits of authority for a decision making forum.

Many companies set up sub-committees to explore issues and report back to the Board but actual delegation of decision making authority to sub-committees is patchy at best. The lack of clarity about 'who decides who decides' is a major factor contributing to organizational inefficiency, sub-optimal performance and impaired leadership. As a consequence many critical decisions actually get made in corridor conversations, executive 'side-bars' or 'off-line' chats. As a new recruit to an executive team it can take a long time to figure out where the power actually sits in terms of decision making. A new executive may for example attend the 'Transformation Committee' meeting which is meant to decide on Capex spend only to discover that people mysteriously seem to be in agreement before the debate even happens. Often the debate has already happened elsewhere in pre-briefings and the Committee become a rubber stamping process where dissenting views are discouraged. Even if this doesn't happen and there is genuine debate the decision making process is often not clear and sometimes the

CEO will step in and autocratically over rule everyone. On a different issue things may be put to a vote or sometimes issues are simply 'parked' for another day, which usually means the decision gets made in secret by a couple of leaders outside the room.

This doesn't mean the wrong decision gets made but it is often very difficult to know who decides who decides, where the decisions get made, what the process for decision making is, how to change or reverse a decision that is not working and who we need to speak to to get things sanctioned or signed off.

In contrast genuinely effective governance involves a series of detailed and robust mechanisms and processes that are thoroughly understood and implemented across the business which can then continuously improve organizational efficiency and the quality of decision making on complex issues as well as precisely clarify accountabilities so as to generate greater executive alignment. As such effective governance is also a brilliant way to reduce pressure in the system because it simplifies *and* clarifies by facilitating answers to key questions that very often stay unanswered or even unasked.

For example, does everyone in your leadership team really know what activities are needed to achieve the group's goals and who will perform them? Do they individually and collectively know how much autonomy each individual has? Does everyone know how decisions will be made, how tasks will be defined and assigned or what overarching guidelines or policies will be followed? Chances are they don't and yet these are all questions of governance, about how the group will organize their work together and the answers to these and other important questions define authority and expectations within the group. An explicit governance framework to answer these questions only exists, if it exists at all, at the top of an organization, but these questions are just as relevant on the shopfloor as they are in the boardroom. Without an explicit governance process for each team at every level the opportunities to improve organizational patterns and performance often remain unresolved or largely stuck at the very top of the organization. And yet, most senior leaders are desperate for improved performance further down in the business.

Effective governance requires a whole host of different processes to be installed, not least:

- Regular governance meetings;
- Clarification on roles and accountabilities;
- A purpose-driven Board.

Regular governance meetings

For most organizations their decision making and accountability agreements are *not* properly defined – usually because the pressing challenges in the 'doing' dimension create such a focus on action that sitting down to decide 'who decides who decides' seems an unnecessary process or bureaucratic time wasting. As a result real governance is often given little executive time or consideration. In fairness some organizations do have some degree of effective governance but even when they do their governance forums and processes are never universally understood and applied up and down the business.

Ironically the really thorny, endemic challenges that leaders wrestle with year in year out are predominantly governance issues. If we scratch the surface on the myriad of issues a leader faces, they are almost always caused by a lack of clarity around who makes what decision and why, where those decisions get made and who is really accountable for delivering certain aspects of the business plan.

We encourage every single team to set aside regular time for proper governance meetings separate from operational meetings and separate from strategic meetings. It is vital to ensure that everyone in the business knows the answers to the critical governance questions:

- What decisions are needed?
- Who will make the decisions?
- How will we decide?
- What processes will we follow?
- What policies will guide our work together?
- How can we change the answers?

The appropriate output of governance meetings are:

- Clarify all decision making forums and create any new necessary sub-forums;
- Define remit and limit of authority of all forums;
- Define reporting process, frequency and quality standards;
- Establish meeting discipline and way of interacting in meetings – 'Team Rules';
- Creation of new roles;

- Establish clear accountabilities and assign any new accountabilities to existing roles;
- Establishing new policies or changes to existing policies;
- Defining ways of working;
- Establish appropriate feedback mechanisms, portal and templates for communication to those people who need to know the outputs of the governance meetings.

Successful businesses are no longer run by a few people at the top who will actually see each other and speak to each other on a daily basis so communication of decisions made in governance meetings is crucial. Globalization, technology and escalating speed and complexity mean the rules of the game need to be redefined, clarified and aligned behind robust governance to ensure everyone is 'singing off the same hymn sheet' and key decisions, issues or discussions don't fall through the cracks. Most leaders are acutely aware of just how much time is wasted in endless meetings where the people in those meetings don't know why they are there, what they are trying to achieve, who can and should make the final decision and who will be responsible for implementation. This confusion is amplified because operational, strategic and governance issues are not discussed in separate meetings and instead are constantly hijacked by the 'urgent'. Too often, meetings descend into operational fire-fighting instead of focusing on what's 'important'. As a result one of the core principles of effective governance is to establish separate meetings, frequencies and meeting disciplines for operations, strategy and governance meetings thus reducing the number and length of meetings while also massively increasing output and performance.

On a human level, governance meetings can also transform the emotional tone of a team. Lack of clarity around governance leaves everyone with implicit expectations about who should be doing what and how they should be doing it. Without a defined governance process the tendency is to make up negative stories about others or blame each other when these unspoken assumptions and expectations are not met. But blame and recrimination do not move a business forward and elevate performance. Regular governance meetings therefore provide team members with a forum for channelling their frustration over misaligned expectations into organizational learning and continual improvement. Playing politics loses its utility, and personal drama gives way to a more authentic discussion of how to consciously evolve the organization in light of its objectives.

Clarification of roles and accountabilities

One of the key early outputs of effective governance is the detailed clarification and definition of roles and accountabilities. Again this sounds obvious and most executive teams believe this is already done well enough or covered in detailed job descriptions. However, in our experience when we look at executive accountabilities in detail it is easy to identify a number of gaps where no one is clearly responsible and areas where accountabilities overlap. Clearly these gaps and overlaps can cause tension and frustration in the team when things fall through the gaps or when executives feel that others are 'stepping on their toes'. Plus the likelihood of accountability gaps and overlaps becomes much greater as the world speeds up and things change so quickly. So keeping accountabilities under continual review in the governance meetings is vital.

In working with Executive Boards and teams on their governance I am continually surprised by how much we are able to improve a team's clarity around their accountabilities and elevate performance even when they have already spent a lot of time working on their 'RACI' (responsible, accountable, consulted and informed) frameworks.

Clarification of roles and accountabilities needs to be done regardless of who is available to fill certain roles and whether the individual in that position has the skill set to deliver. Too many organizations try to fit the role to the person rather than deciding what the business really needs and then recruiting and developing people to that requirement.

A purpose-driven Board

If the 'war on talent' has proved anything over the last few decades it's that the financial ambition of a company is insufficient to attract, retain and motivate the best people. Fluffy mission statements outlining 'visions of future desired states' are also not effective in attracting key people and keeping them because they are too abstract or generic. Increasingly the companies that are attracting the best people are the ones that have a strong 'Why', an emotive *purpose* that attracts and motivates talent and unlocks discretionary effort (Sinek, 2009).

Profit is not a purpose it's a metric. But with a Board composed entirely of shareholder representatives, profit is very likely to get mistaken for a purpose. Great companies are first and foremost purpose-driven, with all activities designed to deliver on that purpose. Defining an organization's purpose is highly skilled work. It takes time and must be done in collaboration with representatives of the key internal stakeholder groups. There are very few organizations that have uncovered a compelling purpose for the business. Most end up not bothering because it is too difficult or irrelevant to operational performance. I have even had a Board member of a FTSE 20 company say to me 'I don't see the purpose of having a purpose'! If you really don't know why you do what you do then you truly are lost. Purpose is the 'Why' that unlocks discretionary effort from the employee base and attracts employees to the business. It can also make the company much more attractive to its customer base and ultimately it is a powerful cohering force. In the companies where we have helped them identify their purpose it has endured over time, acting as a compass that helps guide activity and maintain alignment across the business.

Network analysis

The final tool to help drive up performance in the 'IT' dimension is network analysis. This tool provides important insights into how the business really works as opposed to how the organizational chart suggests it works. And these insights can be used to direct and influence behaviour.

Based on complex social network theory this tool objectifies the connections between people and their patterns of interaction within the business and beyond. By asking senior leaders seven simple questions we can generate thousands of data points in a matter of minutes and those data points can reveal invaluable insights about three critical networks:

1 Functional Network

Q1: Name the people you typically get work related information from.

Q2: Name the people you regularly collaborate with.

2 Emotional Network

Q3: Name the people you feel energized by when you interact with them.

Q4: Name the people you feel comfortable sharing sensitive information with.

Q5: Name the people to whom you turn for support when things are tough.

3 Leadership Network

Q6: Name the people who you feel personally stretch your thinking.

Q7: Name the people to whom you turn for leadership or guidance.

In business, as in life, nothing is achieved alone and the ability to connect with and 'muster the troops' so as to deliver on objectives is largely determined by a leader's networks – functional, emotional or leadership. Once these seven questions are answered by senior leaders the network can then be 'read' using Deep Network Analytics.

Deep Network Analytics (DNA)

Deep Network Analytics allows us to see who is connected to whom, why and the strength of each connection. A unilateral connection (represented by a single arc line) indicates that person A referenced person B but person B did not reference person A. A bilateral connection (represented by a wavy double headed line) indicates that person A and person B referenced each other, which makes that connection or relationship much stronger. The size of an individual node also reveals the importance of that individual in the whole network.

In Figure 2.6 the connectivity in a group of 24 leaders is shown. This is the 'trust sub-network' where leaders answered the question 'who do you trust with sensitive information?' This type of visualization instantly reveals a number of important insights. For example, there are clearly two smaller clusters within the group where a number of individuals referenced each other. These two sub-clusters appear to be connected by just two

FIGURE 2.6   Simple network visualization of connectivity in the trust sub-network

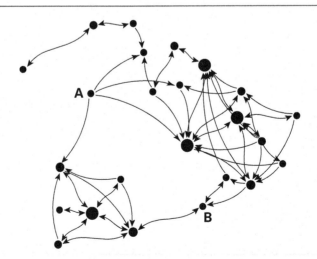

individuals, labelled A and B. These two individuals would be important in 'bridging' the two clusters but they would not be the most central, significant or influential in the network. Such network analysis visualizations can be adjusted so that each node can represent an individual, a team or a whole organization.

Although there is a rich academic literature exploring all manner of social networking concepts the terminology is often impenetrable. Many of the labels to explain the various types of connections, such as 'tightness', 'density' or 'prestige' are confusing to anyone who is not already deeply immersed in the academic topic and the ability to relate this to an organizational context is limited. As a result most organizations have yet to tap into the power of network analysis to transform their business. Our network analysis software seeks to generate comprehensible visualizations of the connections in organizations and our Deep Network Analytics (DNA) simplifies the terminology to create compelling and actionable insights about the real relationships that exist in a business within departments, teams and cross-functionally (Table 2.5).

TABLE 2.5   Full range of insights available via Deep Network Analytics (DNA)

Metric	How it is measured	What it means
Significance	Number of people who referenced you	How connected you are
Symmetry	Number of people who share a bi-directional reference	Reciprocity of your relationships
Centrality	Number of steps to reach whole network	How quickly you transmit to all
Clustering	Number of bi-directional triads you are in	Strength of your alliances
Bridging	Number of clusters you connect	Dependency of the system on you
Influence	Number of high quality connections you have	How easily you influence the system

Normally when people think about their networks they tend to think simply in terms of numbers of connections. In other words – how many people is that person connected to? But the number of connections is not always that important and it's certainly a poor measure of influence or reach. Just because someone has thousands of contacts on LinkedIn or thousands of 'friends' on Facebook, doesn't necessarily mean that person is influential. That said, it's a useful starting point so 'Significance' simply measures the numbers of connections. This data can give us an initial handle on the individual's social connectivity.

For example, the data shown in Figure 2.7 is a snapshot of the 40,000 data points accrued when the top 60 people in a multi-national organization were asked the seven key questions. The Significance graphic shows the number of references each person has across the different networks. You will notice that the CEO of this organization had the most connections with 145 in total. The marketing and operations directors had the next highest number of references at 126, followed by the finance director with 101. In this particular company, this exactly matched the degree of impact each of these leaders were having on the business. The individual, who had the fifth largest number of references, and more than six other Executive Board members, is one of the rising stars of the company and had been identified as

FIGURE 2.7   Significance graphic

Function	Info	Collab	Energy	Trust	Suppor	Guidan	Stretc	Total
	Total	Total	Total	Total	Total	Total	Total	Total
1 CEO	12	6	46	12	11	29	29	145
2 Marketing	16	10	25	12	14	30	19	126
3 Operations	25	12	28	9	13	23	16	126
4 Finance	12	7	16	13	8	26	19	101
5 Marketing	17	15	31	13	10	10	2	98
6 People	11	10	8	17	14	12	14	86
7 Other	8	5	7	8	16	17	20	81
8 Commercial	13	8	12	5	8	17	11	74
9 People	10	9	6	16	17	6	8	72
10 Strategy	8	7	12	4	3	23	3	60
11 Operations	17	6	12	7	5	6	4	57
12 People	5	10	11	4	9	5	6	50
13 Finance	13	5	4	9	8	6	5	50
14 People	7	7	2	9	11	5	6	47
15 Finance	12	3	1	6	4	14	4	44
16 Operations	11	10	5	6	4	3	4	43
17 Finance	7	8	1	7	6	8	5	42
18 Commercial	16	11	2	6	3	3	0	41
19 Operations	12	11	10	3	3	2	0	41
20 Strategy	10	10	5	4	5	4	2	40

FIGURE 2.8   Symmetry graphic

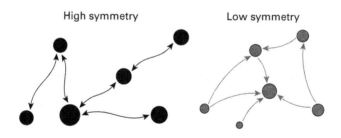

High symmetry   Low symmetry

a future potential Board member. This data helped to confirm the potential of this rising star and the significance of key directors in the business.

The next metric identified by DNA is 'Symmetry' which reveals how many bi-directional connections exist between one senior executive and the other people in the social network (Figure 2.8). In other words, how many people did the executive reference that then also referenced them back? This DNA metric can be quite nuanced because an individual may have a bilateral connection with a person on one of the seven questions but not on all of them. So for example there may be a bilateral connection for trust but not for information. The greater the reciprocity within a relationship, the greater the mutual strength of the bond. This often suggests that the stakeholder and the other person see themselves as peers. Figure 2.8 shows an example of high symmetry in the 'Information' network where every connection is bilateral. In contrast, the right-hand panel shows the connections within the 'Stretch' network and all the connections are unilateral, ie there is a low level of symmetry.

'Centrality' identifies how central the leader is in the network; that is, how many steps would the leader need to make to get to the periphery of the whole exterior network (Figure 2.9). Clearly the closer to the middle the more weight the leader usually carries and the quicker they can then affect the whole network. Person 'A' in Figure 2.9 will clearly have a higher 'Centrality Score' than person 'B'.

Another key DNA metric is 'Clustering' which indicates the number of bilaterally connected triads or how many sub-groups or clusters of three or more people the leader shares a bilateral connection with (Figure 2.10). This indicates powerful alliances that can be extremely useful in solving problems or shifting a system or culture.

In the example shown, the executive labelled 'A' is only connected to one cluster with a single bi-directional link within that cluster. The executive

FIGURE 2.9   Centrality graphic

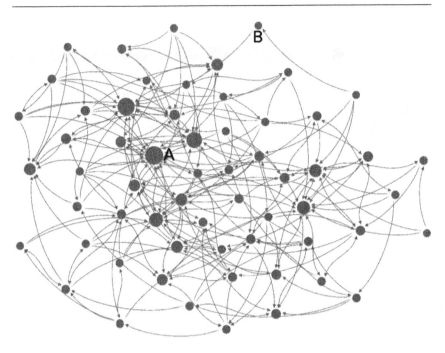

FIGURE 2.10   Clustering graphic

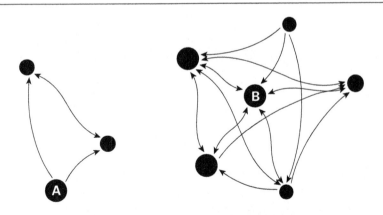

labelled 'B' in contrast belongs to four clusters that have bilateral connections. So the clustering score would be much higher for executive 'B' than executive 'A'.

The 'Bridging' metric is particularly important if your performance improvement initiatives require behaviour change within the network. As

FIGURE 2.11 Bridging graphic

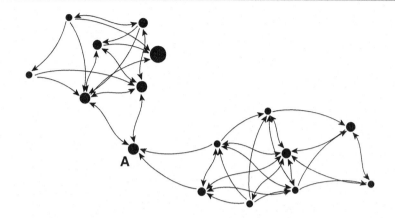

the name would suggest this DNA metric determines whether a leader or senior executive is the bridge between key clusters (Figure 2.11). In the example in Figure 2.11, person 'A' is the only person from one department who bridges the two different departments. Therefore they can have a significant influence on shifting the centre of gravity in both departments.

And finally, 'Influence' seeks to identify a leader's overall impact in a specific network. This DNA metric is really driven by the importance of who references that leader. Thus the number of people a leader is connected to may be relatively low but if those connections are powerful connections then they will be significantly more influential within a network. For example a Communications Director may not be heavily connected in the network but if they have the ear and the trust of the CEO and the Finance Director then they will exert a disproportionate influence because of the nature of those senior connections. A senior executive will always exert far more influence if the people that reference them are 'big fish', even if there are only one or two, than if countless 'minnows' reference them.

Network analysis and Deep Network Analytics allows us to see who is connected to whom, why and how strong those connections are. These insights can be extremely useful in improving individual, team, divisional and organizational performance. Not only does it allow us to make sure the right people are involved in the right discussions but it helps to engage the entire network if we know who we need to get on side in order to do that. The organization chart of any business may tell us who is supposed to report to whom and why, but network analysis shines a light on what is actually happening inside the business in real time and we can then use those insights to deliver our strategic objectives.

Action steps

When it comes to squeezing value from the objective world of 'doing' there is still more that can be done but only if we are smart about it. Below are some suggested action steps that can help extract the maximum value from the 'IT' dimension:

1 Assess the developmental level of all the senior team across the 11 performance driving behaviours.

2 Identify and leverage the 'Strengths' and 'Strategic Strengths' in the team and use those insights to re-negotiate tasks and responsibilities across the team to drive better performance.

3 Identify 'Developing Strengths' and encourage each senior leader to invest in those behaviours to elevate to 'Strengths'.

4 Identify limiting behaviours across the senior team and invest in tailored development to stop those behaviours from undermining individual and team performance.

5 Reduce excess pressure on individuals and the team to ensure performance improves quickly. Monitor pressure to ensure everyone remains on the healthy side of the pressure-performance curve.

6 Identify which of the organizational challenges are problems that can be solved and which are polarities that need to be managed. Actively manage polarities to get the best of both worlds.

7 Institute regular governance meetings separate from operational and strategic meetings and ensure that the governance conversation is not simply compliance or operational oversight.

8 Save time, energy and money by implementing effective governance processes to ensure fast decision making occurs in the right forums at every level across the business.

9 Take the time to clarify roles and accountabilities to a much higher standard. Pay particular attention to identifying accountability gaps and removing ambiguity and duplication.

10 Clarify your organizational purpose and ensure it is compatible with your corporate vision so both can work to attract high quality people to your business.

11 Consider investing in network analysis to look under the hood of your business. See who is connected to whom, why and how strong the connections are. Use the data to flush out hidden talent, high potentials, underperformers and performance blockers. Also use the data to target investment in the right people, track the impact of restructuring, drive initiatives and step change performance.

PART TWO
The subjective world of 'being'

Vertical development of the 'I' dimension

03

Although it's easy to see why we are all so preoccupied with the external, observable world of action, behaviour and results this approach is no longer delivering the results it once did. We are all so busy trying to find answers to the universal business problems of performance, productivity, innovation and growth that we often fail to realize that we are all viewing these problems from the same dimension or perspective ('IT'). We may occasionally explore the interdependent world of 'WE' in an effort to improve team performance but such effort is usually focused on what the team must 'do' rather than how the team functions or how people interact with each other in that team. And as for the subjective world of 'being' ('I') – it's rarely, if ever considered.

It's not surprising that we rarely come up with anything that is truly differentiated or radically innovative. Instead most businesses simply regurgitate the same incomplete and only partially effective answers, the same ideas and the same strategy as their competitors. What's needed is a different vantage point – one which will allow us to see the challenges we face from a completely different perspective, one which will open up our thinking and provide fresh, long-term answers and that's what this chapter is all about.

We will explore the internal, subjective world of 'being', not least because this is where real leadership actually starts. What is happening on the inside makes a huge difference to the results we see on the outside. Consequently this chapter also details a number of practical exercises that can be used to increase energy levels, facilitate better quality thinking, expand emotional awareness and elevate emotional intelligence. All of which can improve stakeholder buy-in and increase our ability to fast track results and take others with us on the developmental journey.

The integrated performance model

For most business leaders all that really matters is results. Objective results tell us how well the business is performing and are often seen as the only yard-stick of success. But, if we are serious about finding long-term solutions to the myriad of complex problems we face then we absolutely must look deeper into what is causing the behaviour from the 'inside' instead of just focusing on the 'outside' surface behaviours. This dynamic is explained visually by the integrated performance model in Figure 3.1.

The results we achieve in business exist in the external objective world and as such they are visible. If those results are not good enough then most of us will immediately look to behaviour which is also visible in the objective external world to see what we need to 'do' to improve those results. But what is driving the behaviour in the first place? A manager can give instruction or incorporate certain behaviour into their KPIs or performance management system but these and many other initiatives are no guarantee that the behaviour will emerge. So what really drives behaviour?

The answer is thinking. What we *think* determines what we do. So if I'm coaching a senior leader and he *thinks* my suggestions are rubbish or

FIGURE 3.1 The integrated performance model

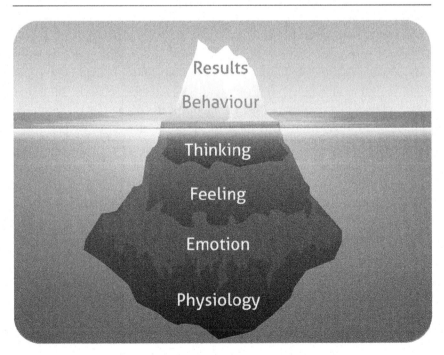

that I don't actually know what I'm talking about then he is not going to *do* what I suggest. In the same way, if what I'm sharing in this book doesn't make rational sense then you're going to close the book and you're not going to *do* anything differently. And if you don't *do* anything differently you're not going to get different results.

So to create a sustainable change in behaviour we actually must change thinking. So the task just got harder. If you believe changing how people behave is tough – try changing what they think! But even if you were some sort of guru able to change the minds of the people that work for or with you unfortunately that is still not enough to guarantee a change in fortunes. Why? Because what we think and how well we think is determined by something more fundamental in the human system – and that's how we feel.

How we feel directly alters what we think. These two phenomena, thinking and feeling, reciprocally affect each other. How we think affects how we feel; and how we feel affects how we think so they are inextricably interconnected. But if 'thinking' and 'feeling' were to have an arm wrestle then feeling would win almost every time because feeling is faster and more powerful than thought. So ultimately feeling not thinking determines what we do. This is heresy to many 'right minded rationalists' who are convinced that thoughts determine all action. But the conviction that thoughts are the primary driver is itself a feeling! An operations manager may *think*, 'I really have to finish that tender document before I go home tonight'. But if it's Friday afternoon and they don't *feel* like it? What wins between thinking and feeling? Feeling wins almost *every* time. The ops manager may be able to complete the tender if he thinks there is enough incentive or is suitably fearful of the consequences if he doesn't but it's unsustainable as an ongoing strategy. What's more likely is that he will simply bend his thinking to justify not completing the tender and convince himself that it is OK (feels right) to go home early instead.

As adult human beings we can all make ourselves do stuff we don't want to do if we think it's important enough but it won't last unless we really feel like doing it and 'feel it is important'. What we feel has a far bigger impact on what we do than thinking does. We all know this. When we are putting on weight for example we know we need to eat less and exercise more but after an initial flurry of well-intentioned activity, we just don't feel like going to the gym and besides we worked hard this week so we deserve that sticky toffee pudding with double cream!

In order to change the quality of someone's thinking, so they behave differently, improve performance and achieve better results, we actually have to change the way they feel. Sustainably changing how people feel is almost an art form. Most marketers can change how people feel temporarily but if we want to change results permanently we need to change how people feel permanently or at least for a longer period of time. But even if you are a gifted marketer or storytelling genius that could successfully change how people *feel* is that enough? No, it's still not enough because what we feel is determined by something even more fundamental in the human system – and that's emotion or more accurately e-motion (energy in motion).

If a colleague is angry and you say, 'look it's fine, just calm down' – does it work? No. It absolutely doesn't work. Even if they realize they have to calm down and actively want to calm down it's incredibly difficult to do because the raw emotion that is occurring in their body is already surging through their veins, nerves and airway. Telling them to calm down once they are angry is pointless – it's too late. And the reason this raw energy is coursing through their body in the first place is because at an even deeper level, down in the basement of the human system there is a multitude of biological reactions and processes that are occurring without their aware-ness. Their physiology has kicked in and it is this that ultimately creates the platform on which performance is built.

The real reason poor performance is a constant problem in business is because everyone is too busy looking at behaviour as a route to improve-ment instead of realizing that behaviour is just a convenient visible scape-goat. What's really driving our behaviour is our internal, invisible thinking. And what we think and how well we think it is largely determined by our internal and invisible feelings which are driven by our internal and invisible emotions which are made up of the myriad of internal and invisible bio-logical physical signals and processes that make up our physiology at any given moment.

Performance drops, poor decisions are made and strategy is executed poorly because the physiology of the people involved changed and they just didn't realize it. If you really want to elevate performance and demonstrate brilliant 4D Leadership then that journey starts in the subjective internal world of 'being' ('I') not the external objective world of 'doing' ('IT').

Leadership is an inside job – the power of 'I'

If you ask a group of senior executives to name the most significant global leader in the last 50 years Nelson Mandela is almost always the first name to be mentioned. I've tested this question all over the world and it doesn't matter which country I am in Nelson Mandela is at the top or very near the top in most cultures. There are of course some who will disagree but the vast majority see him as an inspirational leader.

What's really interesting about Mandela's life journey is that he was locked up in prison for 27 years so he couldn't really 'do' anything. There was virtually no external objective world of 'doing' over which he could exert much control. There was also very little 'relating' because most of his prison sentence was served in a tiny cell on his own on Robben Island. He talked to a few guards from time to time and some fellow prisoners but his interpersonal world of 'WE' was also significantly hampered. The only world that was available to him was his internal world of 'being'.

There is little doubt that one of the reasons Nelson Mandela is universally admired as an outstanding leader is because he spent 27 years cultivating his interior landscape. Right up until his death in 2013 Mandela was a man who knew who he was. When he left prison in 1990 he was not bitter, angry or aggrieved about how much of his life had been spent behind bars. He had every right to be angry; he was imprisoned because of his fight against the injustice of apartheid which will remain a stain on humanity for ever. His marriage failed and he wasn't able to see his children and grandchildren grow up and yet he was able to let go of the hate and recrimination and step up to lead his nation into a new, post-apartheid era. And that was *only* possible because he cultivated his interior world of 'I' over the course of 27 years.

We know leadership brilliance when we see it. Mandela was a man apart, he was different, capable of inspiring millions because he had a very rich understanding of his interior world and yet the vast majority of leadership books don't even mention it. And we can make similar arguments about the impact of interior cultivation for other inspirational leaders such as Aung San Suu Kyi, Gandhi and the Dalai Lama.

Really brilliant leadership is built on a very sophisticated interior landscape (the 'I' dimension).

The role of physiology on leadership

Starting in the basement of the human system it's important to understand what physiology is and how it impacts leadership performance. Physiology is just the word to describe the data or information streams that are occurring inside your body all the time. Your body is alive with vast streams of data being sent and received from one biological system to another in the form of electrical signals, electromagnetic signals, chemical signals, pressure, sound and heat waves. For the most part we're not aware of most of this data and we rarely appreciate its impact. New smart technology in the form of wearable devices and apps are however beginning to make much of this invisible interior world visible. These insights are already having a profound impact on health and personal well-being and they can also have a profound impact on leadership. Using these physiological insights to help master this traffic and generate better quality information flow is the first critical step to facilitate vertical development in the interior world.

In business our appreciation of our interior landscape is often limited to vague expressions of motivation. Before giving an important presentation we may consider it wise to get 'psyched up' in order to try to inspire the audience. Or if the team is beginning to panic about this quarter's financial performance we may need to project a level of steadiness in the face of the crisis. And most of us have the emotional bandwidth to know the difference between the two. But if the extent of our physiological repertoire is restricted to getting 'geed up' or 'steadiness under pressure' with very little in between then our ability to perform will be massively impaired. Beside, whether we are 'psyched' or steady does not predict how well we perform in any given situation anyway.

When we ramp up our energy levels or get psyched up prior to a major event we activate our autonomic nervous system (ANS) and engage the primitive 'fight or flight' response. When flight looks like the best option, our system releases adrenaline (known as epinephrine in the US), which gives us a boost of energy so we can take 'flight' and run away. In contrast when we trigger the desire to fight our body releases adrenaline's sister, noradrenaline which readies the body for battle.

The other main physiological response to a threat is the 'relaxation response' which is usually to freeze, play dead or faint. Possums use this approach as their main survival tactic and thankfully for the possum it works. However, it's not a terribly useful leadership approach.

While most people have heard of adrenaline, the 'accelerator fluid' very few people have heard of acetylcholine – the 'brake fluid'. So in very simple terms adrenaline or noradrenaline heat our system up in readiness to either run away or fight or acetylcholine cools the system down into a relaxed state so much so that we can freeze or faint.

Interestingly it is these exact responses that are the assumed drivers of performance (see Figure 3.2) and as such they are frequently cited as the way to improve performance. Coaches in business and sport regularly tell their clients that they need to get pumped up before a big game or important business pitch or that they need to learn to relax and 'absorb the pressure'.

FIGURE 3.2   The assumed drivers of performance

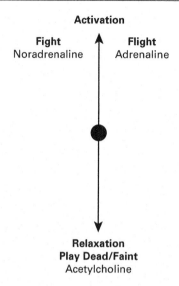

As a result you will see athletes literally banging their own chest before a big race or a swimmer entering the arena with headphones on almost oblivious to the crowd in the stands.

The problem is, performance is not about relaxation or activation. The reason this advice occasionally works is not because it provokes relaxation or activation, rather it may inadvertently trigger a second system. It is this second system, the neuroendocrine system (NE) and not our autonomic nervous system (ANS) that determines the quality of our performance. The NE system determines the quality of our emotional experience whereas the ANS determines the degree of our activation or arousal.

On the right-hand side of the horizontal NE axis (Figure 3.3) we are said to be in a catabolic state or 'breakdown' state. This is an important biological process necessary for repair and regeneration but this breakdown state is underpinned by the catabolic hormones, particularly the body's main stress hormone, cortisol. Science has already proven that there is a strong relationship between cortisol and negative emotion which means that increased

FIGURE 3.3   The real drivers of performance

levels of cortisol are likely to induce more 'negative' emotions. Of course, it's extremely difficult to function at our best and produce consistent high performance when we are feeling negative. And to make matters worse the negative emotions then increase the cortisol levels still further creating a vicious cycle of escalating cortisol and negativity.

On the left-hand side of NE axis we are said to be in an anabolic state or 'build up' state. This is underpinned by a range of 'anabolic hormones', particularly dehydroepiandrosterone (DHEA). DHEA is the 'performance' hormone and our body's natural antidote to cortisol. As such it is associated with more 'positive' emotions. It is the molecule that makes testosterone in men and oestrogen in women. High performance is obviously much easier when we feel positive. These positive emotions then increase the levels of DHEA still further creating a virtuous cycle of escalating DHEA and positivity.

If we put the vertical 'Activation' axis together with the horizontal 'Positivity' axis we get the Performance Grid which depicts the interaction of these two critical physiological systems. Consistently brilliant leadership is determined by how much time we spend in the positive left-hand side of the grid as opposed to the negative right-hand side. It is not determined by how much time we spend in the activated top half or relaxed bottom half of the grid. This is why results are so variable. A leader could assume that getting 'psyched' up before an important meeting works for them but if they don't recognize the difference between positive psyched up and negative

FIGURE 3.4   The Performance Grid

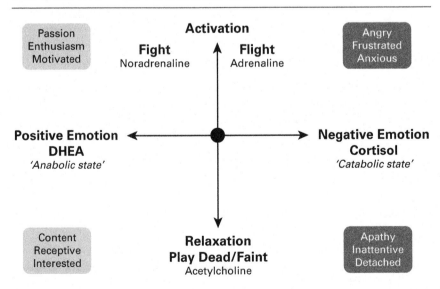

psyched up they will be confused as to why it works sometimes and not other times. They may not appreciate that their preparation worked when they were in the top left of the Performance Grid and didn't work when they were in the top right of the grid. Similarly there are some leaders who mistakenly believe that calm and steady is the approach that works best. But there is a world of difference in terms of output and action between someone who is positive relaxed (bottom left) and negative relaxed (bottom right).

We are incorrectly told that we need to manage our degree of arousal or relaxation whereas what we really need to manage is the degree of positivity and negativity. Unfortunately when we drop into negatively 'relaxed' states such as apathy or boredom we are still producing elevated amounts of cortisol and other catabolic hormones. We already know that persistent high levels of cortisol accelerate ageing. Having high cortisol and low DHEA has also been implicated in obesity, diabetes, high blood pressure, heart disease, cancer, depression and dementia. Clearly producing too much cortisol over a sustained period of time will seriously interfere with our health, our ability to think clearly and ultimately our performance. And this can be especially true for the leaders who appear cool and calm under pressure.

Often leaders who project a calm, in-charge demeanour think they are somehow saving themselves from the vagaries of excess excitement and too much adrenaline but if they are negatively relaxed instead of positively relaxed their body is still creating the cortisol. At least when someone is negatively aroused (top right) they are usually aware of it because they feel angry or resentful. As a result they are more likely to take action to defuse the anger and therefore reduce the cortisol levels. Someone who is negatively relaxed is duped into thinking they have it handled because they are relaxed. However, inside cortisol levels are still causing havoc with their physiology.

It is therefore essential that we are able to distinguish between positivity and negativity not just relaxed and agitated. When we learn how to manage our physiology, we can choose to live on the left-hand side of the Performance Grid more often which will in turn massively improve performance over the long term.

Coherence as the vertical development springboard

The real secret to performance is developing the ability to move over to the left-hand side of the Performance Grid and stay there. As explained in more detail in *Coherence: The secret science of brilliant leadership*, this requires us to establish a new way of being, it requires us to cultivate a state of 'coherence'. Coherence is the biological underpinning of what elite performers call 'the flow state' (Csikszentmihalyi, 2002): a state of maximum efficiency and super effectiveness, where body and mind are one. In *flow* truly remarkable things are possible.

Conceptually coherence is a state of 'stable variability'. There are two aspects of variability that are critical to the optimum functioning of the system, namely the *amount* of variability and the *type or pattern* of the variability. When a system exhibits a predictable pattern of stable variability it is a vibrant, healthy, living system. We need to be able to move coherently (i.e. in a stable and predictable way) between being positively relaxed and positively psyched up. If we slip into negativity we need to be able to appreciate that and take active steps to move back into a more constructive mindset so we can find solutions and maintain strong performance.

Too little variability makes a business vulnerable to threats. When a leader refuses to acknowledge and respond to a changing environment or customer requirements the business will suffer. Too *much* variability is also a threat because the business is too changeable, jumping from one product or market to another. What we need is balance and when we achieve that balance we achieve coherence.

As we have suggested physiology is the foundation of all of our performance, silently, unknowingly altering and determining behaviour and results. It follows therefore that if we are to create coherence we need to start with physiology. We need to bring balance and flexibility to our physiological processes so we can actively manage our energy levels and recuperate properly. This is achieved via the physical line of development. Think of physical coherence as the foundation upon which complete coherence is built. Effectively, physical coherence allows us to turn the clock back to access the energy levels we experienced 10 years ago. Not only will we feel as though we have *more* energy, but we will use it more efficiently and recharge our batteries more effectively.

Developing greater physical coherence increases the likelihood that we can cultivate emotional coherence because we become more aware of our emotional data when we are physically coherent. This greater emotional awareness can facilitate more stable and more predictable (ie coherent) emotional regulation. Using a musical metaphor, physiology is the individual stream of notes that are being played all the time by all of our bodily systems such as the heart, lungs, joints, gut, liver and kidneys. Emotion is the integration and combination of all the individual notes to form a tune. And feelings are the cognitive awareness of what tune our body is playing at any given moment. Unless we learn how to master those physiological notes and recognize the tunes we are playing we are often like the tone deaf contestant on a TV singing show who believes he sounds like Frank Sinatra but actually sounds like a cat stuck under a fence! Health, productivity and performance problems happen when we either don't hear the tune, ignore it or misinterpret it. The continued ignorance and misdiagnosis of the repertoire of emotional 'tunes' our biological systems are currently playing can have serious consequences for our health and emotional well-being as well as our leadership potential.

Learning how to master our physiology constructively is surprisingly simple and I'll explain the process in the next section of this chapter. Physical coherence creates a solid foundation which then makes emotional coherence possible. When we learn to recognize and actively manage our emotions instead of suppressing them or ignoring them we develop greater emotional flexibility, and this can help unlock greater intellectual capacity and maturity. Such emotional coherence also positively impacts our energy reserves. Physical and emotional coherence in turn facilitates cognitive coherence and gives us consistent access to more of our cognitive ability whilst also preventing those 'deer in headlights' brain shut down moments.

But preventing brain shut down is just part of the answer when it comes to improving intellectual horsepower. Real cognitive breakthroughs and superior cognitive processing are only really possible once we expand our awareness and develop vertically along the key lines of adult development (see Figure 3.5), particularly ego maturity.

FIGURE 3.5   Lines of development

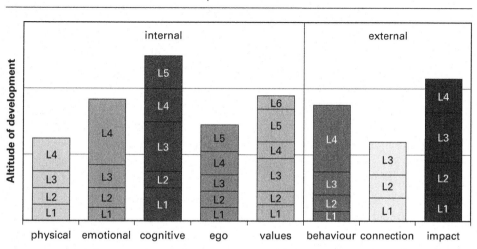

Increased ego maturity is an area that can yield extraordinary improvements in performance and capability. It is so important that the next chapter is dedicated to this critical line of development. For now suffice to say that increased ego maturity allows us to think more deeply and clearly, it allows us to apply the right type of thinking to adapt to complex and challenging problems in real time, therefore we become significantly more creative, more innovative and better able to bring our A-game to the table every day, not just intermittently.

This collective internal coherence across the first three internal lines of development – physical, emotional and cognitive – can facilitate a vast leap forward in performance which begins to manifest in the external world. Ultimately it is the leader's 'altitude' not their 'aptitude' across all the key lines of development that really determines their ability to deliver performance improvements in a VUCA world. In our experience the value to the business of each new level of development varies depending on which lines of development we are addressing. Thus the amount of altitude in moving from level 3 to level 4 in the emotional and social intelligence line (second from the left) is much greater than moving from level 3 to level 4 in the behaviour development line.

While understanding our own values is an important part of expanding our internal subjective world it is especially relevant to how we communicate and relate to others. As a result values will be explored in more detail when we discuss the interrelating world of 'WE' in Chapter 5.

How to cultivate your interior world of 'I'

The rational objective world of 'IT' and what we need to do to deliver results is already squeezed and continued focus on this dimension is insufficient to stay ahead of the competition. Any competitive advantage it still yields takes time to mine and may be relatively short lived. There is however significant competitive advantage available from the internal, invisible world of 'being' ('I' dimension). Even better – generating such advantage is cheaper and relatively simply to achieve. Building such advantage does require some time and effort but the benefits of upgrading our operating system far exceed the investment necessary to achieve this vertical upsurge in capability.

Who we are as individual human beings has a profound impact on the results we achieve in life and yet this dimension is barely even acknowledged in business. If it is acknowledged it's often reduced to some descriptive personality testing that cannot drive development. But how do we develop or expand who we are? How do we create cumulative internal coherence across multiple lines of development to facilitate massive up-surges of productivity? Where do we even start? This section answers these questions.

Figure 3.6 shows the skills and intelligences that can be cultivated in the physical and emotional lines of development needed for 4D Leadership. The rest of this chapter will explain the specific physical and emotional skills we need to master in order to increase our verticality in these two internal lines of development of the 'I' dimension. We teach these skills before skills in the other lines because they are foundational. They create a solid platform that can facilitate vertical development in all the other lines. On their own they can transform our performance, when applied consistently they can unlock unprecedented potential and can literally transform organizational output.

FIGURE 3.6   4D Leadership skills and intelligences

Inter-personal skills

10. Sustain positive relationships drives success = Social intelligence (Appreciation v2)

9. Awareness of others' emotions = Social intuition, empathy and rapport (MAP)

Personal skills

8. Ability to make positive emotions your default = Optimistic outlook (Appreciation v1)

7. Use raw emotional energy to drive self forward = Self-motivation (Purpose)

6. Ability to return to a positive emotional state quickly = Emotional resilience (SHIFT)

5. Control emotions and manage stress = Emotional self-management (PEP and Landscaping)

4. Label and discriminate emotions correctly = Emotional literacy (MASTERY)

3. Awareness of emotions (feeling!) = EQ, Emotional Intelligence (E-diary)

Physical skills

2. Control physiology, especially HRV = Physical management (BREATHE)

1. Awareness of physiological state = Physical intelligence (E-bank)

Developing these skills within individual leaders can step change the quality of the relationship within a leadership team or Executive Board. With much stronger relationships in place the quality of the debate in an Executive Board improves, decision making speeds up and becomes more effective and this often translates to better commercial results. We have seen in a number of organizations that as executive teams develop more altitude in their physical and emotional lines of development, thus increasing their emotional and social intelligence they are much more likely to turn the fortunes of the business around. We have seen this happen in many market sectors with organizations returning to profitability, entering the FTSE 100 for the first time or transforming the quality of the organization itself.

In one company we were working simultaneously with the Operations Board and the Executive Board. Initially the Ops Board committed the minimum two days per quarter necessary to develop themselves as a team. In contrast the Exec Board only invested in two events per year. Within one year the Ops Board started to function at a much higher level than the Exec Board. It was obvious and it became a topic of conversation inside the organization. To their credit the Exec Board recognized that they were simply not investing sufficient time in their development and committed more to their own team journey. Within six months they were eclipsing the effectiveness of the Ops Board and driving the organizational transformation more effectively and starting to deliver what they were capable of and create greater competitive advantage.

In some executive teams we ask the leaders to complete a 360 degree process called the 'Team Energy Grid (TEG)'. Each leader anonymously rates the emotional impact of their peers on a good day and a bad day. The data is then fed back confidentially to each leader as part of their development. Figure 3.7 provides an illustration of two different executives as rated by their peers. The leader on the left generally increases the energy in the system on most days. On good days she positively invigorates most of her peers. On bad days she can have a more negative or agitating effect and she can drain three of her colleagues. In contrast the leader on the right has a more energetically neutral effect but on a good day increases the positivity in the team and on a bad day adds to the negativity in the team.

We do, of course, perform a lot of sophisticated analysis on this data but at the simplest level it can be extremely useful for leaders to see the energetic and emotional footprint they are leaving on those around them. Such objective evidence can help leaders see clearly whether their intended impact is matched by their actual impact.

FIGURE 3.7 The team energy grid

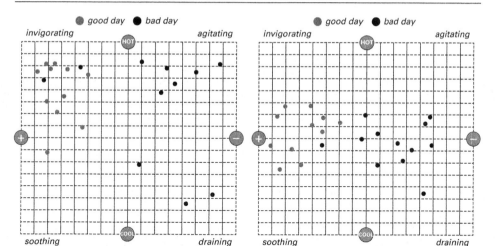

Physical skills

Often a leader's start point for creating a more positive impact and cultivating verticality across the key lines of development is to create a solid foundation of physical coherence. Physiology is ground zero when it comes to vertical development. If it is skipped past or ignored then any progress in other lines of development can evaporate if a leader becomes exhausted by the pressure of the VUCA world. Becoming aware of our physiology and learning to manage it allows us to increase our energy levels, recuperate faster and positively influence everything above physiology in the integrated performance model, ie emotion, feeling, thinking, behaviour, results. In business an individual's physiology is considered irrelevant and yet not being aware of it and not learning to manage it can diminish our energy reserves leading to exhaustion and illness.

I explain how this works in more detail in *Coherence: The secret science of brilliant leadership*, but essentially in order to get anything done in the external objective world of 'IT' we need the energy to do it! Senior leaders must show up day in day out and pour their energy and effort into the business, they need to inspire and energize those around them and they need to renew their reserves so they can do it all again tomorrow. If we don't have that energy then we will never be able to crank out our A-game every day and performance will remain inconsistent.

Energy is created automatically through the physiological processes that are occurring in our body all the time and the heart creates more energy than any other bodily system. The heart is the body's main power station with a power output of anywhere between 1 and 5 watts – considerably greater than the power output of the brain or any other system in the body (Muslumova, 2003). Electrically speaking the heart generates about 40 to 60 times more electrical power than the brain and 5,000 times more electromagnetic power than the brain (Deepu *et al*, 2012). And it is claimed that the information the heart carries in this electromagnetic field can be detected not only in the brainwaves of other people in close proximity but also has measurable physiological effects on them (Childre and Martin, 2000).

Physical coherence is made possible through the conscious control of your heart beat through rhythmic breathing which in turn facilitates something called entrainment, a synchronization of multiple bodily systems. Dutch physicist, Christiaan Huygens coined the term entrainment in 1656 when he invented the pendulum clock. He noticed that even if he deliberately pushed some of the pendulums out of sync with the other clocks in the room they would sync up within a few minutes. He discovered that the driving force for this synchronization was always the largest pendulum in the room. Entrainment is now a well understood mathematical phenomena or fundamental principle of how complex systems with inherent vacillation work. Thus any complex system that has a number of centres or units that generate a repeating signal, pattern, beat or a rhythm will synchronize to the strongest and most powerful 'pendulum' in that system. The heart is the strongest and most powerful 'pendulum' or beat in the human system.

When we train our heart to generate a coherent signal (using the BREATHE skill below) instead of a chaotic signal it gives us greater control over our energy reserves and how we chose to utilize them. In addition physical coherence then creates a stable platform from which emotional and cognitive coherence can emerge which in turn can improve the quality of our thinking.

In order to access more energy and recuperate more quickly we must first gain a greater appreciation for what is currently adding to and draining our energy levels. The E-bank allows us to do that. Second we need to learn to control our physiology and generate a coherent signal from our heart and the easiest and quickest way to do that is through the BREATHE skill.

E-bank

The E-bank helps us become more aware of how our energy is currently used. There are certain events, situations, people, experiences or even thoughts that boost our energy reserves and others that deplete it. We need to know which is which so we can manage the energy inflow and outflow more effectively.

Draw a line down the middle of a clean sheet of paper. Write 'Deposits' at the top of the left-hand column and 'Withdrawals' at the top of the right-hand column. Take a few minutes to write down all the decisions, events, situations, people or thoughts that increase your energy (deposits) and everything that robs you of energy (withdrawals). For example deposits might include the ability to listen to your favourite music on the drive to work, or being able to take a walk at lunch time or you may enjoy working with a particular colleague – all these experiences or situations add energy and should be recorded on the positive side of your energy ledger. Withdrawals may include an unpleasant commute such as road works or a crowded train, it may be working with someone you don't like or having to manage an irritating employee – those types of situations consume your energy and should be recorded on the negative side of your energy ledger. Your deposits and withdrawals can be things from the past, present or even the future. When writing them down however take a few extra minutes to relive the positive deposits so you get an additional 'hit' of energy from their memory. For your withdrawals, don't relive them, simply write them down and let them go.

This simple exercise provides useful insight into what is currently adding to or diminishing your energy levels. Once you have completed your list look for patterns in the timings, the people, or the type of work or thoughts that rob you of energy and vitality. Is there a common denominator between the experiences or events that add to your energy levels? For example a director we worked with looked at the issues she highlighted on her E-bank and saw her propensity to focus on the past. She realized she was wasting a great deal of her energy stressing about whether or not she had made the correct decision and what she could or should have done differently. Her over emphasis on the past was therefore robbing her of the energy she needed to better manage her present and future. Alternatively you may notice that there are two or three people who provide a boost to your energy and a couple of others who trigger all the drains. You may also notice most of the boosts occur at a certain time of day or part of the week etc.

Now reflect on the whole list. What conclusion do you reach about how your energy ebbs and flows? Write this conclusion down and think about how you are going to change your account. Do you need to spend more time with the people who boost you? Do you need to grasp the nettle and deal with that person who creates a 'standing order drain' from your account?

Have you got sufficient boosts during the week? Have you dealt adequately with the drain? Are there any drains that could flip over into boosts? What action could you take to add more positive energy to your account or minimize the drains on your energy reserves?

Often bringing these things into conscious awareness is the first step to changing the dynamic. You may for example realize that taking the time to walk your dog in the evening or going for a run recharges your batteries but you rarely have time to do it. Knowing how much it nourishes you could help you to make the necessary changes to find the time. Alternatively you could realize that daily contact with a certain person in your team is depleting your energy reserves, which would be enough to prompt a re-shuffle so that person reports into someone else. Just because you find someone draining doesn't mean everyone else will! Finding a better match for the individual involved *and* the person they report to could improve the situation for everyone.

When protecting your energy levels watch out for self-criticism and self-judgement as they are particularly powerful and effective energy drains in your system. They act like direct debits going straight out of your account on a daily basis.

Also be aware that you can make deposits and withdrawals in other people's E-banks. Acknowledging someone's effort or simply being kind during a difficult time can add a huge energy boost to others, and also your kindness to others can boost your own reserves. Conversely moody silence, irritability and constant criticism can wipe out large chunks of energy.

The BREATHE skill

One of the main ways we lose energy is through incoherent or erratic breathing. Think about a time when you were angry, shocked or frustrated. You got some news from the outside world, that news was processed by your brain and your physiology automatically went into chaos. One of the first things to 'go' in a situation like this is your breathing. For example, if someone is frustrated their breathing tends to become a series of mini breath holds or what is known as 'glottic stops'. The same is true of panic, anxiety or anger – all of which involve a different type of disordered breathing.

When your breathing is chaotic the energy the heart generates also becomes chaotic. Such chaotic cardiac signals influence other bodily systems with the net result that you start to 'leak' significant amounts of energy. It is possible to see this happening live by watching your own heart rate variability (HRV) patterns during a normal working day (Figure 3.8).

FIGURE 3.8   Different ECG signals and heart rate variability patterns

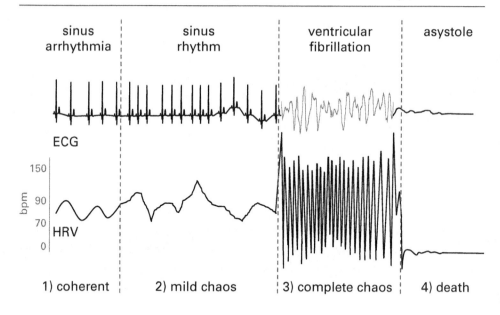

Contrary to popular belief your heart rate changes all the time. In fact your heart rate changes every single beat because the distance between one beat and the next is constantly changing (see Figure 3.9). It is this variability or perpetual change in the interval *between* each individual heart beat that is measured by HRV.

FIGURE 3.9   Heart rate variability

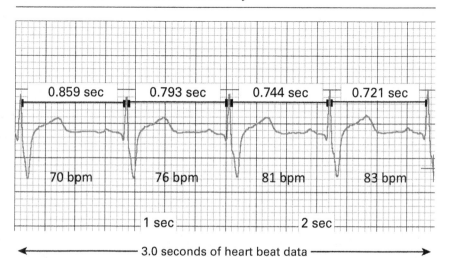

When we perceive a threat, usually subliminally, we will react and instantly create a chaotic, erratic HRV signal and leak energy. When we control our breathing we generate a coherent HRV signal, waste less energy, burn less 'fuel' and don't flood our body with excessive amounts of cortisol or other 'breakdown' hormones.

The BREATHE skill is designed to enable us to generate a rhythmic breathing pattern which increases the power output of the heart and drives other biological systems to synchronize with it. Effectively we are using our breath to consciously control the output of the body's power station. This may then trigger entrainment with all the other bodily systems, conserving energy, optimizing physiological efficiency and establishing the high performance 'flow' state.

The conscious control of breath is taught in many disciplines such as public speaking, playing a musical instrument, sport, yoga, martial arts and meditation. There are 12 aspects of breath that can be controlled and these are documented more fully in *Coherence: The secret science of brilliant leadership*. However the aspects that alter HRV the most and promote positive emotions are:

1 Rhythmicity – fixed ratio of in:out breath;

2 Smoothness – even flow rate in and out;

3 Location of attention – particularly focused in the heart area.

First we need to control our breathing so that there is a fixed ratio between the in breath and the out breath. So for example you may decide to breathe in for the count of 4 and then breathe out for the count of 6, then repeat this in a fixed rhythm. All that matters is that whatever ratio you choose you maintain that ratio consistently – 3 in 3 out, or 4 in 6 out, or 5 in 5 out.

The second step is the smoothness of the breath. Technically we could breathe rhythmically but in a staccato 'jumpy' fashion. Coherence requires a smooth rhythm. This means we need to ensure a fixed volume of air is going in and out of our lungs per second.

And finally the third step to coherent breathing is the location of attention. It's important to focus our attention on our heart, or the centre of our chest. Often when we are angry or upset and our HRV is chaotic our mind gets scrambled so focusing on breathing through the centre of our chest helps to get us out of our head and drop into the body. Plus shifting our attention to the area around the heart also makes it more likely that we will drift into a positive emotional state because the heart is where most human beings experience positive emotions. For example, we feel the sensation of love in the centre of our chest, courage is a quality of the *coeur* or heart,

FIGURE 3.10   Impact of correct breathing

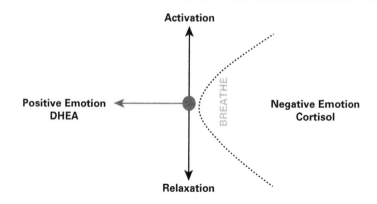

when we feel connected we often talk about having a 'heart to heart'. As a result consciously shifting our attention to the centre of our chest can facilitate the experience of a positive emotion which in turn moves us toward the positive side of the Performance Grid. Rhythmic and smooth, heart focused breathing helps to get us to the midpoint of the grid (see Figure 3.10). Ultimately we need to engage and use our emotions constructively to get over to the positive side and stay there but breathing creates the platform on which 4D Leadership is built.

When we breathe rhythmically and smoothly we create a coherent HRV signal. This then stabilizes our physiology and creates cardiac coherence – turning our HRV signal from chaos to coherence. Coherence allows us to establish a much higher degree of self-control in highly charged situations; prevents our brain from shutting down and enables us to think clearly and be more perceptive. Seeing the world from a coherent standpoint also gives us a better chance to actually change how we feel. In addition generating coherence enables us to stop the unconscious expenditure of our most precious resource – our energy.

The breathe technique is an acronym so it's particularly easy to remember:

- **B**reathe
- **R**hythmically
- **E**venly
- **A**nd
- **T**hrough the
- **H**eart
- **E**very day

Once you master this technique you are in control of the most powerful signal in the body – the HRV signal. Events, situations or other people won't be able to scramble your thinking. You will be less reactive and less likely to make off the cuff decisions that can lead to failure. Knowing that no one can scramble your physiology, because you now control it using the BREATHE skill, will help you feel much more confident and your confidence won't be affected by the external environment because you know how to remain coherent.

Although simple and really easy to do, this skill does require practice. Don't underestimate its power or how quickly the skill can desert you when you need it most. Start by practising alone with your eyes closed and work your way up to more challenging situations. Don't use it for the first time in a hostile shareholder meeting!

You should be able to generate a coherent pattern within a couple of minutes, especially if you use the CST biofeedback kit to guide you (see below). We have used this biofeedback kit with children as young as 3-years-old and people as old as 80 years with equal success. Practise whenever you remember. Use any 'dead' time you have such as waiting to board an airplane or travelling to and from work. If you find just 10 minutes a day to practise this BREATHE skill then rhythmic breathing and physical coherence will soon become your default pattern. When it does you will discover that you are much less reactive and you'll have much more energy. And perhaps most importantly you'll have the solid, stable foundation you need for vertical development across all the lines of development that facilitate 4D Leadership.

CardioSense Trainer™ (CST Mobile) biofeedback kit for iPhone and Android

To help leaders take control of their breathing and perfect the BREATHE skill we've developed some biofeedback software, the CardioSense Trainer™ (CST) which can be used on your computer, iPhone, tablet or Android device. The CST works with a variety of heart beat sensors to let you see what is happening to your HRV throughout the day. You can see how it works by visiting **http://www.complete-coherence.com/what-we-do/apps/**. The software has a breath pacer that you can follow to ensure that you can actually shift your HRV from a chaotic signal into a coherent signal. The CST is designed to help you train your breathing pattern to generate greater levels of coherence and develop the right breathing habits. Plus it allows you to test just how much control you can have over your heart beat and how different it can feel when you achieve coherence.

Although we've been measuring HRV in executives since 1996 it never ceases to amaze me how dramatic this information can be for people. I've literally seen grown men cry when they realize that they can in fact control their own response to pressure and see the immediate effect correct breathing can have on their system and how easy it is to generate coherence when they know how to do it. Suddenly, they have access to a skill that can change something they didn't think they *could* change.

Personal skills

Mastering the BREATHE technique allows us to bring stability and coherence to our physiology regardless of the external environment or situation. In effect it nullifies the chaos and pulls us from the negative side of the Performance Grid to the mid-point (see Figure 3.4 above). The next crucial step is to strengthen the 'emotion' line of development to enable us to live on the positive side of the Performance Grid. Without rhythmic breathing to stabilize the system the move from negative to positive can be harder to achieve.

Every line of development is important in the journey towards 4D Leadership. They all contribute to creating greater altitude across all three dimensions of doing, being and relating. But when it comes to vertical development in the subjective internal world of 'I' the 'emotional' line provides a quantum leap in leadership capability.

Traditionally the whole subject of emotions has been dismissed as irrelevant to business. We are taught to keep our emotions in check or leave them at the door when we come to work. The only trouble with that idea is – it is completely impossible! Emotion is simply e-motion or energy in motion. The physiological signalling between the different bodily systems is occurring in your body whether you are aware of it or not. So 'leaving emotion at the door' is no more possible than leaving your head at the door.

The real E-myth in business is not the one author Michael Gerber talks about (2001), it's the universal dismissal of (E)-motion in favour of intellect. Business is still predominantly run by men. Most cultures, East and West still condition their sons to be the strong, un-emotional protectors that need to provide for their family. From a very young age boys are told not to cry or show any outward displays of emotion. As a result what we instinctively assume about business is often nothing more than an expression of the out-dated and inaccurate assumption we hold about men and how men should behave. Emotion is seen as a demonstration of weakness preserved for the 'weaker sex' and is often cited as the whispered although invalid justification for why women shouldn't be in business in the first place.

If we ask a man what he feels, he will tell us what he thinks. For example, if we ask a male CEO to explain his feelings around a recent dismissal he will explain his decision. Often he won't even understand the question and even if he does he's so used to ignoring and suppressing his feelings that he doesn't have the self-awareness or language to answer. The challenge for men is to improve their low levels of emotional awareness.

For women, it's slightly different because they tend to be more aware of their emotions in the first place. The challenge for women is therefore not lack of awareness but insufficient control over their emotions. Women can sometimes be more easily affected by the energy because it's always bubbling away closer to the surface and this is a widely perceived 'female' issue, especially in business. As a result men and women continue this endless dance of misdiagnosis. When a woman loses control of her emotions this reinforces the male belief that emotions are unhelpful, which in turn causes men to suppress their emotions even more. When a man stifles his emotions, even in situations that warrant an emotional response this reinforces the female belief that men lack empathy and have little emotional literacy. Even worse some women, in an attempt to survive or succeed in the male-dominated C-suite often start suppressing their emotions in the exact same way men do. They can often become even worse examples devoid of warmth, empathy or sensitivity. We are not suggesting that men and women become 'bleeding hearts', crying at the drop of a hat or exploding into rage. Rather that they should become more emotionally intelligent and masterful of a much wider range of emotional states, that they can express in healthy ways enabling them to be effective leaders and engaging human beings.

Emotional and social intelligence is, in truth, not gender based. Emotional suppression is just as unhelpful as emotional excess or over expression. And contrary to popular opinion there are no emotional differences between men and women. Every human being – male or female has emotion. Everyone has physiology which is in a constant state of flux and this energy in motion creates signals that are being sent continuously and simultaneously around the body across multiple biological systems. The fundamentals of the physiological reaction to the world is therefore no different between the sexes; the triggers and intensity of emotions and the degree of self-regulation vary by person but the fact that emotions occur every second of every day is true of men and women. The only thing that *is* different is the weight of thousands of years of gender based expectations and social conditioning which can manifest as unhealthy biases inside and outside business. This in turn has created a mistaken belief that emotions are commercially irrelevant and do not belong in a modern business context.

Nothing could be further from the truth. Of course it is possible to be a powerful business figure with low levels of emotional and social intelligence (ESQ). But individuals who become more emotionally and socially intelligent will significantly improve results because emotional mastery:

1 **Improves clarity of thought and ability to develop.** Chaotic physiology and turbulent emotions cause the frontal lobes of the brain to shut down. So mastering your emotional state (not suppressing it) creates more coherent physiology which facilitates clear thinking and the ability to develop yourself, your ideas and your business.

2 **Improves the quality of decision making.** Neuroscience has demonstrated that the emotional system and logical system are inseparable. It is therefore impossible to exclude emotion from the decision making process. All decisions are actually driven by how we feel first and then we look for logical data to justify what feels right to us. So rather than trying to remove emotions from the decision making process (which is not even possible) we need to understand them and the information they bring us so we can make more effective decisions.

3 **Improves relationships at work.** Very often commercial success comes down to our ability to develop strong relationships with others – even if you don't like them. The quality of our relationship is often based on how we make others feel and our ability to empathically connect, which involves emotion.

4 **Facilitates effective management of change.** Change of any type is an emotional rollercoaster so being aware of the emotional dynamics and what to do about them can significantly improve our ability to successfully manage change.

5 **Increases leadership presence.** Emotion has a huge impact on leadership presence because other people can feel positive or negative energy radiating from the leader.

6 **Improves health and well-being.** There is now considerable scientific evidence that *mismanaged emotion* is the 'superhighway' to illness and unhappiness. (See *Coherence: The secret science of brilliant leadership* for more detail.)

7 **Increases enjoyment and quality of life.** In the end, our ability to enjoy our life comes down to our ability to access our emotions and feel

our feelings. That means understanding the emotional signals our body generates, consistently feeling them, correctly interpreting the information they provide and learning to act on that data effectively.

8   **Ignites meaning, significance and purpose.** Ultimately what we feel about a person, situation or accomplishment is what gives those things and life itself meaning.

9   **Improves motivation and resilience.** The word motivation comes from the Latin word 'movere' which means 'to move'. Emotion comes from the Latin word 'emovere' which means 'to move out'. So the core of motivation is emotion. Motivation is literally the process of changing the internal energy.

10   **Expands our sense of self.** To be authentic we must understand ourselves. Consciousness and emotions evolved together so when we collapse or suppress emotion we ignore an essential part of being human so a smaller, less authentic 'you' shows up. Conversely when we activate more positive emotions the bigger, more expansive, more creative, more authentic, smarter 'you' shows up and consciousness (and capability) expands too.

Clearly, it's essential that we take emotion seriously inside and outside business and the following tools and techniques can help:

- E-diary;
- Universe of Emotions app;
- MASTERY;
- MASTERY app;
- Positive Emotion Practice (PEP) and Landscaping;
- The SHIFT skill;
- Identify your purpose;
- The appreciation skill.

E-diary

The E-diary enhances emotional intelligence by cultivating an awareness of our emotions. After all we can't use emotions constructively or do something about them if we have no awareness of our inner emotional states and patterns.

Human beings cluster different emotional states in the same way most of us cluster our music. Some people love classical and may only ever listen to classical. Others may enjoy rap or dance music and some people may enjoy a wide eclectic mix. The most important initial observation around emotion is whether we tend to cluster around positive or negative emotions. And seeing as most of us don't really know what emotions we feel on a daily basis expanding our emotional intelligence is the starting point.

This can be achieved very easily and relatively quickly by keeping an emotions diary (E-diary) to keep track of exactly what emotions you feel over the course of the day, week and month. Simply insert a column on the left- or right-hand side of your existing diary or meeting note pad and document any emotional states you notice during the meeting. At the end of the day review your notes and notice how many of your feelings were positive and how many were negative. If you don't keep meeting notes or have a diary then set your watch or phone to beep at a few different times throughout the day and record your emotions in your phone.

Unfortunately, most people are much more aware of their negative emotions than they are of their positive ones. It's likely therefore that your initial observations may appear to be weighted toward the negative. Most executives who complete this exercise only recognize, on average, around 12 different emotions that they feel on a regular basis (Table 3.1).

TABLE 3.1   Most commonly reported emotions in business

	Commonest positive emotions	Commonest negative emotions
1	Focused	Tired
2	Determined	Worried
3	Relaxed	Anxious
4	Happy	Frustrated
5	Fine	Stressed
6	OK	Annoyed
7	Content	Irritated
8	Curious	Angry
9	Good	Confused
10	Excited	Sad
11	Interested	Bored
12	Pleased	Disappointed

And most of the time these 12 come from a stock of about 20–25 emotions. Twelve is a pretty impoverished emotional palette when we know that there are actually 34,000 distinguishable feelings (Goleman and Dalai Lama, 2004). Knowing just 12 distinguishable emotions is the equivalent of your actual palette barely being able to tell the difference between sucking a lemon and eating chocolate.

Taking the time to notice the emotions you feel so that you can bring them into conscious awareness is the first step to gaining control over your internal emotions. After all you can't change or utilize something if you aren't aware of it.

Universe of Emotions app

To make this process even easier we have released an app for use on people's phones or tablets called 'The Universe of Emotions' (Complete Coherence, 2015a). The app enables people to identify which emotion they are feeling. The app equates feelings to planets and prompts you to answer the question, 'which planet are you on?' It offers you 2,000 different emotions and shows which 'galaxy' and which 'solar system' each emotion exists in. You can see what the nearest planets are to your current emotional state, in case you want to change how you feel. You can create an audit trail of which planets or emotions you have experienced in any one day, week or month. You can share this data with whoever you want via social media. You can see where your colleagues tend to 'live' and compare that to your own emotional gravity map.

The Universe of Emotions app can be downloaded for £0.99 from our website: **http://www.complete-coherence.com/universeofemotions/**. It is also available from Google Play and iTunes.

MASTERY

The MASTERY skill is used to step change your level of emotional self-regulation because just being aware of the feeling is not enough to change it. We need to be able to distinguish between different (and similar) emotions and accurately label each one.

Think of this technique like a wine appreciation course. Wine experts have developed very sophisticated palettes that can easily differentiate between a shiraz and a malbec. Often they can tell where the wine was made, what year it was made and even the type of soil the grapes were grown in. But that level of sophistication required training and practice. The same is true of emotions. Being able to differentiate and discriminate between a range of emotions allows us to appreciate how each emotion feels in our body. This can, in turn, make it easier for us to access that emotion and re-create it when needed. Plus the purpose of emotion is to provoke action and every emotion is designed to provoke a different action. If we are unfamiliar with our emotions and tend just to cluster them as positive or negative then the action that results is often blunt, clumsy and ineffective. We need to be able to differentiate between the signals we receive so we can interpret their meaning more accurately and therefore make better choices more often.

MASTERY develops our emotional repertoire and ability to self-regulate so we can tell the difference between the emotional data we are privy to. To achieve MASTERY:

1 Stop what you are doing and take a moment to reflect on the energy that exists in your body right now.

2 If you are not feeling a distinct emotion, try triggering an emotion through the use of music, a memory or even a picture.

3 Once you can start to feel the energy try and identify the emotion, give it a name or label and write that word down.

4 It doesn't really matter what you call the emotion at this stage, you are simply trying to familiarize yourself with the energy of that particular state.

5 Explore the features of the emotion within your body. How does the energy feel? Follow the structure in Table 3.2 and use the worksheet to capture some of the descriptive features of that emotion. Write down as many 'basic features' as you can. There are no right answers so just document the features that you can feel.

6 Having captured the basic features write down some descriptions on the movement features. Describe how the emotion moves through your body. Does it stop at your skin or does it radiate off your body? How does it move through you and how does it radiate?

7 Finally does the emotion have any special features that bring it alive?

8 Make a note of any insights that may have surfaced during the MASTERY process.

TABLE 3.2 MASTERY structure

Emotion map for...

Type	Guide	Your description
Basic features	Location	
	Size	
	Shape	
	Sound	
	Temperature	
	Colour	
	Intensity (0–10)	
Movement features	How it moves through your body	
	How it moves off the body	
Special features		

I've been using this process with seasoned and occasionally sceptical business leaders and senior executives for many years. Most find it a bit weird to start with, not least because emotion had long been considered something to avoid in business. Using a little humour I can usually manage to get them to try it and although they may start off thinking emotion don't have a colour, shape or location they soon discover that it does! Once they run through the MASTERY process they are usually surprised and fascinated to realize that their feelings can be objictified in this way. This can be really interesting because while some emotions may be objictified in a similar way, using similar colours, they are always uniquely experienced. Even if five executives experience joy, their objectification may have the same feel but the details are almost always unique.

When you use the MASTERY skill repeatedly it allows you to build your understanding of the emotions you experience the most and makes it easier for you to differentiate between similar emotions for greater accuracy. And perhaps more importantly you can consciously build up a repertoire of positive emotions you can call on to improve the outcome and how you feel.

MASTERY app

To make this process even easier we have released an app for use on people's phones or tablets called 'MASTERY' (Complete Coherence, 2015b). This app works alongside the Universe of Emotions app. The MASTERY app enables people to draw, colour and keep notes on the emotions they experience in detail and share them and compare them with other people's descriptions of that same emotion. The more we are able to objectify what are normally subjective experiences the greater control we can achieve over our emotions. Until we can effectively objectify our feeling states they have 'got us', we are 'subject' to them. We have no sovereignty. When we become proficient at objectifying our emotions we take control, we have now turned the tables on our emotions and we have 'got them'. We are in the position of being able to control how we feel. This is a game changer. Most human beings simply cannot control their own emotions. For most people emotions are things that happen 'to' them. Once we have mastered our emotions we never have to feel anything we don't want to feel again – ever!

The Mastery app can be downloaded from Google Play, iTunes or our website – **http://www.complete-coherence.com/what-we-do/apps/**.

Positive Emotion Practice (PEP) and Landscaping

The PEP and landscaping tools help to further improve an individual's emotional self-management. All the previous techniques to facilitate vertical development in the dimension of 'I' require time and effort through repetition and practice. This can be an additional challenge for leaders who are already beyond busy. PEP and landscaping were therefore developed to help leaders 'practise without actually practising'. The idea is that we practise by inserting the rehearsal of positive emotions into our existing routines or habits.

PEP works by acknowledging that most of our lives are made up of hundreds of unconscious daily habits or rituals. These rituals largely exist at the various 'transition points' that occur as we move from one activity to another. So for example most of us have a 'getting up ritual' that smoothes the transition from being horizontal to being upright. Similarly we may have a specific breakfast ritual that enables us to transition from lower energy sleepy state to a higher energy 'refuelled' state. We will have various 'going to work' rituals. In fact there are hundreds of rituals throughout our day that we can plug into.

If you identify some rituals that you already engage in then you can enhance them by adding some Positive Emotion Practice (PEP) as part of the ritual. The best rituals are the simplest and most frequent and the best PEPs are emotions that relate directly to the ritual. For example, I was coaching the Creative Director of a children's TV company some years ago and she had a great idea for a PEP – opening a door. It was perfect and really simple. Every time she went through a door – up to 50 times a day – she was going to practise the feeling of excited anticipation. It was brilliant and as she pointed out, 'In truth I never know what I will find the other side of that door – it may be something great or it may be something disastrous, so for a few seconds I get to feel that frisson of excited anticipation'. So after a few days of rehearsing the feeling of 'excited anticipation' when she went through every door this executive really had a sophisticated idea of what it felt like to experience 'excited anticipation'. As a result she could then turn this emotion on whenever she wanted or whenever it was appropriate or going to help her or others.

Similarly when I was coaching a teacher he also came up with a very useful PEP. He said he had noticed that when he was driving, every time he was stopped by a red traffic light he was inadvertently rehearsing frustration because he had to wait. Once he noticed this he decided to PEP up the ritual of slowing down and stopping at a red light with 'patience'. Once the light turned red he deliberately induced the feeling of patience in his system.

In fact he had started to enjoy the 1–2 minutes of patience that he hoped the traffic light would turn red as he approached so he could enjoy a moment of patience.

By inserting a few minutes or even a few seconds of positive emotion practice into your existing rituals you make the space for the necessary rehearsal. I was working with one senior executive who was sceptical to put it mildly but he identified his 'going to work' ritual and promised to give it a go. Instead of putting the radio on as he drove to work, for the first five minutes of his 30 minute journey he listened to his favourite CD. While listening to his favourite music he rehearsed the feeling of exhilaration and sang along at the top of his voice! After five minutes he put the radio on as normal. He was genuinely shocked at how this tiny little change to his morning ritual resulted in him arriving at work feeling much more energized and optimistic which in turn had a positive impact on his day and the people around him.

Identify your existing rituals from getting up to leaving a meeting to unwinding after a long day and enhance them by rehearsing an emotion for 30 seconds to a few minutes. Ultimately you don't need any additional time to set aside for specific practice – life becomes practice.

Landscaping

The other way to embed emotional self-regulation practice into your life is to build practice time into your week around events or situations in your diary that would benefit from that positive emotional energy. Known as 'landscaping' it just ensures that you (a) practise the skill and (b) benefit from the practice every time you practise. If for example you have a very important client pitch or are presenting to the shareholder meeting then schedule in 5–10 minutes before those events to practise a specific emotion that is helpful to that specific event. In this case, for example, you might want to practise 'resolute' or 'energized' or whatever is most appropriate given what you know about the people you are going to meet and what you would like to project.

This might sound silly and you might think, 'I've got a really important meeting to attend, I don't have time to waste practising a positive emotion'. But consider Amy Cuddy's powerful TED talk on body language (2012). Cuddy, a social psychologist, reminds us that we make sweeping generalizations and assumptions based on nothing more than initial impression. A researcher at Tufts University, Nalini Ambady, demonstrated that a doctor's likelihood of being sued was directly linked to his likeability and the assumption was made non-verbally within 30 seconds. Princeton researcher Alex Todorov has shown that our judgement of political candidates' faces in just one second predict 70 per cent of US Senate and gubernatorial race outcomes.

Cuddy goes on to explain the two-minute 'life hack' for improving the odds of a meeting, interview or high pressure situation going well – engage in a high power pose for two minutes before the event. There are a few high power poses including standing like a super-hero with your legs hip distance apart with your hands on your hips or sitting with your feet up on a desk and your hands clasped behind your head. All high power poses expand the physical space you take up with your body. Low power poses do the opposite so they reduce the physical space you take up with your body and they include hunching your shoulders, looking down and basically anything that makes you smaller.

Cuddy, along with her main collaborator Dana Carney from Berkeley, wanted to know 'Can you fake it till you make it?' To test the theory a group of volunteers were told to spit into a vial and their baseline testosterone (confidence hormone) and cortisol (stress hormone) levels were measured. Half the group were then told to engage in certain poses. The volunteers were not told anything about the poses but one group were engaged in high power poses and the other in low power poses. Then they were immediately tested again. What's remarkable is that with just two minutes' practice their physiology had changed. The high power pose group experienced a 20 per cent increase in testosterone and a 25 per cent reduction of cortisol, whereas the low power pose group experienced a 10 per cent decrease in testosterone and a 15 per cent increase in cortisol levels.

Would a conscious increase in confidence, assertiveness and positivity be useful in an important Board meeting or critical negotiation? Absolutely it would and if you can get that from a two-minute hack by shifting your body shape imagine what you can achieve if you also consciously practise emotional self-regulation so you choose what emotion to feel before you even enter the room.

Through landscaping you can build up your practice time without it feeling like practice and ensuring that you get the most real world benefit from that practice at the same time. Remember this is not something you do in the meeting or important negotiation, it's a process of self-direction *before* the big event that puts you in the best possible frame of mind for a positive, constructive outcome.

Landscaping is a tool that acknowledges that leaders are already busy while encouraging us to incorporate the practice into our normal business day rather than some hypothetical situation. That way we can experience the benefits of emotional self-regulation in situations that really matter while fitting shorter practice sessions around situations and events that are less important. I have taught this skill to a number of Olympic athletes to allow them to become much more conscious of what they are rehearsing in the crucial couple of minutes before the start of a race. If an athlete consciously engages a more positive energy state they will get closer to their personal best whereas if they do not consciously manage their internal state they may be on the start line feeling intimidated or nervous. It is a complete myth to say 'that it is good to be nervous before the race starts because if you are not nervous you will not perform well'. Nervousness, or negative arousal, will inhibit performance. Excitement or positive arousal will improve results. So it is vital to make the distinction and ensure that you are in the right state before you start 'performing' whether you are an Olympian or a CEO.

The SHIFT skill

Once you have built a larger emotional repertoire and you are better equipped to live or experience life from whatever 'planet' you choose then a second skill becomes vital to develop. That skill is the ability to change the planet you are on whenever you want. As a leader it's critically important to be in the right frame of mind when we are dealing with challenges, creating strategy and working with others. And being in the right frame of mind requires you to be in the right emotional state. This is ultimately what determines the quality of thinking and yet for the most part it's left to chance.

The SHIFT skill is a technique that shows us how to consciously move from a negative emotion to a positive emotion at will. This can be incredibly helpful in business, especially once we've mastered a range of positive emotions to move into.

In order to test this skill, try the following process: First describe an area in your life or work that is currently challenging you. Write down the associated thoughts, feelings and behaviours around the challenge. Then work through the SHIFT process. SHIFT is an acronym:

Stop everything that you are doing and simply shift your attention to your ...

Heart, breathe through the centre of your chest and

Induce a positive emotion.

Feel it in your body, enjoy how it moves through your body for a good 40 seconds or so and allow it to ...

Turn the brain back on. Notice your insights and write them at the bottom of the page.

If you think about it many of the steps of this process have already stood the test of time and we use most of this process when we try to solve problems. Normally when we are faced with a difficult situation or thorny decision we will stew on it for a while. Eventually we'll decide to do something different because we are not making any headway. So we may decide to go outside for a walk, have a coffee break or simply sleep on it (ie the first step is that we 'Stop' what we are doing). If this break from the challenge induces (I) a positive emotion then we can come up with new ideas. If the coffee makes us feel good, or calling a friend diffuses our tension or the sleep makes us feel more rested then the technique will work. The critical thing here is that we don't just induce a positive emotion but we really feel the feeling (F). The stronger we feel the positive nature of the emotion the better the technique works. Feeling the positive energy turns (T) our brain back on and we may even have a 'light-bulb' moment. We now have far greater access to our cognitive capabilities and new thoughts and perspectives flood in. As a result we go back to our desk with the solution and press on. All this occurred because we inadvertently shifted our emotional state from a negative state to a positive state.

The problem is that we can't always go for a drive and nip out of the office for a coffee or a chat. Nevertheless we still need to get ourselves into a more constructive state of mind and do what needs to get done.

And that's where the 'H' in SHIFT comes in. If you breathe smoothly and rhythmically while focusing on your heart in the way I explained in the BREATHE skill you rely only on yourself. And you can do this anytime, anywhere. Remember your heart is the location of most of your positive emotions so paying attention to the centre of your chest will help to induce a positive emotion.

The SHIFT skill allows you to move from a negative emotion to any one of the positive emotions that you've mastered through the emotional MASTERY skill. Once you have embodied the new positive state and held on to it for 30 seconds you will then get access to new insights. After just 30 seconds you can then go back to the challenge you originally wrote down and write down any new ideas or insights that emerge. You will be amazed at how often your perspective changes as a result of this process and ideas flow.

Where emotional MASTERY adds to your collection of more positive emotions the SHIFT skill allows you to consciously move into one of those emotions rather than just hoping it shows up. By taking back conscious control over what and how you feel you are no longer at the mercy of external events, situations or people.

Identifying your purpose

There is no doubt that being a leader in the modern business world can be exhausting. The increasing complexity, pressure and rate of change can take its toll on the physical well-being of many leaders. It is therefore hardly surprising that many senior executives become quite motivated by money in an effort to build a significant pension pot in case their career comes to an abrupt end through C-suite politics or personal fatigue. In the VUCA environment maintaining motivation can be a struggle particularly during tough market conditions.

One of the most powerful ways you can step change your desire and ability to keep yourself going, especially in tough times is to identify 'Why' you do what you do. Discovering your own personal purpose can be a game changer for motivation and happiness. When what we 'do' all day in the external observable world of 'IT' brings us joy and fulfilment because it's aligned to our personal purpose the work is considerably easier than if we are simply 'going through the motions'. This clarity of purpose and direction also speeds up and simplifies decision making because every course of action is either taking us closer to that purpose or further away from it. When we know where we are going it's much easier to stay on track and make the right decisions without the stress.

Clay Christensen, the Kim B Clark Professor at Harvard Business School, suggests that often, 'We pick our jobs for the wrong reasons and then we settle for them. We begin to accept that it's not realistic to do something we truly love for a living. Too many of us who start down the path to compromise will never make it back. Considering the fact that you'll likely spend more of your waking hours at your job than in any other part of your life, it's a compromise that will always eat away at you' (Christensen, Allworth and Dillon, 2012).

Uncovering your life purpose is a subtle process. For most people the real reason for their existence is obscure. Most people know what they do and how they do it, but why they do it is often a mystery. Most senior executives just ended up in the C-suite through persistent effort, hard work, skill and some degree of career management. But when you ask them 'What is the point of you? Why do you do this particular job and not some other kind of job?', most of them can't give you a good answer. Despite what the newspapers say about 'fat cat salaries' I have yet to meet a leader whose purpose was 'I make money'. Money is a by-product of what you do, it is not why you do it. This is one of the reasons why money is a relatively poor motivator. In the same way most people's reason for their personal existence is not 'to be a good husband and father/wife and mother', that is more to do with the purpose of being a man or a woman. We are all here for a unique reason and uncovering that reason takes careful reflection and skilful guidance and it is neither money nor procreation.

One of the reasons many executives have a 'mid-life crisis' is that they were not clear about their personal purpose in the first place. The good news is there is a reason; a meaning for your existence and it can be uncovered. Your life is littered with clues that can help you clarify your personal purpose.

Your talents are almost always something that you yearn to do, learned to do easily, love to do or that bring fulfilment and that you do with ease. Often it is this last characteristic that can throw you off the scent – because you probably use your talents effortlessly you may wrongly assume that it's nothing special, not difficult or that everyone can do it. Actually it is often perceived as special and difficult by everyone other than you. A skilled developmental coach can bring what is unconscious into your awareness, and help you uncover your core purpose, which is about you and not the people around you.

As Steve Jobs so rightly pointed out, 'The only way to be truly satisfied is to do what you believe is great work. And the only way to do great work is to love what you do. If you haven't found it yet, keep looking. Don't settle' (Christensen, Allworth and Dillon, 2012). Joseph Campbell, the great scholar of myth and mythology also suggests that the route to fulfilment and happiness is to 'follow your bliss'. Adding, 'If you follow your bliss, you put yourself on a kind of track that has been there all the while, waiting for you, and the life that you ought to be living is the one you are living.'

The appreciation skill

One of the most critical elements to driving behavioural change in the 'IT' dimension is cultivating a belief that change is even possible in the 'I' dimension. This can be achieved, in part, by practising the art of appreciation so as to foster an optimistic outlook. When we appreciate everything – the good days and the bad – and convert every experience into a development experience then we open ourselves up to life and we can cultivate our wisdom much more quickly.

The journey toward 4D Leadership is not always easy and vertical development means going beyond the traditional learning approach. This can be challenging enough but it is especially challenging for adults because as we grow up we move from curious, optimistic and eager children absorbing new knowledge like a sponge to less optimistic, cynical adults who often dislike learning because it highlights what we don't know instead of what we do know.

This less open disposition means that most adults are poor learners. Too many of us leave school and university and think, 'That's it – job done, I've completed my education'. We assume that aside from a few skills picked up on the job our learning days are behind us. But if we are to survive and prosper in the VUCA world such abdication is inadequate and will keep us locked in out-dated and unhelpful thinking. Or as William James put it, 'A great many people think they are thinking when they are merely rearranging their prejudices.' If we want to continually add value and ensure we are not simply rearranging our prejudices then we must embrace life-long learning and ongoing vertical development.

One way to transform your ability to learn and therefore develop is to learn how to appreciate yourself, others and life in general. The rule of thumb is that we must first learn to appreciate before we can truly appreciate what we learn.

Of all the thousands of emotions available to us appreciation is one of the most powerful because it allows us to wake up every morning and see the world anew. The appreciation skill is therefore about learning how to cultivate the state of appreciation as a default emotion which can massively enhance your ability to impact others and drive results.

The first part of the appreciation skill is learning how to appreciate ourselves. Often we are our own worst enemy – our destructive self-talk and self-criticism can rob us of vital energy and limit growth and opportunity.

To make this exercise easier think about what you appreciate about yourself across six distinct areas:

- Mentally – What do you appreciate about your mental abilities?

- Emotionally – What do you appreciate about yourself emotionally?

- Physically – What physical attributes or abilities do you appreciate about yourself?

- Socially – What do you appreciate about your social skills and how you interact with others?

- Professionally – What do you appreciate about your professional skills and capacity?

- Spiritually – What do you appreciate about your sense of meaning, ethics or morals?

Think of this as a private stock take of the things you appreciate about yourself and are grateful for. Convert the resulting list to bullet points and record them on a credit card sized piece of paper. You could even laminate it if you were feeling particularly creative. If anyone finds it, it won't make any sense to them but you will see it every day and be reminded of your best qualities.

The idea is that even if you've had a really bad day you can take a moment to look at your list as you go home at night and you can remind yourself that you're still 'creative' or 'kind'. What you appreciate about yourself doesn't change with the ups and downs of life. You don't stop being thoughtful, you may get irritated at times but that doesn't mean you are no longer a thoughtful person. You might have behaved like an idiot shouting at your partner but you can still appreciate that you are still an 'energetic and loyal' person deep down. You may have used your 'quick wit' in an unhelpful and hurtful way but you didn't stop *being* quick witted. And, you can still appreciate that quality.

Psychologist Sonja Lyubomirsky from the University of California at Riverside found that people who took the time to count their blessings, even just once a week, significantly increased their overall satisfaction with life (Lyubomirsky, 2007). Psychologist Robert Emmons from the Davis campus of the same University also found that gratitude (which is in the same 'galaxy' as appreciation in the *Universe of Emotions*) improved physical health, increased energy levels and for patients with neuromuscular disease, relieved pain and fatigue. Emmons added, 'The ones who benefited most tended to elaborate more and have a wider span of things they're grateful for' (Wallis, 2004).

The reason this skill is so important and so powerful is because people spend vast amounts of time in self-judgement and self-criticism. Personally directed negative emotions do not facilitate clear and creative thinking. Plus self-judgement and self-criticism are the hallmark of mismanaged emotions and are extremely toxic to our health and happiness. Many of us have a natural drive to succeed but when that spills over into excessive concern about our own performance it can and does contribute to ill-health. One 10-year study of over 10,000 managers and professionals suggested that those characterized as 'perfectionists' were 75 per cent more likely to have health issues including cardiovascular problems (Rosch, 1995).

We simply must learn to appreciate what we *are* instead of berating ourselves over what we *are not*. Forgiveness is not something we give to others; it's a gift we give to ourselves. When we truly forgive someone (and ourselves) we release the unhelpful energy or emotional charge from our body.

As a result that negative energy no longer wreaks havoc with our health, thinking or performance. We don't forgive someone to let *them* off the hook – we forgive them to let ourselves off the hook (Dowrick, 1997).

If we learn to appreciate then we are much more likely to be able to appreciate what we learn. If we can appreciate what we learn then we are much more likely to be able to change our behaviour. We see other options, we feel good about ourselves and this optimism enables us to make different choices.

Action steps

For most people the interior work necessary to facilitate vertical development in the 'I' dimension is unusual. And it certainly doesn't appear in leadership books. In order to really unpack performance and genuinely elevate executives to 4D leaders we need to explore a number of scientific discoveries from all the levels of the human system; including the fields of medicine, cardiology, neurophysiology, evolutionary biology, quantum physics, signal processing and systems theory as well as organizational performance, sports psychology and emotional intelligence. What's perhaps surprising is that what we've covered is largely agreed upon facts from these disparate fields. Unfortunately they are usually only known in academia or reported in obscure medical or scientific journals. Very few of these key insights have made it into mainstream discussion and almost none are taught in business school or published in business literature. And yet when we integrate these insights they lead us to an exciting conclusion about ourselves – we *can* be brilliant every single day. We can regain the energy level we enjoyed 10 years ago, we can be considerably smarter, happier and healthier. We can be more successful, have much better relationships and have a greater impact on our business, our society and the world. But only if we embrace the world of 'being' with the same commitment and gusto we've already applied to the world of 'doing'.

Below are some suggested action steps that you can take to help you extract the maximum value from the 'I' dimension:

1 Develop the ability to control your physiology through the BREATHE skill, to ensure that your brain doesn't shut down under pressure.

2 Identify the origins of the boosts and drains to your energy levels using the E-bank and proactively manage them to ensure you have boundless energy every day. (The E-bank app is available from complete-coherence.com, Google Play and the App Store.)

3 Recognize that emotions play a vital and positive role in business and are central to decision making as well as creating competitive advantage. Use the Universe of Emotions app to significantly expand your emotional literacy and keep track of which emotional planet you tend to operate from. (The Universe of Emotions app is available from complete-coherence.com, Google Play and the App Store.)

4 Practise the MASTERY skill and use the MASTERY app to step change your ability to access whatever emotion you need to drive high levels of performance in any situation. (The MASTERY app is available from complete-coherence.com, Google Play and the App Store.)

5 Use PEP and landscaping to ensure you're able to turn on the right emotion in the right situation and ensure that emotional regulation is baked into your daily routine.

6 Practise the SHIFT skill to ensure you don't get stuck on any unhelpful 'emotional planet', and you have the emotional flexibility to engage any emotion on demand.

7 Foster an optimistic outlook by practising the art of appreciation. Appreciate the people, situations and events in your life – even the tough ones. Everything can be turned into a development opportunity if you shift how you think and feel about it.

8 Work with a developmental coach to identify your purpose and clarify how to align your daily activity in the 'IT' dimension to that purpose for improved productivity, happiness and well-being.

The untapped potential of adult maturity

04

There are literally thousands of books on leadership. Why? Because if you include the word 'leadership' in the title of the book it's more likely to sell. But most of these books have nothing to do with leadership. Referred to amusingly as 'Leadership Tourette Syndrome' (LTS) writers, executives and consultants will blurt out statements on leadership constantly but often don't have a clear definition of what it actually means (Logan, 2011). Consultants often diagnose 'leadership' as the problem and then offer a narrow set of programmes, plans or processes as the 'fix'. It's not that leadership is not the issue. As John Kotter pointed out most organizations are over-managed and under-led (Kotter and Heskett, 1992). Rather, the problem is our definition of leadership is usually far too limited.

Some commentators are scathing about the proclamations of Covey, Chopra, Goldsmith, Maxwell, Tracy and other leadership authors, claiming that their LTS and insights from religion, self-help, personal transformation, psychoanalysis, and neuroscience are at best 'fringe' (Logan, 2011). Others, having dismissed the views of their peers, make the very same mistake they criticized their peers for and offer an equally narrow, albeit different, range of solutions as a substitute. Usually the critics' answer is to identify a single cause such as culture (Logan, King and Fischer-Wright, 2008), a lack of emotional courage (Bregman, 2013) or leadership behaviour as the real problem. But the real problem is none of these – it's that we have a partial understanding of what leadership actually is and therefore we can only ever implement a partial answer. This chapter seeks to expand our definition by looking at leadership from the perspective of adult development and maturity. When we understand the evolution of adult maturity a great many of the challenges we face in leadership are explained and a proven path through becomes clear.

We have argued here that there are four dimensions to leadership. It is not just about behaviour and what leaders 'do'. It is not just about emotional courage and how leaders show up – their internal 'being'. And it certainly isn't just about culture and how leaders 'relate' to others. It is about all of these three dimensions and even more importantly it's about the development of a compatible degree of altitude in all three dimensions. This altitude provides the fourth dimension. Leaders need to develop simultaneously in the dimensions of doing, being and relating.

We have already explored some of the developmental skills that can increase the altitude of 'being'. In this chapter we want to unpack, in more detail, one specific line of internal development – namely ego, identity or 'Self'. The reasons for focusing on this line in particular are that it has a disproportionate effect on performance, it is widely misunderstood and aspects of ego are frequently mentioned in the leadership literature. As mentioned in Chapter 3 leaders are often encouraged to 'be authentic' or 'just be yourself'.

Of course, it's sound advice. The only problem is that most of us have done virtually no detailed study into the nature of our 'Self'. So most of us don't really know who we are outside of what we do and what we own. We don't really know what makes us tick and we don't understand ourselves to any great extent other than a few superficial 'likes', 'dislikes' or maybe a few preferences and style choices. We have not studied the phenomena of ego, identity or Self. We have not thought deeply about how the Self is constructed or deconstructed or how it can change, evolve or develop. As a result we will often believe that how we are right now is how we have always been and will always be. So if we don't know who we really are, what our core purpose is and what determines how we show up in the world then how can we possibly be 'authentic'?

Developing authenticity is vital for effective leadership but many leaders find the exploration of their inner world, the 'I' dimension, uncomfortable, challenging, unnecessary or even irrelevant. It's just not something most executives consider important and it's certainly not a priority when they are completely consumed in the external objective dimension of 'doing'. When we believe that 'doing' is everything we often fail to appreciate that the ability to change how we are 'being' is just as critical to commercial success as the actions we take *and* has an immeasurable impact on the actions we take in the first place. There is a widespread lack of recognition of the profound connection between the two dimensions of 'being' and 'doing' and how much the former influences the latter. Even when we walk executives through the logic and they fully acknowledge that if they are angry, depressed or upset for example their ability to 'do' the job is significantly impaired, most will still immediately revert back to the world of 'doing'. They also realize that when they are positive, optimistic and inspired who they are as a human being rubs off on others and makes the doing easier and usually much more enjoyable. However, they don't appreciate that the outcome – either good or bad – largely depends on how they show up and they certainly don't reflect on how they show up because it's not a spontaneous or natural part of an executive's thought process.

We really need to embrace the fact that the outcome of any event or situation is profoundly enhanced or polluted by who we show up as and who we show up as is largely determined by our identity or who we believe our 'Self' to be. So let's explore the issue of 'Self' and how it matures, or doesn't, over time. Our ability to recognize ego maturity as a commercially critical phenomenon and take conscious steps to increase verticality in this line of development can disproportionately improve our lives and the returns we achieve. It can increase our ability to drive transformation in our business because it allows us to proactively break down 'silo' structures, change behaviour, increase our ability to manage complexity and increase our ability to facilitate stakeholder collaboration and communication. It also increases our perspective, makes us less reactive, more perceptive and emotionally aware. We tend not to get so worked up about the ups and downs of business life which can alleviate stress and fatigue and improve our well-being and quality of life.

That said, ego maturity can be a controversial topic to discuss in the C-suite and one that can be met with hostility and resentment (a fact that only serves to illustrate the dire need for us to address this internal line of development). No one is going to enjoy having their maturity questioned and yet we must all have our maturity questioned, or at least be prepared to explore the issue, if we are to achieve altitude in this critical line. The key is to consider maturity as simply a part of our identity that can, and should, evolve as we develop our leadership capability.

Identity and the disease of meaning

For most of us, our identity is almost exclusively wrapped up in what we do. When asked, 'So who are you?', most people will state their name followed almost immediately by what they do – 'I'm a lawyer', 'I'm an accountant' or 'I'm a teacher'. But what we do is not who we are. Most people don't or can't make the distinction because if they are not a lawyer, accountant or teacher then who are they?

If we disallow a job title, then the next response is usually a series of personal qualities. But such a description is usually plucked out of thin air rather than a result of careful reflection on the nature of 'Self'. If you ask slightly different questions – 'why should I be led by you?' or 'what leadership qualities do you have that can create followership in others?' – most executives would struggle to provide a well thought out answer that characterizes who they are and also matches what their closest friends would recognize.

It's easy to reject such explorations as commercially irrelevant, touchy-feely nonsense that has nothing to do with generating profits or quarterly returns. However we would do well to consider the words of Jim Clifton, CEO of Gallup, who, following the Gallup World Poll states, 'What the whole world wants is a good job. Humans used to desire love, money, food, shelter, safety, peace, and freedom more than anything else. The last 30 years have changed us. Now people want to have a good job, and they want their children to have a good job. This changes everything for world leaders. Everything they do, from waging war to building societies, will need to be carried out within the new context of the need for a good job.' Drawn from deep advanced analysis from Gallup's US and World Polls, macroeconomic data on job creation and trends in world economics, what people want in their lives is meaningful work (Clifton, 2007, 2011). And yet, if we don't know who we are, why we exist and what our lives are really about how can we identify and engage in meaningful work? And who says that what we are doing is or is not meaningful? Meaning is a personal journey of exploration. If we have never asked the hard questions about who we are then we are probably just following a set of rules about how to live our lives that have been imprinted on our brain by someone else without our awareness or agreement.

We are all conditioned to see the world in a certain way, to interpret reality according to a set of rules. Our parents or care givers train us to give certain events or sensations 'signal importance', ie they teach us what matters and what we should ignore. And this conditioning occurs before we are really aware that it's happening or our brain is fully developed. None of us can escape the conditioning process although the content of the conditioning depends on our birth conditions, our family context, our culture and when and where we are born. That said, we can become aware of all the ways we have been trained to interpret the world around us and decide whether we want to stick with those rules, beliefs, values and ways of viewing the world or change them. If we don't even appreciate that these deeply embedded structures, or 'codes of the mind' exist then how can we possibly change them?

Plus, our minds are not just conditioned to interpret reality in a certain way but also to believe certain 'facts' about ourselves to be true, regardless of whether they are or not. If parents constantly tell their child that they are clumsy or 'not good enough' the child will eventually believe they are clumsy or 'not good enough' and their self-confidence can be permanently impaired. Too many people have extremely low opinions of themselves and what they are capable of – just because of repeated 'stories' they were told as children that they accepted as fact. This sense of not being good enough is often more common in women than in men. On top of the normal conditioning process that affects all of us, women have also had the weight of thousands of years of faulty, but deeply ingrained, gender based assumption to deal with. That's not to say men don't feel it too; it's just they learn to mask their feelings of doubt or insecurity with façades of bravado, invincibility or aloofness as a protection for an underlying fragility.

This fundamental lack of self-awareness usually ends up rocking our world as we suffer what American philosopher Ken Wilber refers to as a 'disease of meaning' (2003). This particular affliction is often recognized as a 'mid-life crisis'. Whether brought on by a particular event such as redundancy or the end of a marriage, or it creeps up on us as a growing sense of dissatisfaction, the 'mid-life crisis' can be bruising. Usually there is a mismatch between 'how things are meant to be' and how things actually are and this is often enough to jolt us out of our sleepwalking and begin the process of 'waking up'. We start to realize that we have been following a set of rules and playing certain roles for decades in the belief that it would yield a certain reward. Only the reward doesn't materialize, or if it does materialize we don't feel the way we thought we would feel.

We are despondent because we kept our side of the bargain. We worked hard to get the good grades so we could get into a good university. We then worked hard again to get a good qualification and secure a good job. We followed the organizational rules and toiled away at nights and weekends to complete the MBA and worked even harder to secure the next promotion. We made more money, we were a dutiful husband/wife, father/mother, leader, worker, friend and colleague and it *still* didn't work out the way we envisaged it. Even if some of the rewards did materialize the 'high' they created was short lived and the happiness was transitory. We may have followed all the rules that society said we should, built a career, bought a house, had a family, worked hard and then one day woke up and still felt empty on the inside for no obvious reason.

In an attempt to fill this void people will often make even more effort in the external world of 'doing' and set their sights on the next promotion, the next pay milestone, the next car, the new affair, exercise regime or the next luxury panacea. In effect they seek an external answer to an internal problem. They may even achieve these external objectives only to feel even more despondent because the wealth and success doesn't actually fill the void that prompted the pursuit of wealth in the first place. Often they can end up feeling even more distraught and unhappy than they were before they became wealthy. At least before they reached their destination there was hope that out in the future once certain milestones were achieved they would get to feel fulfilled. That hope would drive them forward into hard work and late nights. Only the milestones are achieved, the money is in the bank but the meaning they were seeking does not materialize and that realization can be crushing.

Until the penny drops that we can't solve an interior problem with an exterior solution we will remain in pain. The emptiness, loneliness and isolation so often felt by senior leaders is an interior problem in the 'I' dimension. At best the external solution may act as a sticking-plaster or distraction but it won't solve the interior problem.

This also works the other way too – you can't solve an exterior problem with an interior solution. If you can't pay the mortgage, thinking about it and deciding to visualize a sudden windfall is probably not going to be very helpful. If you can't pay the mortgage you need to find another exterior solution to solve that exterior problem. The only solution to an interior problem is an interior solution and the only way to cure the disease of meaning is to face it head on, understand that it is simply a stage of development and move through it.

For all of us there is much to explore and understand about our true nature. And this work is critical if we want to enjoy meaningful work, live fulfilling lives and mature into the person we are truly capable of being. Some of our deepest moments of unhappiness, confusion and disappointment occur when we don't have a sense of our own interior or we feel disconnected from our own purpose and other people. In these instances we are often just 'going through the motions' of life without any real meaningful connection to the work we are doing or people we are doing it with. This lack of meaning in our lives can make us feel empty and lonely. In fact, new insights into drug addiction have indicated that it may not be the drugs that are causing the addiction but the isolation and loneliness of the people taking those drugs. Take those people out of the desperate, disconnected environment and rehabilitate them with social skills and encourage them to bond with other human beings and the addiction disappears (Hari, 2015).

Men are particularly at risk at this stage. Suicide is more than three times more common in men than women and suicide is the leading cause of death in men under 50 years of age (NHS, 2014). This disparity is thought to be largely due to the cultural conditioning that encourages men to 'man up' and keep their fears to themselves whereas women are not so encumbered by such nonsense and are more likely to share their distress with someone else which can alleviate the pressure, reduce cortisol levels and help to find a solution.

This desire to end their own life is driven by the sense of helplessness, meaninglessness and an inability to talk effectively about what the person is experiencing. But as Winston Churchill once said, 'If you are going through hell, keep going' (Loftus, 2012). Keep going because hell is always temporary, it's just a stage of development so it's absolutely possible to come out the other side, particularly if the person receives quality guidance.

The road to salvation: forget, distract or mature?

Often our isolation and dissatisfaction can be amplified because we look at friends and colleagues and assume they are somehow immune from the disease of meaning. There are usually two possibilities. They are either presenting an elaborate front and actually feel the same as we do or they just haven't realized it yet! It can be tempting to look at other people's lives and assume they are ahead of us on the journey but often the reverse is true. Most of the people around us have not yet woken up to their own potential. They are at risk of the same disease of meaning we may be suffering from but they just haven't reached the stage of development we are struggling with. Many people remember the unbridled enthusiasm and optimism of their late teens for example when they felt invincible, confident and ready to take on the world. The only difference between your current self and your 19-year-old self is that at 19 you'd probably never really questioned your life yet. It comes to us all eventually – but instead of getting stuck in that developmental stage we need to keep going and find people who can help us transition through the stage. And we can't be helped by an individual who has not yet reached our stage of development because they are behind us on the journey. The thoughts and feelings that come with the disease of meaning may not even be arising in that person yet so how can they possibly help us navigate them successfully?

Without the awareness that how we are feeling is just a developmental stage we simply put on a brave face and learn to live with it. The most popular methods for 'living with it' are anaesthetics and distraction.

Most, therefore, choose to either numb or anaesthetize their pain through the excessive use of alcohol or drugs – prescription or otherwise. Alcohol is especially popular with busy executives who will regularly exceed the safe intake on an almost daily basis. Alternatively many go for the distraction method which includes everything from having an affair or multiple affairs to excessive materialism to obsessive fitness or beautification. Although not necessarily conscious the logic is 'well if I can't have meaning and can't therefore feel genuinely happy then …', 'at least I can get laid', or 'at least I can drive a killer car', or 'at least I make a million dollars', or 'at least I can live in an amazing house', or 'at least I can look amazing' etc etc …

Over time the pain of this life crisis can become so intense it leads to a breakdown or a breakthrough. But not before the individual hits 'rock bottom' and enters a very dark place. They know their life isn't working but often they have absolutely no idea what to do about it because they still believe that the disease of meaning is a permanent condition rather than simply a developmental signpost. Although intensely painful this moment often heralds a turning point. We are on the cusp of a genuine transformation – perhaps *the* transformation of our entire life. To break through we need to realize our life is not the way we want it to be, we are not happy and perhaps more importantly no one can fix it but us.

This is one of the most important and transformational moments in any life. When an individual finally comes to the conclusion that their parents aren't going to fix them; their boss isn't going to fix them; their spouse or kids are not going to fix them; society or the government isn't going to fix them and for things to get better they need to 'grow up', mature and take ownership for where they are and who they have become.

This moment is what Joseph Campbell called 'crossing the threshold' (2012) – the liberating realization that we are each on our own 'Hero's Journey' that calls us to move from the safe, known world into the unsafe, unknown world so we can find out who we really are and what we are truly capable of. We must all eventually answer the 'call to adventure', move from ignorance to enlightenment and take personal responsibility for that transition. Just as I am responsible for my personal growth and vertical development, you are responsible for your personal growth and vertical development.

Adult ego maturity

Wilber suggests that there are two key processes in human development, 'waking up' and 'growing up'. First we must individually and collectively 'wake up' from the delusion of control and power. When we talk about a spiritual (as opposed to religious) awakening we are talking about an individual's growing realization that their truth, or how they interpret reality, is just one of many possible perspectives and that what we believe is right or 'the truth' is just a single expression of many possible truths. There is no such thing as *the* truth – only your truth and as we evolve as human beings our truth does and should change to transcend and include our growing awareness of the nature of reality. As such we become more in every sense of the word. We are able to access more creativity, more intellect, more perspectives and as such we are much more capable and much more sophisticated and flexible in our approach. We are, as Newton suggested, able to 'stand on the shoulders of giants' (1676).

Crossing the threshold and 'waking up' is just the start of the real journey of self-discovery. On its own 'waking up' is not enough. We must also do the work necessary to 'grow up' and mature as an adult human being. The upper reaches of growing involves us 'owning up' to past behaviours, personal failings, addressing our 'shadow' or 'darker side' and looking at the parts of our nature that we don't like so much. As human beings we all make mistakes and poor choices but it is the denial of those mistakes that keeps us locked into the same frame of mind that created the problem in the first place. If our ego is so fragile that we can't admit that we make mistakes then we are destined to repeat the same errors over and over again. When we 'own up' to our own shortcomings we can re-integrate them into the whole, become more mature. This evolution from 'wake up' to 'grow up' can result in a quantum leap forward in capability because growing up makes a dramatic difference to how we show up as a leader, a parent, a partner, a sibling or a friend. It fundamentally expands who we are and what we are capable of.

Doing the work necessary to develop the ego line of development is some of the most potent work any leader can do to step change commercial and organizational capability. While stabilizing our physiology is a critical first step and developing our emotional and social intelligence is a crucial second step, cultivating our ego maturity can transform the internal, subjective world of 'being' and add significant verticality in the vital dimension of 'I'. It can also yield serious competitive advantage because this work massively increases cognitive sophistication which allows us to more effectively manage the escalating complexity and intensity of modern business. If we are to prosper and genuinely thrive in a VUCA environment we need to expand our awareness and ego maturity so as to raise the calibre of leadership exponentially.

That said, awareness or self-awareness is not simply an on/off phenomenon. Even if you wake up to the nature of reality, growing up is an ongoing evolutionary process that moves through many levels and degrees of sophistication. The way that we think and lead an organization is fundamentally altered by our ego maturity.

Child to adult to mature adult

If you have ever watched a child grow up it's very obvious that they move through various well-defined developmental stages. These stages encompass their physical, emotional, cognitive, moral and many other developmental lines. The specific stages of development are often visible and vocal! Numerous authors have provided detailed descriptions of how each stage differs from the previous stages but we don't need to go into too much detail here. Initially a baby has no real appreciation of the fact that they are alive and a unique, separate human being from their parents or environment. Gradually this changes as they start to recognize that the thing staring back at them in the mirror is, as it turns out, 'me'. At the most basic level this is the emergence of the 'physical self'. The second level of awareness is often prefaced by a period parents call the 'terrible twos'. This stage is so named because the child is incredibly ego-centric. The child can't understand why, if they want ice-cream and they are yelling at the top of their voice for ice-cream, we don't want ice-cream too. They are utterly bewildered that we are not every bit as upset at the lack of ice-cream as they are! This is because the child believes that their emotional needs are identical to ours. They have yet to differentiate their emotional needs from ours. With this distinction comes the emergence of the 'emotional self', the second level of development. As the child develops they discover words and evolve still further until eventually at aged 14 they have most of the necessary skills and capabilities that they require to function in the adult world. (If you want more detail on these levels of development you can find it in *Coherence: The secret science of brilliant leadership*.)

If there is no 'burning platform' or strong need for us to develop further we are likely to maintain the maturity of a teenager into later life. Most people therefore leave school or university thinking that their development is finished. But we've only achieved the most basic levels of ego maturity from baby to child to physical adult. The move from immature adult to mature adult is, however, where *all* the magic happens. Society and the law consider an 18-year-old to be an adult and yet the truth is we are really adults with 'P plates' on. We are essentially baby adults – we may look physically mature on the outside but we are 'stuck' at about 14-years-old on the inside. There is no doubt that we may have scaled various 'learning curves' at school, university, through apprenticeships or at work but essentially we are far from developed. We have not really 'woken up' and developed much self-awareness and we are certainly not 'grown up' and mature.

What is required is a concerted effort to elevate our internal maturity to match the external sophistication of the world around us, but this rarely happens. It is this internal, invisible work that constitutes vertical 'I' development and holds the key to unlocking the vast reservoir of human potential.

When it comes to maturity and adult development there have been many significant contributions from the early days of Piaget (1972), Kohlberg (1981) and Loevinger (1996) to luminaries such as Ken Wilber, Robert Kegan, Eliot Jacques, Kurt Fischer, Susanne Cook-Greuter, William Torbert, and Clare Graves – each describing the vertical evolution of maturity and adult development from a slightly different perspective. For example, Wilber looks at the evolution of awareness or consciousness of Self. Cook-Greuter takes the perspective of ego development which is related to Self and helps to explain maturity. Torbert's Action Logic looks at how those stages play out in business and his collaborations with Cook-Greuter have been especially insightful when looking at behaviour. Graves' model of 'Spiral Dynamics' explores individual and collective values. Understanding someone's values can be transformational in relationships and will be discussed in greater detail in the next chapter. And more recently Wilber and others have offered more details around the key developmental stages that most people are stuck in. This makes the developmental frame especially helpful in moving people up the ego line of development.

Whilst undeniably brilliant many of these developmental theories sadly never make it out of the world of academia and they almost never reach the areas that desperately need them such as business, government and politics. Our goal has always been to bring some of the very best thinking to areas that could benefit and make it commercially relevant to business. To that end we use a tool – the Leadership Maturity Profile (LMP) – to help CEOs and senior leaders assess their current developmental location and where they could progress to.

The Leadership Maturity Profile (LMP)

Drawing on the best of the various developmental theories the LMP provides leaders with an accurate insight into their own leadership maturity and personal integration and that of their C-suite colleagues. The various 'locations' are illustrated in Figure 4.1. When leaders understand these ego maturity developmental stages and the characteristics and capabilities associated with each level much of the dysfunction in modern business makes sense. This assessment helps the leader and the executive team to understand why employee engagement may be low; why union negotiations may be stuck; why growth is stalled in emerging markets; why investor relations are so difficult; why executive team meetings are sub-optimal and all manner of people challenges exist inside and outside the business. The LMP also provides a clear explanation for why people behave as they do, where they can fall back to under pressure and where the greatest growth opportunities are for the individual and the team. As a result the LMP explains why individual performance often falls short, why a team isn't working and most importantly, what to do about it.

The model itself is made up of three main tiers, although we have alluded to the possible emergence of a fourth tier. We have adapted the terminology used by other developmental theorists to make them more business friendly. Each new level is capable of embracing a more sophisticated perspective and within each tier there are two levels. In each tier there are also four sub-stages (denoted 1.0 to 2.5; or 3.0 to 4.5; or 5.0 to 6.5). In every tier each of the four developmental sub-stages emerges from the previous stage and that emergence follows a specific developmental process which I will explain in more detail later. But for now it's enough to know that the biggest jump in developmental capability in most organizations is reaped when a leader makes the leap from 3rd person perspective to 4th person perspective. Although the leap from 4th to 5th person perspective is also significant as I'll explain shortly. These transformational hurdles are illustrated in Figure 4.1 by the thick dark lines.

One of the key factors that characterizes the progression from 3rd to 4th person perspective taking is the shift from 'concept awareness' to 'context awareness'. In the 3rd person perspective all issues tend to have a 'right answer'. Things are black or white, right or wrong and the world is very concrete. At the 4th person level all answers tend to sit in a specific context. So when dealing with any challenge the solution usually 'depends' on a number of factors.

For example, a few years ago I was coaching the marketing director of a FTSE 50 company who definitely operated from the context awareness level.

FIGURE 4.1 The LMP model

7th person perspective individual	7.5	7.0 'Non-dual'	
6th person perspective collective	6.5 Illuminated	6.0 Embodied	Tier 3
5th person perspective individual	5.5 Unitive	5.0 Alchemist	
4th person perspective collective	4.5 Integrator	4.0 Pluralist	Tier 2
3rd person perspective individual	3.5 Achiever	3.0 Expert	
2nd person perspective collective	2.5 Conformist	2.0 Self-protective	Tier 1
1st person perspective individual	1.5 Ego-centric	1.0 Impulsive	

When presenting to the Executive Board he would offer several options for them to consider and explain that the one they should choose depends on what balance of outcomes they wanted to achieve. The Executive Board would ask him to give them a steer on which was the correct answer given the current market conditions. His reply would be 'it depends on what we are trying to achieve'. With increasing frustration the Board would usually respond with: 'Yes but we don't have time to debate the options and as the marketing director we need you to recommend an answer'. In the absence of knowing what they felt was most important it was impossible for him to answer their question. This stand-off occurred a number of times and after 12 months the Board's impatience with what they perceived was his indecisiveness ran out and the marketing director was compromised out of the business. The marketing director was happy to depart as he felt the

Board was not considering all the options appropriately. He subsequently went on to become a successful CEO at another company that did appreciate that in modern business there sometimes isn't a neat one-size-fits-all answer. It's not that the marketing director was right and the Board were wrong or vice versa, it was simply that the marketing director's ego maturity meant he saw more of the complexity and could appreciate that the answer was dependent on the context.

This story is a classic example of the misunderstanding that can occur between different levels of development. The leap from 3rd person perspective to 4th person perspective taking is the most significant transformation in maturity that needs to occur in most businesses. However, the leap from 4th to 5th also represents a major evolution and this latter transformation holds a great deal of promise especially as we move into an increasingly VUCA world because it allows a step change in a company's innovative capability.

The leap from 4th to 5th is the shift from 'context awareness' to 'construct awareness'. In the 4th person perspective all answers are seen in a specific context. There are no absolute truths, rather a whole series of relative truths. However when leaders develop 5th person perspective taking capability they are able to transcend context. They start to understand that all contexts are created or 'constructed'. In fact all phenomena are 'constructions' including personal identity or Self. A leader that truly embodies such understanding is completely liberated from all constraints. This can unleash an incredible surge in creativity and innovative capability.

Such a transformation can often be seen in how musicians talk about their ability to write a hit song. At 3rd person awareness most live in fear that their creative capability will dry up. Their song-writing capability appears to them to be a 'gift'. It is a concrete concept and in the absence of any deep understanding of how creativity really works and how to unlock their potential and genuinely develop such ideas their fear often becomes self-fulfilling. If the musician has matured to the next level of adult development they will tend to see their song-writing capability as more context dependent. Thus if they are in the right studio with the right people and the right frame of mind they can create the conditions that enable them to be creative. In the optimal context they can sustain their own career. But of course maintaining these conditions can become a challenge particularly if they lack altitude in other developmental lines such as emotional and social intelligence.

There are a tiny number of song-writers who operate with construct awareness. They are exceptional people who seem to be able to almost permanently generate new ideas, new songs and new concepts regardless of context, changes in musical tastes or styles or cultural memes.

So the development of adult maturity represents a huge opportunity for business because currently 85 per cent of the planet operates from the 3rd person perspective or below. Don't get too caught up in the labels of each maturity level. Sometimes it's easier and more intuitive to think about the progression between levels of maturity as upgrades to the operating system of a computer. In this case we simply move from Human Being Version 1.0 (HBv1.0) to Human Being Version 6.5 (and beyond). Each upgrade improves the software, fixes some of the glitches from the previous version and expands its capabilities and sophistication. Some upgrades such as the ones between HBv2.0 and HBv2.5 represent small developmental tweaks while others, as we have discussed, such as the upgrade from HBv3.5 to HBv4.0 represent a quantum leap forward.

HBv1.0: Impulsive

At HBv1.0 the individual is only concerned with 'me, my, I'. These individuals are immersed in the 1st person perspective; as such they are impulsive, driven only by their own needs and impulses. My autistic son, Sam operates largely from HBv1.0. At times he is completely consumed and overwhelmed by his interior subjective experience. So much so that when he feels an internal urge he has to satisfy that urge otherwise he gets really upset. At the Impulsive level the individual doesn't have any awareness that he's driven by his own subjective impulses or urges, he just has the impulse or urge.

We can also see this behaviour in a young child going through the 'terrible twos' stage. They want that ice-cream and will happily (or not so happily) ask for it 50 times or more. In that moment *all* that matters is the ice-cream. Learning at this stage is largely through imitation and repetition. At this stage there is no awareness that other people see a different view of the world. So if you hold up a mobile phone screen to a person at this stage they will assume that you are also seeing the screen rather than the back of the phone.

HBv1.5: Ego-centric

HBv1.5 is still operating from the 1st person perspective and is still therefore concerned with 'me, my, I' but they can start to objectify or witness their own impulses. In other words they have some awareness about the fact that they are being a bit self-absorbed and ego-centric but they are still largely driven by their own egoic needs and desires. When someone is operating from HBv1.5 you may hear them say, 'I know I'm being selfish but ...'. They can appreciate they are being self-absorbed but it doesn't really affect the outcome – they still want what they want! 'Mine' is a very strong concept in children at this stage. They tend to believe everything is 'mine'. Given this, there is an interesting philosophical debate as to whether they can really understand the concept of theft. If their sister's pencil is 'mine' then how can they be wrong for taking it? Adult gang leaders that operate from this stage will believe that they are often simply taking what is rightfully theirs and would have little remorse about any of their actions. Symbolism, rituals and luck play a large part in the life of HBv1.5. Adults stuck at this stage have usually experienced some sort of significant trauma which has then arrested their development. They often need a lot of compassion and strong boundaries if they are going to successfully develop any further. It is possible that many adults have developed further but they have a 'shadow' pattern that is trapped at this stage and this will emerge under certain circumstances.

The shift from being subject to (in this case our own impulses) at stage 1.0 to being able to objectify (our own impulses) at 1.5 is the pattern that repeats in the first two sub-stages of every tier. This stage is sometimes referred to as 'late first person perspective'.

There are many people operating at HBv1.5 in business. For example much has been written about the narcissistic boss (Banschick, 2014); whether CEOs have sociopathic tendencies (Babiak and Hare, 2007) and the degree of hubris in the C-suite (Owen, 2012). In conversations HBv1.5 aren't really listening that well – they are only listening to the extent that they can pick up bits and pieces of the conversation that will allow them to bring the conversation back to them or what they want to talk about. They are always working to their own agenda.

We've all met people who operate at HBv1.5 – it doesn't matter what we've done or where we've visited or who we've met they will have a similar story and use the similarity to hijack the conversation and make it all about them again. HBv1.5 will reject the very idea of coaching and will certainly not become a coach themselves, although they will never shy away from telling people what the answer is – albeit their answer from the vantage point of this stage of development.

HBv2.0: Self-protective

As we start to interact with others it begins to dawn on us that other people actually exist and they don't necessarily share our 1st person perspective. We realize that there is more to the world than 'me, my, I'.

In order to succeed it is necessary to start to understand the rules that govern other people's perspectives because they are different from 'mine'. The emergence of this 2nd person perspective is a big step forward that is absolutely crucial to successful relationship building. A person operating at HBv2.0 has shifted from a largely individualistic view to being more concerned with the collective. Children at this level move from parallel play to 'playing with' others, although there is now a battle of wills and tantrums occur if the will is thwarted. The goal at this stage is still largely to protect self-interest although the sense of Self is still immature and merged with personal desire, ideas and wishes.

In the world of self-protection the rules of others are only followed to ensure personal advantage or avoid punishment. Thinking is generally binary right or wrong, judgements are simplistic, physical gratification is central and emotions are often expressed as simply single words – OK, bad, sick or tired. As such, people at this level have little insight into their 'Self' or others and tend to only look at the surface of things. Other people are now things that need to be controlled and 'self-respect' is largely based on how much control we hold over them. Opportunities are normally seen as a way to get their own way. Since people at HBv2.0 are still learning the subtle rules of social interaction they often feel like outsiders, loners and are unsure of how to relate effectively to others. They often experience feedback as an attack, react badly and go on the offensive.

Because it is unclear how to control others, the world is now more hostile and they have to be ready to fight or flee. In this dangerous world of others it is necessary to be wary and assume the worst. There is low trust, hyper-vigilance and reactivity. Relationships are mainly based on power and are fragile. With low social awareness it is easy to over step the mark. Conflicts are always the other person's fault. So blame is common and it is vital not to show weakness.

Poor ethical decisions or action is deemed 'bad' only if they are caught. Even if caught, people at this stage of development still show little remorse or shame. This is partly because they still do not yet have a sophisticated understanding of causality. Being caught is often just 'bad luck' but it won't stop them trying to get away with as much as possible. They struggle with ranking the importance of rules so may want to punish transgressions with equal severity regardless of the 'crime'.

At the slightly later evolution of this stage individuals may start to become more preoccupied with social rules and the need to be respected becomes increasingly important. Disrespect can become a big deal very quickly. This may shift into a desire to be liked or accepted by the collective. At this stage of development individuals may deliberately choose not to express an opinion and just go along with whatever the consensus is either to fit in or as a self-protection manoeuvre. At the later stages fitting in can trump doing the right thing. Those operating at HBv2.0 can easily be led astray by the collective. In business they may agree to poor or unethical behaviour because 'everyone else is doing it'.

Coaching HBv2.0 or being coached by HBv2.0

The main thing someone operating at HBv2.0 wants from coaching is to feel safe and supported. For example if an athlete is operating from HBv2.0 then they will feel supported if their coach makes sure their kit is clean and has sorted out all the logistics. The coach may help with some suggestions of how to perform better but this has to be done in gentle and encouraging ways for it to work. An individual operating from HBv2.0 will need to understand how what their coach is doing is helping them; otherwise the input is likely to be rejected.

A coach operating at HBv2.0 tends to be more of a helper than a coach. They will clear a path towards their objectives in very tangible, often simple terms. Coaches at this stage of maturity will often rely on specific systems to guide their work whether these are religious systems, psychological systems or frankly any approach which possesses a lot of structure.

According to Dr Susanne Cook-Greuter, approximately 4 per cent of the American population operate from this stage or below. It's likely that these statistics would therefore hold true for all developed populations.

HBv2.5: Conformist

A person at HBv2.0 has the ability to choose whether to go with their gut instincts (HBv1.0) or rationalize them (HBv1.5). The ability to choose to follow our instincts or objectify them differentiates HBv2.0 from HBv1.0 or HBv1.5. This ability to choose characterizes the third stage in every tier but the content of that choice varies as we develop through the tiers. At the next stage up at HBv2.5 individuals start to understand what determines the choices they are making more clearly. This ability to understand the 'system' in which the choices are made characterizes the fourth stage of every tier.

At the Conformist stage our identity becomes much more strongly identified with a specific group. The group, gang or tribe we belong to provides protection and power. Self-identity may actually recede somewhat as this is replaced by the identity of the group. Thinking for 'yourself' is not common. Any tension in the relationship with the group is perceived as a threat to survival. The price paid for inclusion in the group is loyalty and obedience. In return for their loyalty, HBv2.5 expects to be rewarded with visible signs of approval – which may be status symbols, explicit acknowledgement, trophies or money. They often feel massively underappreciated if these do not materialize. The fear of rejection by the group often leads HBv2.5 to go into conflict avoidance or play a smoothing and soothing role. If these abilities are cultivated the individual becomes skilled in diplomacy. In fact HBv2.5 is often called the Diplomat. Managers operating at this level are often overly agreeable or polite and rarely question authority. They find it difficult to reprimand or criticize others and believe there is limited scope to be creative as this would involve challenging the status quo. Leaders who operate from HBv2.5 often subordinate themselves in service of the group. Shame comes online at this level of development and when things go wrong this can be quite intense. Shame can also come from being different from the rest.

HBv2.5 struggle with ambiguity because this makes it difficult to conform to the rules of the group. The other person is either a friend or a foe and there is a 'them versus us' mentality rather than the 'me' versus 'them' that occurs at HBv1.5. Standing out from the group or taking personal initiative is frowned upon. As a result of the need for acceptance the language is often impersonal, overly positive and full of platitudes. Whitewashing problems, looking on the bright side and the absorption of all sorts of abuse occurs in an attempt to keep the peace. Strong negative emotions are often suppressed which can lead to passive aggressive tendencies. Blind conformity is common but often with a dark side of generalized prejudice ('all of that group are cheats'); emotional polarization ('you either love me or hate me'); or literalism (rigidly sticking to the party line or agreed 'truth'). HBv2.5 likes to offer unsolicited advice based on the simplified morality that exists at this level (from social etiquette to codes of honour) and these rules are often forcefully imposed. Although, at this level punishments are more likely to fit the crime.

HBv2.5 often judge people by looks alone, so 'looking good' is important and success is often measured in material terms or by the amount of 'bling' someone has. There is a tendency to pigeon-hole people into simple categories with statements such as 'there are three types of people'. Self-esteem is usually based on status within the group. As personal reputation and prestige is so highly valued HBv2.5 can become increasingly worried what others might think and engage in legal fights to protect their image. Feelings are often described unsubtly in stereotypical and clichéd ways but without any awareness of the clichéd nature of their own descriptions. In fact they will often adopt group jargon in order to fit in as 'one of the guys or girls'.

Coaching HBv2.5 or being coached by HBv2.5

When someone is operating from the conformist HBv2.5 their goal is to fit into the team or organization. So they respond well to knowing exactly what is expected and what rules need to be followed.

A coach operating at HBv2.5 will probably function more as a counsellor than a coach. They will often become somewhat of a disciplinarian with a strict code of conduct. They can become emotionally involved in the process and lay down the 'law' to the person being coached. Compliance is a big issue for them and they like to enforce the norm believing this is what delivers results. Obviously if the person being coached operates from an advanced level of maturity the coaching relationship will be difficult at best and possibly ineffective.

Approximately 11 per cent of the population operate from this stage and 15 per cent are at this level or below.

HBv1.0–HBv2.5: Concrete stages

All these first four stages operate in the concrete world of the here and now. They are primarily focused on the definable, touchable, concrete reality. There is nothing terribly subtle about these stages. It's all observable phenomena.

We see this concrete stage play out in business all the time. The junior manager will usually focus on fitting in to the organization so they can get themselves up the corporate ladder. Initially they will do whatever is asked of them and find their feet in the role. This blind acceptance of the group will almost always backfire a few times so they will endeavour to learn the rules of the group so they can consciously conform or at least appear to conform. Conformism is an essential stepping stone in many careers. The individual may realize that he or she needs an MBA for example so they will busy themselves getting an MBA because that's the rules they need to follow to get to the top.

Even when a leader has managed to transcend the concrete stage and operates from a higher maturity level, under pressure they can still collapse back down to HBv1.5 and become a bully. Excess stress can make a normally more mature executive demanding and show little care or concern about the impact of their actions and decisions on others or the relationship. They just want what they want. And this can happen all the way up to Board level.

HBv3.0: Expert

Moving from HBv2.5 to HBv3.0 unlocks a whole new set of capabilities that are enabled by 3rd person perspective taking and the pendulum swings back to a more individually orientated view from the collective leaning of HBv2.0 and HBv2.5. This leap into 3rd person perspective taking is transformational particularly for businesses as it unlocks rational objectivity. The ability to view things from a distance and make them an 'IT' step changes an individual's ability to work with every type of phenomena. Ironically the ability to work with any phenomena had its biggest impact not in the concrete world of tangible 'IT' objects, but in the world of 'I' and 'WE'. HBv3.0 has the ability to objectify their own interior and examine their own thoughts, feelings, beliefs, attitudes as well as their own identity or Self. This was truly transformational and takes HBv3.0 into the foothills of transpersonal awareness with the realization that things exist beyond their own Self. Experts are able to think about thinking and therefore able to come up with better answers. This ability to objectify phenomena also extends to the interpersonal world. So relationships with customers, colleagues and stakeholders can be explored in some detail when maturity has reached HBv3.0. The content of awareness in this second tier shifts from the very concrete tangible things in the first tier to more subtle intangible things. And at this first stage of this tier the tendency is to experience these intangibles or be 'subject' to them. Thus feelings and thoughts while they can be objectified often overwhelm the individual at this stage of development.

With this rational objectivity comes the ability or tendency for constant comparison and measurement. Standard setting also kicks in, which brings with it continuous improvement, competitiveness, perfectionism, compulsion and all manner of operationally relevant behaviour.

The emergence of 3rd person perspective taking also spawns an explosion in information and knowledge, which means people start to develop well-defined areas of expertise. And this expertise itself becomes a sellable or tradable commodity. HBv3.0 understands the power of ideas compared to the idea of power that is central to HBv1.5 and HBv2.0. One of the critical capabilities unlocked by HBv3.0 is the ability to more effectively differentiate one thing from another. So conversations about USP or what is unique about an individual, a company, a team, a product, a process, a strategy or all manner of commercial phenomena are now possible. This desire for uniqueness is in direct contrast to the conformity of the previous stage.

Unfortunately expertise has its own dark side. Standards enable a sense of superiority, intellectual aggression, hostile humour and ridicule. Interestingly

HBv3.0 don't mind giving others unsolicited 'feedback' and they can be highly critical of others and themselves but usually resent feedback because it threatens their self-image as an Expert.

In order to protect the 'unique' value of their own expertise HBv3.0 are often very insular and resistant to change. It is said, 'you can always tell an expert but you can't tell him much'. In business, Experts are often the hardest people to coach or develop because they operate from an 'I know' or 'you can't tell me anything' stance. Experts are rarely lost for an answer. To defend their position they will often try to discredit material that does not fit their model, dismiss counter evidence, belittle others or engage in one-upmanship. They often suffer with 'yes but' syndrome. Trading in knowledge, Experts ask lots of questions and want to know 'the facts'. This can often come across as criticism. They like a good argument and generally feel entitled to impose their views and expert opinions on others often in an unsolicited fashion.

Experts are also often fascinated by 'descriptions' of people. People are pigeon-holed using typologies such as Myers-Briggs Typology Indicator (MBTI); alternatively they may be defined by their 'strengths' or some dimension of their personality using instruments that assess aspects of the 'Big 5' personality dimensions. So managing the talent pool is often driven by descriptive methodology. As fascinating as these descriptions are, these typologies can become a swamp that actually prevents executives from unlocking new levels of capability, potential and effectiveness. Unlocking new levels of capability, potential and effectiveness requires a completely different approach – a developmental methodology. The irony is that the 'war on talent' is often perpetuated by 'experts' inside and outside the organization who stall development by offering assessment instruments that produce all manner of descriptions but can't guide the development of capability. We need instruments that can quantify what level of development the executive is operating from and therefore what level they need to unlock next – not some blanket 'solution' based on typography. Unfortunately most companies are stuck in the swamp of description and mis-measurement (Watkins, 2014).

Experts are adept at seeing alternatives, experimenting and creating options which can add a lot of value. They are able to conduct sophisticated comparisons but are less able to prioritize, sequence or synthesize. The ability to synthesize through analytical weighting doesn't strongly kick in until the next stage of development – HBv3.5. Experts are more aware of time than previous developmental stages and start to think more about past, present and future, although the future focus rarely extends much beyond the next 1–3 years. They tend to see time as a linear fixed phenomenon. However, in their push for project perfection Experts will often lose track of time and frequently find it difficult to predict how long things will take.

Most businesses, particularly at the executive level, are awash with HBv3.0. In fact no organization could run without experts handling the technical running of the day-to-day operations. Experts rise up the business because of specific expertise such as finance, law, operation, marketing etc. They follow a particular training discipline and build their career based on that expertise to get them into the C-suite. They see themselves as 'movers and shakers' in charge of themselves and their environment. Unfortunately their belief in their own expertise often creates a misplaced confidence that they are experts in everything – even areas where they have no formal training.

The individual operating at HBv3.0 will automatically assume they are right and others should defer to them. They can build a mighty reputation as an expert and as a result many people stop developing at HBv3.0. Instead they just learn how to leverage that expertise to get to the top of a company. The financial expert eventually becomes CFO and then CEO. Or the sales expert becomes the Sales Director and then the CEO. But as an expert each of these new CEOs is also very resistant to input around finance or sales respectively because they are an expert in that area. As a result they can often take a very narrow, incomplete or partial view of the challenges they face, they may fail to transcend their own expertise and that can be their downfall. We have seen many CFOs become CEOs and then run the company from a spreadsheet as though they were still the CFO.

Coaching HBv3.0 or being coached by HBv3.0

When coaching someone who operates from the Expert stage of development it is important to recognize that what really engages them is the ability to acquire more knowledge and demonstrate their expertise. As such they tend to respond better, at least initially, to learning rather than development. If they do engage with coaching they will respect and respond much better to someone who can demonstrate their own expertise in a relevant area or someone who has impressive academic credentials often regardless of whether they are an effective coach or not. To get the best out of an Expert it can help to set high goals and encourage them to seek perfection.

Expert coaches like to mentor more than coach. They tend to talk at their clients rather than to them. The Expert coach sets very high standards, presents evidence in order to convince their clients of the accuracy and veracity of their argument and then offers guidance on how to master specific skills or developmental steps.

Approximately 40 per cent of the population are at this stage of development and therefore 55 per cent are operating from this stage or below.

HBv3.5: Achiever

Particularly in the West, Achievers are often mistakenly considered to be the most sophisticated and mature version of an adult human being in terms of conventional development despite the fact that there are at least seven more stages beyond HBv3.5. Helping executives and leaders develop from HBv3.0 to HBv3.5 can however completely transform individual, team and organizational performance. This shift involves a significant broadening of capability and focus and tends to liberate leaders from the narrow confines of the silo and helps cultivate a much stronger cross-functional capability. One of the reasons HBv3.5 become significantly more capable is they can operate as an expert and also stand back and think about their own expertise. This gives them much more control over their abilities and allows them to broaden their skill set beyond the original area of their expertise and focus their abilities on achieving a specific goal.

This subject-to-object (S_2O) manoeuvre that occurs when moving from the first to the second stage of Tier 2 is the same S_2O manoeuvre that occurs in the shift from the first to the second stage of Tier 1. The difference is that in Tier 1 the focus of the objectification is an individual's basic impulses and in Tier 2 it is their expertise. There is a saying that typifies the subjective absorption with our own expertise that 'if all you have is a hammer everything looks like a nail'. At HBv3.0 the hammer is an individual's expertise and the executive will try to solve every challenge with that hammer/expertise. When a leader develops to HBv3.5 they start to perceive the limitations of their own expertise so they broaden out their abilities and the metaphoric hammer can be exchanged for pliers, a spanner or a screwdriver.

The ability of both Experts and Achievers to objectify any phenomenon is driven by the development of 3rd person perspective taking and results in something called 'concept awareness'. People at HBv3.0 and HBv3.5 live in the world of either/or. Experts tend to believe that either my idea or concept is right or your idea/concept is right, but since we can't both be right the likelihood is the other person is wrong. Experts love to argue and show other people the variety of ways they are mistaken. In contrast an Achiever, while sharing this same basic belief about either/or answers, tends to take a slightly more nuanced and less absolute view. They are likely to suggest that one of the answers was 'better' than the other. This makes Achievers very adept at choosing what they consider to be the 'best option' and prioritizing that. This is enhanced by their passion for differentiating things. What both Experts and Achievers struggle to see, however, is how two apparently opposing views can both be correct at the same time. This would not even make sense to HBv3.5 or earlier stages. As a result Experts and Achievers struggle with conflicts of interest.

When F Scott Fitzgerald said, 'The test of a first-rate intelligence is the ability to hold two opposed ideas in mind at the same time and still retain the ability to function' (1945), he was clearly talking about someone who had matured beyond HBv3.5.

An Achiever's reductionism or power to break a problem down to its component parts in order to help comprehension or resolution is greater than an Expert's because they are able to embrace a wider data set. And this ability is further enhanced by their ability to objectify the value that others can bring and rope them or their skills into the problem-solving process. Achievers are very driven to uncover what they consider to be the 'truth'. Although since they understand that there are better and worse versions they will often call it the 'deeper truth' or even claim an 'absolute truth'.

Achievers' ability to relate to time has also matured compared to Experts, often making them more reliable around delivery as they understand the consequences of not achieving the goal. Whereas Experts tend to resist and even reject feedback, Achievers tend to be more open to it and they will often adhere to the sentiment, 'feedback is the breakfast of champions'.

The greater the Achiever's ability to objectify all phenomena, including their own expertise, the more able they are to deal with change of any sort. They realize that they themselves are a work in progress as is the success of their team or business. So the kind of 'Immunity to Change' (Kegan and Lahey, 2009) that we frequently see in many leaders, teams and organizations suggest that the individual or collective maturity level is probably stuck below HBv3.5.

The belief that everything can get better can be a powerful transformational force and if properly harnessed can shift the focus from 'learning' (much loved by Experts) to vertical development. This single fact is possibly the most powerful competitive advantage – because it enables a completely different orientation to the phenomena of change.

Most change programmes are conceived by Experts or individuals operating from the same developmental level as the leader who has the problem. Therefore the best that can be hoped for is a small-scale improvement in efficiency or effectiveness. Generating an answer which is at the same level of sophistication as the problem often simply reinforces the problem and keeps the team or organization stuck at the same level they were already at. This is sometimes referred to in the developmental literature as 'auto-poiesis'. The system tends to self-organize and remain stuck at the same level of development. With Achievers it becomes possible to flip the ability to change vertically and create 'vertical autopoiesis', ie the ability to perpetually change as the world around you changes. This is a really big deal and sows a powerful seed of future-proofing the individual, team and organization.

The self-confidence of Achievers is normally also more deep rooted and stable compared to an Expert because it is not driven by internal expertise but by the implemented outcome of that expertise in the world – by results. This is further supported by the Achiever's emerging understanding of their ability to not only determine the commercial outcome but also their own personal destiny. Interpersonal relationships at HBv3.5 become richer, more textured, more intense and diverse. It becomes possible to 'agree to differ'. Other individuals can be valued for who they are, or their belief system rather than their loyalty to a person.

The participation in any group is less about self-protection, identity or gathering more knowledge and more about purposeful participation in service of a specific objective. Alliances made are driven by tasks and their fear about either becoming too conformist, dependent or submissive, or simply being absorbed by the group exacerbates their drive for action. However the Achiever's perpetual focus on goals, targets, objectives and outcomes means they risk becoming overwhelmed and even more trapped in one dimension – in the world of 'doing'. This relentless drive to perform means HBv3.5 rarely take the time to stop and reflect on their action and the intensity of their drive can cost them in terms of their health and their relationships.

With the ability to objectify the content of their own thinking HBv3.5 become more sceptical and start to appreciate the complexity of things. They also start to see the contradictions within any system, including their own business, as well as within themselves. Statements about themselves start to become more nuanced rather than clichéd and they can, at times, be somewhat contradictory: 'I am relentlessly laid back'. They defend their point of view by using the power of their rationality and can become a little intellectually aggressive. But what they often fail to see is the inherent subjectivity that sits behind all objectivity.

In most organizations, Experts and Achievers are responsible for the day-to-day business success. Both enjoy experimentation and working things out. While Experts focus on the details of doing the job extremely well and improving procedures, Achievers will often design whole new methods and approaches to solving a problem and streamlining processes. Achievers focus on output measured in terms of turnover, volume, profit, return on investment, market share, and personal career satisfaction. Achievers become increasingly enthusiastic about outcomes, evidence and metrics because this allows them to repeat their success.

If leaders don't make the shift from Expert to Achiever as they get promoted to larger and larger roles there is a high risk they will fail. If they get to the top as an Expert and continue to be an Expert then the narrowness of their perspective, inability to embrace a wider data set particularly in larger more complex organizations usually means that they are eventually removed from office.

The very best leaders understand the importance of broadening their perspective and recognize that it may be necessary to let go of whatever expertise got them to the top. And that requires real courage and also explains why there are significantly more Experts than Achievers leading businesses around the world. We spend significant effort in working with organizations helping executives develop from Expert to Achiever and beyond so they can reap the significant rewards for themselves, their team, their organization and ultimately society itself.

Coaching HBv3.5 or being coached by HBv3.5

In coaching Achievers it is important to remember their main goal is results rather than knowledge. Exactly how the results are achieved is secondary to 'the win'. They need to see immediate returns otherwise they will start to assume that the coach doesn't have the requisite ability and believe that there may be someone better that can help them. It is therefore not uncommon for Achievers to switch coaches frequently even though the new coach will almost certainly be at the same developmental level as their previous coach. After an initial 'honeymoon period' where there may be some short-term benefits the new coach's ability to transform the outcome is discovered to be no greater than the last one and the cycle starts again. Of course, what is really required is a coach who has developed beyond HBv3.5 themselves and can therefore go beyond results to create a more sustainable outcome.

Coaches operating at HBv3.5 tend to see themselves as facilitators of the outcome. They use logical arguments; play the role of the teacher, the task master and 'contract' with their clients on what is required. They are open to experiment and are prepared to re-evaluate their approach in the service of the client's primary goal. They tend to come from a specific 'school' or philosophy and will try to leverage their beliefs in order to deliver. When they encounter alternatives they may filter those alternatives through the beliefs of their current approach, either rejecting or subtly co-opting anything useful.

About 30 per cent of the population are at this stage of development and 85 per cent are at this stage or below.

HBv4.0: Pluralist

Less than 15 per cent of individuals make the quantum leap in capability from HBv3.5 to HBv4.0. It is this ego maturity that unlocks the 'post-conventional' stages of development and brings 4th person perspective taking online.

The most profound capability unlocked by 4th person perspective taking is the ability to 'take a perspective on a perspective'. This means that HBv4.0 is aware that there are three perspectives, 1st, 2nd or 3rd, and they can choose to operate from any of them. The ability to step in or step out of any of those views and simultaneously be aware that we are doing so is the essence of 4th person perspective taking. The ability to step in or step out is also what characterizes the third stage of Tier 2. The focus of this ability in Tier 1 was the subject-to-object (S_2O) move. In Tier 2 it is a little more sophisticated and involves the ability to choose perspective. The impact of being able to choose perspective cannot be underestimated. The power of choice means that we don't have to be overwhelmed by the subjective view of the 1st person vantage point, with its inherent lack of awareness; we don't have to be stuck in the hyper-rational stance of 3rd person perspective taking with its tendency to be disconnected; and we don't have to get stuck in the swamp of 2nd person perspective taking protecting or conforming and potentially losing our identity. I will unpack the incredible power of perspective taking more in Chapter 6.

With the move from 3rd to 4th person perspective the whole world of context also opens up properly for the first time. This marks a shift from the 'concept awareness' of 3rd into 'context awareness' of 4th and means that HBv4.0 is able to evaluate their own answers to a much more sophisticated degree. Answers are no longer 'right' or 'wrong' and not even 'better' or 'worse', rather they are now all contextually dependent. Because HBv4.0 sees so many possible answers people at this stage are often called Pluralists. They not only realize that there are multiple possible answers but they are motivated to find a way to embrace disparate and diverse opinions. In fact they frequently use the 'and' rather than 'or' option to allow multiple answers to be considered.

With the opening up of 'context awareness' comes a realization that everything is relative, the 'truth' is culturally conditioned and nothing is ever 'totally objective'. This spawns a realization that things are not what they seemed at the earlier stages, interpretation depends on the observer's perspective. As a result Pluralists often distrust 'conventional wisdom' and 'hyper-rationalism' and at times they may distance themselves from all that has gone before. With the realization that reality has been culturally conditioned certainty and judgement break down. They realize the limitations of rational analysis and look for other ways of 'knowing'. There is an increased interest in the here and now and 'head trips' seem less interesting. This can disconnect Pluralists from their Achiever and Expert colleagues as they prefer to mix with more reflective less driven individuals.

At HBv4.0 the brakes finally come off creativity. There is an increased desire to seek out the new and question conventional wisdom. Learning has been truly ignited, more rapid development is possible and a profound inner freedom starts to emerge. One of the real benefits this allows in an organization is much better situational leadership.

With the opening up of new cognitive capabilities comes a greater social awareness. This results in a greater respect for others, a desire to understand and a reticence to impose their interpretations on others. The subjective world takes on a new fascination and there is more of a shift from the world of 'doing' ('IT') to the world of 'being' ('I'); from outcomes and results to relationships and non-linear phenomena. HBv4.0 enhanced ability to sense the interior world of others also brings an understanding that others can 'see' them more deeply too. This greater reciprocity means relationships can become quite intense with lots of vivid emotional expression (often with lots of exclamations). Relationships deepen and trust is amplified particularly if the HBv4.0 can sense something about the other person that they are not yet aware of.

However, HBv4.0 is not without its own challenges. With so many new views to embrace it is easy to become confused by the contradictions. Tension may arise as a result of increased ambivalence and the struggle to prioritize. As a result HBv4.0 may privilege horizontal learning over vertical development but at the same time rail against the notion of hierarchy preferring everything to be given equal consideration. Of course the blindness of this view is that preferring horizontal over vertical is itself a hierarchy. The ability to see many answers and the struggle to settling on any one, as they all have a piece of the truth, can foster a subtle cynicism. HBv4.0 can be very effective at deconstructing other people's answers without having anything better to take its place. Pluralists can be somewhat difficult to manage. They can be less consistent than Achievers or Experts, tend to engage 'on their own terms' and therefore generate less certainty. Because of their greater sophistication if their boss is at a lower stage of development they may find Pluralists 'difficult to fathom'. The confusion that can occur at HBv4.0 can also extend to their own identity. This can spawn a desire to find 'my True Self'. Concurrent with this HBv4.0 can start to worry about the ever present danger of self-deception and indecisiveness.

HBv4.0 are more collectively orientated than the previous level and they see groups not so much in concrete terms but as contexts in which things can become true. Culture, cultural norms and cultural contexts can be a source of fascination at this stage. Because everything is relative and the context is continually changing HBv4.0 realizes that no amount of meticulous planning, scientific measurement and refined reasoning can make them immune to the biases and peculiarities of a specific context. The greater appreciation of diversity can make HBv4.0 so inclusive of others that meetings can become stalled in consensual hell and decision making slows right down. This can be exacerbated by excessive political correctness and a desire to allow everyone to be heard.

Coaching HBv4.0 or being coached by HBv4.0

When someone is operating as a Pluralist their goal is learning. They realize that if they keep learning then the results will come. So learning trumps outcome. A few years ago I was working with a very thoughtful Premiership football manager. He said something very interesting: 'It is not about whether we win or lose. Rather we focus on the quality of our passing. If we can learn to pass better – most of the time we will win. Occasionally we may get beaten by a wonder goal but the results will come if we simply pass better.' Coaching a leader who operates at HBv4.0 requires subtlety and the ability to flex. It is important to point out progress, not in results, but in learning that can underpin results.

Coaches operating at HBv4.0 tend to take the role of co-learner with the person being coached. They are willing to put their theories to the test, try different approaches and adapt them for the best results. They see themselves as part of the development process; they take an eclectic approach, run innovation labs, adapt things and ignore or invent rules if needed.

About 5 per cent of the population are at this stage of development and 90 per cent are at this stage or below.

HBv4.5: Integrator

The final developmental stage of Tier 2 unlocks another level of sophistication and capability. Whereas the Pluralist has awareness of which perspective they are operating from and can choose whether to step into 1st, 2nd or 3rd person perspective individuals at HBv4.5 understand the phenomena of perspective taking within a wider context of other phenomena such as time, societal evolution and other dimensions of vertical development.

Integrators go beyond the multiple answers of the Pluralist and look for patterns and relationships between the different phenomena so they can create an integrated whole. They can see how multiple perspectives impact and interact with each other. Also they are likely to connect different systems together and build meta-models and meta-maps of reality. In science this type of Integrator thinking has been the driving force behind the acceleration of interdisciplinary research over the last 30 years. In business Integrator thinking has driven the cutting edge of organizational design and development. Where the Achiever may advocate matrix structures as an organizational response to the complexity of the commercial world; and Pluralists may promote a more organic approach with cross-functional working and collaboration, Integrators look at the dynamics that are currently driving business systems and seek to facilitate a more comprehensive set of outcomes across all areas of that system by addressing all the workings of the system on all levels and all dimensions. HBv4.5 seeks to create a powerful new meaning through their integration and ability to inspire a new story.

The primary new capability that comes online for those that develop from a Pluralist to an Integrator is their ability to see a more complete picture of reality. This is reminiscent of Rumi's 'blind man and the elephant story'. A group of blind men are encouraged to touch the elephant to learn what it is like. Each of the men feels a different part of the elephant and tells the others what they feel. The first man touches the elephant's skin and says, 'Wow, it's so wrinkly and tough'. The second man who has been touching the elephant's tusk immediately disagrees, 'No it's not, what are you talking about – it's completely smooth'. Meanwhile the man at the back of the elephant is objecting again as he describes the tail, 'That's not correct either – an elephant is long and tapered with coarse hair sprouting from the end'. And finally the man who has been touching the trunk says, 'You're all wrong; the elephant is like a large wrinkly hosepipe'. Of course they are all right because they are each experiencing a different perspective or truth about the elephant.

An Integrator seeks to constantly see this more complete picture; they understand that two people taking a different view can still be right and that duality doesn't strike them as strange. Furthermore Integrators, more than any previous stage, are also aware of the potential limitation of their own perspective and the fact that they may only be experiencing part of the whole reality. This latter realization is a critical breakthrough and marks a significant development in thinking. The Integrator is the first stage of development to explore not only what they believe, but how they come to believe it. As such HBv4.5 are happy to expose the reductionism of the traditional scientific approach, to unearth hidden social and cultural assumptions and to make these visible to themselves and to others. They are able to tolerate ambiguity and uncertainty, a fact which enables them to be more patient when the way forward is not yet clear. Being more attuned to time they can more easily see the trajectory of things, be they lines of reasoning, sales, strategic initiatives or relationship dynamics. They are also more able to identify the unintended consequences of any plan and avoid the negative consequences.

With the much greater awareness of time and systems HBv4.5 are able to see clearly how much they have changed during their own lifetime, regardless of whether they know about developmental theory or not. As a result they may, for the first time, become truly aware that there are likely to be levels of development beyond where they currently operate from. So their motivation to unlock these levels may ignite, and vertical autopoiesis may begin in earnest. HBv4.5 may also start to become much more interested in how they support the vertical development of others (and the world), whether others have themselves awoken to this possibility or not, because they see how this clearly confers competitive advantage in a VUCA world.

In their excitement about the 'much bigger picture' they are now able to see they may find themselves evangelizing, interrupting others or monopolize the floor with their prodigious knowledge of the interconnectedness of things. The fact that most people have not yet reached this stage of development paradoxically exacerbates this tendency as it can create a sense of isolation. This isolation can foster an even more ardent desire to connect with others. Not just to share the exciting information they have discovered but sometimes out of a sense of loneliness. The significant expansion of their understanding and ability to explain a much wider set of phenomena may also create a very subtle, and often unnoticed, inflation of their ego. It is as though by achieving HBv4.5 they may also partially inflate HBv1.5. If this immaturity is avoided then humility is often present.

There is a risk of misinterpretation when the mild indecision that can occur at the Pluralist stage gives way to the ability to preference a view and project greater certainty with clarity and insight. This shift can often be completely misinterpreted by people at earlier stages of development as arrogance which is often exacerbated by HBv4.5's lack of conformity to the cultural norms.

HBv4.5 are also more fine-tuned to their own emotional well-being and may notice how much less cynical and mistrusting they have become over the years. They understand that communication can be a personal projection or personal bias particularly if it is reflected back to them well. There can also be a much greater awareness of how not to offend others. This often manifests as a greater ability to deliberately create a narrative arc and use language that resonates with others who may be operating from the earlier stages. This can make the Integrator very engaging although the danger is they could, in appealing to multiple audiences, lose some of the quality and contour of their views and appear too generic.

Rather than operating with a set code of conduct HBv4.5 works with an evolving set of principles as new data enables them to update and improve their models of the world. Rather than break the rules (HBv1.5); conform to the rules (HBv2.5); or bend the rules (HBv3.5), Integrators prefer to reframe the rules. HBv4.5 embraces paradox and personal projections as unavoidable. They consider feedback as essential as it provides a more complete picture but mainly from people who are at their level or beyond. This means there are only a small number of people whose feedback can make a difference to them. Many people at earlier stages of development find HBv4.5 too complex and not grounded enough. Integrators' ability to play a variety of different roles and show up differently often confuses people from earlier stages of development.

The independence seen at HBv3.0 and HBv3.5 is replaced by a desire at HBv4.0 and HBv4.5 to co-create the future and work in collaboration with others. Integrators are often relaxed in the face of conflict seeing it as an inevitable dimension of most relationships. HBv4.5 with good people skills can motivate staff, clients and consumers towards culture change, integrate values and more sustainable globally responsible business practices and social entrepreneurism.

Coaching HBv4.5 or being coached by HBv4.5

Coaching someone at HBv4.5 requires you to recognize that they are essentially trying to build a system that can deliver. So framing your suggestions in the context of their existing models is crucial for them to be able to integrate your ideas.

An HBv4.5 coach sees their role as an integrator of multiple options into an effective tailored plan for their client. They sense what is going on and what may be required and respond spontaneously rather than trying to predict and control for every eventuality. As a result they tend to be less preoccupied with planning and more alive to the dynamism of the moment and how to leverage that. They often play a crucial role in helping their clients positively reinterpret the story, see a bigger picture and look at the situation in terms of the interplay in multiple systems.

Approximately 4 per cent of the population are at this stage of development and so 94 per cent of the population operate at this stage or below.

HBv5.0: Alchemist

The jump from Tier 2 to Tier 3 is rare and genuinely life changing. It liberates a level of ability that is difficult to imagine at earlier stages of development. It enables an individual to transcend context, the constraints of time and releases a level of innovative potential that can provide an almost inexhaustible stream of ideas on any topic. This may seem far-fetched but elevated ego maturity to Alchemist can produce genuinely astonishing results. This is because 5th person perspective taking comes online for the first time. This new perspective enables an individual to move from the world of ideas (concept awareness) and the understanding of the wider system in which ideas fit (context awareness) to a fundamental change in the way reality is perceived (construct awareness). The central nature of reality at this stage leads some authors to refer to Tier 3 as the 'causal' tier implying that it is concerned with an even deeper, more subtle 'causal' origin or 'source' code for existence.

Whilst an Integrator connects the dots in an ever more complex and exquisite web of relationships the Alchemist sees the dots and the connections differently. This transformation in the perception of reality is deeply rooted in the Pluralist and the Integrator stages of development. At the Pluralist stage there is a realization that all phenomena are culturally constrained. There are no absolute truths anymore. At the Integrator stage a deeper understanding about how thinking and ideas are created emerges. Ultimately at HBv5.0 the penny drops that all of reality and all phenomena in our awareness are artificial constructions of the mind. That is not to say that a table is not actually 'there' in reality but the concept and understanding of what a table is has been created as our mind developed from the earliest days of conception. So everything is constructed, even our own identity or sense of Self. As one of America's leading Zen Masters said to me a few years ago, 'when you have sat, as I have for 40 years, exploring our true nature and the mystery of who we really are eventually you realize that the "Self" is just a collection of ideas held together by spit'.

Basically our identity or Self is a construction, built up over years like a beautifully lacquered jewellery box. We then become identified with the construction and start to believe 'this is who I am'. A construction based on a collection of experiences and things that have been said to us about us. All of which is largely determined by the happenstance of our birth, the family we were born into; the geography we developed in; the culture we experienced; the moment in human history we came into existence at; our gender; the things our parents drew our attention to when we were learning what mattered and what deserved our focus. Our mind was conditioned to make sense of reality in a certain way. And had we been born in a different family at a different time, in a different culture in a different part of the world we would believe ourselves to be a very different person.

That is not to say that who we are does not have purpose, significance or importance. Just that it is a construction and as such it is not permanent, fixed or even solid. At HBv5.0 construct awareness we realize this and it completely liberates us. We are no longer held hostage by a series of made up stories around which our identity was constructed.

It changes our relationship to 'the truth'. I remember helping a client to understand this stage and she said, 'So you're saying that the fact that I am not good enough at something or that I am not worthy is not true?' Of course the answer is yes – it's not true. It may be a very strongly held belief but it is based on years and multiple layers of conditioning none the less. Although it seemed very real to my client the idea that she wasn't worthy was simply imprinted in her mind without her knowledge or permission. And this 'fact' may have been based on the flimsiest of evidence – a fluke of circumstance or the random juxtaposition of a series of experiences. But the good news is that if this idea of her lack of worth is an artificial construction it doesn't really have the validity that she thought it did. And therefore she didn't need to be attached or stuck with this idea about herself anymore. She was so much more than this very narrow description or idea that she had of herself, capable of so much more than she thought. And if she acknowledges that this is true (which it is) then she can completely let go of all the recrimination, doubt, guilt and judgement she was hanging onto about her 'Self' and discover who she really is. There were tears in her eyes as I finished by saying, 'And who knows you may just fall in love with that.'

This liberation from our ideas about ourselves extends to our views about how the world works and reality itself. We can let go of all of our ideas and as a result move completely freely from one idea to another, from one perspective to another, picking up and putting down anything that serves us and those around us. Even the idea of 'us' is constructed and therefore can change. This level of impermanence can sound terrifying particularly to earlier stages of development who may need certainty, stability or the security of 'no change', but to individuals who have developed through every stage it is genuinely exciting. Much of the excitement flows from the realization that in the construct aware world we can put things together in unique and novel ways unencumbered by cultural rules, system connections or anything at all. This is why HBv5.0 is called the Alchemist. Some people prefer the terms Magician but for me alchemy retains the magical quality but implies a methodology. And this makes sense because even at this stage when we are unfettered by the normal constraints there are still principles of operation at play.

It is quite possible that you don't know anyone who operates from this level as they are extremely rare. Because Alchemists are liberated from their attachments to phenomena there is often a lightness of being coupled with a paradoxical ordinariness. In fact they often simultaneously embody complexity and simplicity; can be visionary with an attention to detail; seem very intense yet also laid back; magnetic and intimidating in equal measure; humorous and witty but very hard working; comfortable in chaos while promoting coherence; take a very long-term view but live very much in the present moment; project certainty and embrace polarity. They can often turn around what appeared to be a hopeless situation by the strength of their insight and the power of their personal courage. This may seem far-fetched but only because you have yet to experience this stage yourself. Once we start to inhabit this level consistently then it becomes possible to take conscious control over many dimensions of ourselves that we were led to believe were beyond us. But we have to get here to really test the validity of such statements.

HBv5.0 are also unusual in the relationship dimension as they can often be quite friendly to competitors and share ideas that most others would not dream of doing. Given their paradoxical nature it is difficult to describe HBv5.0 in any consistent fashion – they perpetually surprise. Although one quality that has often been commented on is that they take 'just in time' to a whole new level and have an uncanny knack of being able to do the right thing (often unexpected) at the right time.

Historically, Alchemists have been the kind of societal catalysts and visionaries who have been rejected, ignored or characterized as simply out of touch with 'reality' – ironic given they probably understand reality better than most. Fortunately as society evolves and more people reach HBv4.0 and HBv4.5 they are likely to find a somewhat more receptive audience for their insights.

You may be forgiven for wondering what an Alchemist can offer leadership. But, such a question evaporates if you ever meet one. However, since HBv5.0 is no longer attached to a precious identity, job title, position or even strategy then they can increase their flexibility, fluidity and capability exponentially. This results in a huge energetic release which allows the freedom to fail fast, break down and build up really quickly.

This openness and dynamism is absolutely necessary if we are to thrive within a highly adaptable, highly complex system. Knowledge doubling alone means that what works today will not work or will be superseded tomorrow. Hanging on to the way things were, fighting lawsuits to protect intellectual property, sticking to an agreed strategy because it worked in the past or assuming a market leading product will remain so indefinitely is crazy. The market is changing constantly and incredibly quickly so either we learn to adapt in real time and deconstruct what's not working to make way for the reconstruction of a better way or we simply won't survive.

When we mature to HBv5.0 and become construct aware we finally appreciate that on some level all of it is just a made up story anyway! If something isn't working, change it. If your strategy isn't working, deconstruct it and reconstruct something else. If there is a way to improve the business then collapse the old way and reconstruct a new, better way. Personally I'm really proud of my previous book *Coherence* but I've moved on. I'm not attached to it because I know it was a construction. So while it is packed with really helpful details and I believe it has real longevity I can let it go and construct new cleaner ways to define and rise to the challenges that face leaders today. So I created *4D Leadership* to represent the evolution of our thinking.

The leader who is capable of operating at HBv5.0 has transcended and included all the previous levels. As such they are more than capable of dropping down to Achiever to deliver results or exercise autocratic leadership if it's needed in a crisis but they operate from a much higher more sophisticated level of maturity. These individuals are totally and utterly unconstrained. If they want to formulate strategy, they are unconstrained by history, time, space, competitors, and perceptions of what the business is or is not. In the VUCA world this presents a massive advantage. HBv5.0 also have far greater influence because they're not pushing their own agenda. Rather they are suggesting one of the most advanced levels of thinking that will produce a better outcome for a much greater proportion of the people more of the time.

In business we have two options – we can either constantly create better products and services so as to stay ahead of the pack or we can steadfastly deliver the products and services we already have until a competitor copies them and undercuts us and our customers go elsewhere. In that situation we can choose to complain and fight competitors in the courts in an effort to hang on to our competitive advantage. The problem with that is that everything is moving so quickly that the competitive advantage we are fighting tooth and claw over is like a metaphorical iceberg. By the time the lawsuit is over all that's left is a pool of water! The business has been leapfrogged by other competitors, probably many times.

The only sensible option is to elevate our senior leaders to HBv5.0 and continuously re-invent the business – if someone copies a product, make a better one. If someone steals an idea, come up with a better one. Instead of hanging on to the past the leader and their team open up to profound opportunity. The only way to truly stay ahead in a VUCA world is to move key people up the levels of ego maturity so that they can continuously create, new, better stuff. If everyone or even a few key people are construct aware it doesn't matter if others copy. Take it as a compliment and move on. Your business can never be caught.

Coaching HBv5.0 or being coached by HBv5.0

It is highly unlikely that you will find yourself coaching someone operating from HBv5.0. Partly because there are so few of them about and partly because they are more than likely to already be driving their own vertical autopoiesis.

Being coached by HBv5.0 can be a fascinating and varied experience, and may not be everyone's cup of tea. They may show up in a highly grounded pragmatic way happily sifting through the nuts and bolts of your 'to do' list or challenge the precision and differentiating nature of your strategy. Equally they may take on the role of a mirror reflecting back to you the shadow side of your nature that you don't see and questioning whether you are really living up to your core purpose. One thing is for sure, personal growth and development is almost inevitable.

HBv5.5: Unitive

As you will see from the LMP model there are several more stages beyond the Alchemist. However the chances of you encountering people operating from these stages is extremely small so I have shortened their description. In addition, because of the diversity of expression of how these stages show up, it becomes increasingly difficult to capture an accurate explanation of what it is like to operate from HBv5.5 and beyond. It is however important that you know these stages exist.

As with the first two stages of Tier 1 and Tier 2 the shift that occurs in moving from HBv5.0 to HBv5.5 is a subject-to-object (S_2O) transition. In Tier 3 the focus of this S_2O development is reality itself. Thus an Alchemist is free to move between disciplines, different phenomena and even versions of themselves. They achieve their magic by working with the constructed nature of reality to innovate in any area. An individual operating from HBv5.5 has a much better understanding, and therefore control, over this fluidity and indeed their own alchemy because they can objectify it. HBv5.5 can also see the subtle meanings embedded in the constructions, appreciate the quality of the connections and profound reciprocity between different constructions and therefore see which relationships are more likely to be sustained. With their deeper understanding of the interconnected nature of all phenomena they often turn their alchemy to the service of reality itself giving rise to the name for this stage – the Unitive.

From their more objective vantage point Unitives are able to perceive the spaciousness within and around reality's constructions. In fact spaciousness or 'emptiness' is a characteristic feature at this stage and can imbue all individuals in Tier 3 with a transcendent quality of inner stillness or peacefulness which is most often misinterpreted as some sort of disengagement from reality. This is ironic given Tier 3 are the most connected to reality but the time frame they now work with and how they engage with phenomena is baffling to earlier levels. Because of their ability to perceive all of reality without attachment to any of it they have little to defend and much to observe. They are not natural self-promoters and may be found behind the scenes doing incredible work but in an unassuming way often with forensic precision and great compassion. They will normally quietly work on themselves through some type of spiritual or disciplined practice cultivating their wisdom and ever-present awareness of multiple aspects of reality. They can be very tough and incredibly kind and have the courage to stand out, not for their own egoic reasons, rather because the situation warrants it.

While Unitives are incredibly mature and sophisticated human beings your experience of them may be very ordinary. You may often feel that they are 'nothing special' and that they are on your level. But don't be fooled. People from many different levels describe them this way because they can show up at many levels from HBv1.5 to HBv5.5, and will often do so simply to make you feel more at home. They are not concerned with status symbols, honours or plaudits (although they may accept awards graciously if bestowed). The complexity that clearly exists at this stage starts to recede into the background as HBv5.5 brings the simplicity of the whole into sharper focus.

HBv6.0: Embodied onwards

The further north you go up from HBv5.5, the fewer people are operating at that level. By the time we reach HBv6.0 Embodied there are probably less than a couple of thousand people on the planet who have reached this rarefied stage of maturity. I will keep the description very brief as it is likely to sound strange! As with the third stage in all tiers comes the ability to step in or step out of the first two stages of that tier – so HBv6.0 can bring the magical qualities of the Alchemist or the inclusive qualities of the Unitive as they embody both. They have overcome the loneliness that can surface in the early stages of construct awareness. This loneliness is driven by the realization that there are not many people around who understand reality as they do. Coming to terms with this fact can take a while. Ultimately its resolution relies on the deeper experience of 'non-separation' from all things. HBv6.0 have resolved the paradoxical fullness of emptiness and the space within fullness. As a result of all this developmental work (although it is unlikely to be perceived as work) there is often an easy engaging charm and a beguiling warm bonhomie. People operating at the Embodied stage often experience themselves as a conduit or porous channel to the entire universe. Sometimes they feel like they are receiving 'downloads' from the collective consciousness that drops a zip file into their mind for the benefit of others. Language may be vivid and eloquent with powerful metaphors easily mingling with simple truths and allegorical stories. An Embodied individual's lightness of touch belies a deep wisdom and compassion for humanity, the planet and beyond.

It is easy to be completely inspired by HBv6.0, not so much by the breadth or depth of their knowledge or wisdom (although this may be prodigious). Rather by the complexity, nuance, focus and friendly generous selflessness which they can bring. You may feel they are simply one of the most interesting people you have ever met and being in their presence can feel like a spiritual meal that lifts your energy and sustains you without you necessarily realizing why.

Beyond HBv6.0 is the last stage of Tier 3 – Illumined. It is likely that you may not be able to tell whether the person in front of you is at this stage of development or not. In fact it is probably fair to say that only Alchemist or above could accurately determine whether the handful of people on the planet that operate from here are actually doing so.

Illumined individuals embrace all that has gone before and transcend it. Illumined individual's practices, interests and trajectories cover the entire Universe. There is immediacy to their wisdom and the depth, breadth and scope of their insight often require some time to unpack. As a result it is not unusual for them to be able to speak engagingly for days without drawing breath. The scope and scale of the design can feel grandiose but there are very few people who can legitimately put such a comprehensive wisdom to the test. All of this wisdom is held together with the minimum of scaffolding and their ability to access distributed insights scattered in the far corners of their mind or indeed of existence is awesome. This is the fourth stage of Tier 3 and with the fourth stage in every tier a systematic capability focused on the central concept of that tier comes online that facilitates an upsurge in horsepower. With all this comes a surety of articulation that can create all manner of projections and misunderstandings in others from earlier stages.

Being coached by HBv6.0 or HBv6.5

It is highly unlikely that the person coaching you is operating from this stage of maturity. Even if they were it is unlikely that you will be able to tell. You would probably need to spend some time asking them questions to discover the depth and breadth of their humanity and even if you did they may not share simply out of a desire not to overwhelm you, sound pompous or distract from the fact that they are there to help you. One quality you may notice strongly is that they are a living example of what they are talking about. They have gone beyond walking their talk – they walk their walk.

The key thing to remember about maturity and coaching is there needs to be a sufficient match between coach and client. So if a leader decides to hire a developmental coach to help them and their business develop vertically they need a coach who is at least at the same level of maturity or higher than they are otherwise the coach will not add sufficient value. For example if a leader is operating at HBv4.5 (Integrator) and their coach is operating at HBv3.0 Expert then the coach's solutions will be too formulaic and prescriptive to resonate with the HBv4.5 who is functioning at a higher more sophisticated level than the coach. When they try to communicate they will often be speaking completely different languages. Unfortunately only the more mature person is likely to notice – which is a problem for the coach if this is the client!

If the coach is Integrated (HBv4.5) and the leader is an Expert that can work because HBv4.5 transcends and includes all previous levels. So an HBv4.5 coach can still operate at the Expert level when needed. They will therefore have enough sophistication to show up at this stage and communicate with the Expert leader in a way that can facilitate vertical development and step change results.

Focus on what matters

At Complete Coherence we focus only on what matters. We measure and improve only the lines of leadership development that we believe are the most commercially relevant. So whilst there are additional levels of maturity beyond HBv5.0 they are largely irrelevant to most people in business today. When I explain the LMP model most people understand everything up to HBv3.0 Expert and HBv3.5 Achiever. They usually appreciate the jump to Pluralist and Integrator. There is a general rule of thumb that most people will only understand one level above their current maturity level. So if someone is currently operating at HBv2.5 they will understand the explanation of everything up to HBv3.5. They won't however appreciate the distinctions at HBv4.0 and above.

There is therefore no point getting bogged down in an intellectual exercise about the subtler and more nuanced distinctions between those upper levels of ego maturity. Besides, the biggest opportunities for development that will yield the biggest upsurge in capability in most organizations are the transitions from HBv3.0 to HBv3.5; from HBv3.5 to HBv4.0 and from HBv4.5 to HBv5.0. The jumps between levels may look similar in the model but the uplift from one tier to the next usually unlocks the greatest gains.

It's worth noting here that we can't jump levels – so it's not possible to jump from HBv2.0 to HBv5.0 without travelling through the incremental stages in between. This is just the nature of human evolution. A child must learn to stand up before they can walk and walk before they can run. They must learn how to make noise, before they can form words before they can speak. And we simply can't operate from the higher levels of maturity without first working *through* the lower levels of maturity. It's all an evolution, where we transcend and include what goes before. However, considering that 85 per cent of the current population is at HBv3.5 or below there is still a huge opportunity for senior leaders to increase their vertical development of the ego line and step change their capability.

The commercial value of investing in development to move up just one level in ego maturity from where we are now is disproportionate. If everyone in business moved up just one level the results would be staggering. If that single level development took some of the key players into construct awareness then organizational ability to create competitive advantage would explode off the charts.

The goal of the LMP is to allow leaders to put a marker in the sand as to where they are currently located, appreciate the behaviours that emerge from their current level of maturity and more importantly what additional benefits and opportunities exist if they take the time to consciously move up even one stage. When a leader is currently at HBv3.0 or HBv4.5 there are huge developmental gains to be achieved if they move to HBv3.5 or HBv5.0 respectively. Everyone has the capacity to increase at least one stage and the uplift in capacity will transform results and performance.

It's important to remember that this, or any other maturity model, is not a competition or an assessment of good, bad or ugly. The merit of this map of ego maturity is in giving us a framework for additional development rather than a tool for comparison. The stages simply relate to the various ways we gain wisdom, maturity and make meaning from the world around us. Each stage is simply an expansion from the previous level. With each increase in maturity level we become more aware of who we really are and we become more capable, more sophisticated and more able to manage increasing levels of complexity. Considering just how complex business is already and how unprepared many leaders believe they and their team are for the future, vertical development of the ego line provides us with a phenomenal opportunity to rectify that shortfall. The conscious development of maturity is effectively a 'lifeline' into the future that will not only allow us to cope with the changing nature of business but to thrive and excel in that volatile environment.

Action steps

It's impossible to overestimate just how significant the maturity line of development is – not just business, but society as a whole. Indeed the fate of our species may very well depend on our collective ability to develop vertically up the ego line. If we were to look out into the world today we would see the fighting, the terrorism, the refugees fleeing for their lives, the war, the violence, the environmental challenges not to mention the constant battles in business – imagine how different these situations would be if the centre of gravity of the global population was not at HBv3.5 Achiever and below but at HBv4.0 Pluralist or above. For some 30 per cent of the population that's just one level of maturity from where they are now. Even if a third of the population was operating from that space the world would be a very different place. Imagine if you could do that in your business – the results would be beyond anything you could currently imagine.

Below are some action steps to develop vertically up the ego line of development:

1 Consider assessing the ego maturity level of your entire senior team to identify how many are operating from the Expert or Achiever level or below and how many are operating above HBv3.5.

2 Understand the value that Experts, Achievers and beyond bring but also their limitations. Engage your senior leaders in a conversation

around the competitive advantage available when they embrace vertical development and encourage them to drive their own development.

3 Actively work with the executives operating at the Expert level and encourage them to take a much broader perspective, transcend their technical expertise and embrace a multi-siloed Achiever approach. This can be achieved by:

- Giving Experts a cross-functional responsibility including budgetary responsibility;

- Encouraging them to work with their peers in small groups to deliver collective outcomes;

- Reviewing the reward mechanics so that success and reward can only be achieved and maximized through collaboration with others.

4 Actively work with the executives operating at Achiever level and encourage a much greater degree of reflection and openness to diverse or dissenting views. This can be achieved by:

- Encouraging them to explore the value of different perspectives and how they can be integrated to enhance the quality of the answers generated within the team.

- Encouraging them to move away from right/wrong, either/or thinking to greater inclusivity, plus adopting 'and' in their thinking.

PART THREE
The interpersonal world of 'relating'

Vertical development of the 'WE' dimension

05

Leadership starts from the inside out through vertical development in the 'I' dimension. However it is said that we can only really know ourselves when we are in relationship with others. So developing altitude in the 'WE' dimension can significantly accelerate our maturity in the 'I' and transform our personal performance. Vertical development in the 'WE' dimension can also step change our effectiveness in the 'IT' dimension as our relationships with our colleagues and customers improve.

If leaders start to develop their interior 'I' dimension to match the altitude in their exterior 'IT' dimension they must also develop a compatible degree of verticality in their 'WE' dimension otherwise their progress may be as unbalanced as a two-legged stool. So 4D Leadership requires investment in the interpersonal dimension of 'WE'. This chapter will explore why we so often find relationships difficult and what we can do to improve our results in this critical interrelating dimension. By unpacking the values line of development we can truly unlock customer and employee insights which can in turn greatly facilitate better, stronger and more productive stakeholder relationships.

We are defined by our relationships

We may believe that we are defined by our role, our expertise, our qualifications, our heritage or our culture. And yet we are actually defined by our relationships. The Sanskrit dictum 'So Hum' translates as 'You are, therefore I am' and is the title of a wonderful book by Satish Kumar (2002).

Positioned as a 'declaration of dependence' Kumar reminds us that we are only able to truly know ourselves because of the other. I can only know myself as an 'author' if you are a 'reader', I can know myself as a father through my relationship with my sons. I can only understand my role as a husband through my relationship with my wife Sarah. A speaker is only a speaker if he or she has an audience. We are therefore able to know ourselves better because we are in relationship with others. In a very real way who the other person or people are makes us who we are.

And yet we are notoriously bad at relationships. We only need to turn on the news or flick through a newspaper on any given day in any given country to be reminded just how bad we are at them. Our inability to really connect to others is causing fighting within marriages, families, companies, communities and countries. The gulf between individuals, religions, nationalities and cultures seems to be widening all the time. Too often people are wedded to their opinion and an unwavering belief that they are right and the other is wrong. And sadly they are often willing to die and kill others to demonstrate just how 'right' they are. As we've discovered, the belief that 'I am right and you are wrong' is only a perspective and it comes from a certain level of ego maturity. Unfortunately this limited perspective is shared by about 85 per cent of the global population. We live in unprecedented times – whole regions are teetering on the edge of disaster, others are already waist deep in challenges of epic proportions. We face many intractable complex and seemingly impossible problems – wicked problems (Watkins and Wilber, 2015). If ever the world was operating on a burning platform for change then surely we are on that platform right now.

Ironically, this disconnection is driving us further and further away from what we need and really want. As human beings we need connection. Our need for connection and relationships is as necessary to survival as our need for food and water and this has been known academically since the 1940s. Institutions such as orphanages have always had disproportionally high death rates compared with 'normal' child mortality. But it wasn't until the 1940s that the cause was attributed to anything other than poor hygiene. Austrian psychoanalyst and physician Rene Spitz proposed that what was killing these children was not contagious disease but lack of love and connection. British psychologist, psychiatrist, and psychoanalyst, John Bowlby later presented 'Attachment Theory' to explain the profound importance of early childhood care and the need for a baby to form a strong physical bond to at least one primary care giver. Quite simply if human beings are not able to form early parental connections and feel loved and connected to at least one parent or carer then their chance of survival and ability to thrive is significantly and measurably impaired. And the scars of that early neglect can run incredibly deep and be very difficult to heal.

Renowned physician Dean Ornish, states: 'I am not aware of any other factor in medicine – not diet, not smoking, not exercise, not stress, not genetics, not drugs, not surgery – that has a greater impact on our quality of life, incidence of illness, and premature death from all causes' (1998). Human beings need connection as surely as they need air to breathe. The problem is relationships are tough.

Relationships are tough

Relationships are the hardest thing we do as human beings.

For a start no two people are the same. They bring with them a vast range of beliefs, opinions, values and perspectives that mean that we are almost always talking at cross purposes. Each of us has different needs and objectives that we may or may not even be aware of and we are not always very good at communicating these things clearly in a language that the other person understands.

Add the fact that CEOs and senior leaders are usually complex individuals who have almost never studied psychology or human development or have any desire to do so and relationships at these levels become even harder. Most leaders are highly individualistic and are more likely to be task or goal orientated instead of people orientated. Since most corporate leaders are men social and emotional intelligence is almost always considered secondary to cognitive intelligence. Leaders are not taught and rarely study relationships as a phenomenon because they are too busy wading through their day-to-day responsibilities in pursuit of the quarterly results. To exacerbate the situation still further senior leaders frequently fall back on fast superficial methods of 'communication' such as email, company-wide bulletin, video presentation, PowerPoint etc instead of the detailed telephone discussions or face-to-face interaction that are still so crucial for building strong relationships.

We may understand the importance of relationships and social connections but we have no idea how they really work. In business there is a huge industry around employee engagement, looking for ways to build productive working relationships and develop trust and camaraderie that can transform results. But the vast majority of it makes little difference. Employee engagement is notoriously poor. According to Gallup's study into global workplace engagement only 13 per cent of employees across 142 countries worldwide are currently engaged in their jobs – that is, they are emotionally invested in and focused on creating value for their organizations every day

(Gallup, 2013). Clearly the vast majority of employees are just going through the motions to get paid.

Improving engagement in organizations is a massive task not least because its measurement is so problematic. The current approach to engagement surveys requires some focused data collection interpretation and some months later a report is generated that is then argued over as to the meaning of a shift in scores from 4.5 to 4.6. By the time the meaning of the data is agreed by the companies' leadership many months have passed and engagement levels may have completely changed anyway. Fortunately, new technology, such as engagement heat maps have enabled a much more rapid and precise assessment of the real feelings of employees or customers as seen in real time.

Ultimately relationships are critical to everything we do in life. They are, in many ways, the ultimate prize in life – the real 'finishing line'. Success without connection – colleagues, friends and family to share it with – can often feel hollow and unfulfilling. Such connection can occur at a physical, emotional, intellectual or conceptual level. It can occur at the level of values or beliefs, professional, social, way of being or higher purpose. But at whatever level we all need to connect better to each other.

Ironically once leaders reach a certain level of seniority within an organization their ongoing success at that level and beyond is almost all about relationships and not technical competency. It's like the rules of the game that elevated leaders up the corporate ladder, ie high technical expertise and low people focus is immediately inverted on entry to the C-Suite. Often the skills that facilitated their successive promotions are now almost entirely obsolete and they need a completely new set of skills just to survive, never mind prosper. And it can come as a nasty shock to realize that they are poorly equipped for the demands of people leadership. Some never realize this or realize it too late before they are removed from office by the Chairman, their peers, colleagues, workforce, shareholders, stakeholders or the market itself.

Spiral dynamics and the evolution of value systems

Most people's experience of professional relationships is patchy at best because we are never really taught how to build and sustain productive working relationships. The frustrating part of business is the people, because we don't all think, feel or act in the same way. We are by our nature beautifully complicated human beings.

When we fail to understand or appreciate the impact of individual and collective difference we can end up steamrolling through the changes we wish to make which rarely works. When insufficient attention is paid to the people involved and the relationships they have and how they will change then people simply disengage. But if we take the time to understand what makes people tick and engage with them as individuals rather than just employees then we can unlock a massive amount of discretionary effort and amazing things are possible.

One of the most commercially relevant and useful tools for facilitating this shared understanding is the Leadership Values Profile (LVP). The LVP, based on the work of a number of academics but particularly Clare Graves, allows us to profile how an individual's value system varies depending on the situation they are involved in. In other words an individual can approach strategy from a different value level to the way they approach people management or implementation and these variations can have a profound impact on effectiveness and the relationships with others in those situations.

While a psychology professor at Union College in New York, Graves noticed that his students' responses to an essay assignment could be grouped into four main ways of answering the question. He concluded that there were four 'world views' that determined the way students wrote their essays and what they emphasized. His model developed over time to identify initially six and subsequently eight levels or value systems, each emerging to transcend and include the previous ones.

Two of Graves' students, Chris Cowen and Don Beck, went on to build on his work and named the framework, Spiral Dynamics. Spiral Dynamics is now one of the most widely used and cited cultural assessment tools on the planet and offers some genuinely useful insights when it comes to developing functional relationships.

What we value changes and evolves over time. What you valued as a 15-year-old is (hopefully) significantly different from what you value today. As we evolve up the spiral we don't lose access to the capabilities we had at lower levels of the value systems, we simply expand to transcend and include them into our new capabilities. Thus when we learn the ability to run we do not lose the ability to walk. We become more sophisticated, more capable and more perceptive as we mature and evolve up the spiral because we understand more values and are able to see situations from more sophisticated perspectives. That evolution doesn't mean we are 'better' than those who operate at the lower levels of the spiral and it certainly doesn't mean the higher levels will be happier or more successful. It is simply an expression of the breadth and depth of our embrace. The higher up the spiral we travel the more options we have in terms of how we behave, interact with others and the number of different things we can see value in.

Unsurprisingly the impact of each value system is also affected by the maturity of the individual involved. There is therefore a significant correlation between maturity and spiral dynamics. For example the Expert HBv3.0 and the Achiever HBv3.5 tend to operate from the 'power', 'order', 'wealth creation' value systems (see below). In business we can find mature and immature people operating at every level in the spiral. This is why ego is a distinct line of development from values and a leader's altitude up both lines can be objectively quantified. A mature individual is usually more driven by the positive characteristics of their value system whereas an immature individual is usually more driven by the negative characteristics of that level.

The stimulus for cultural evolution is nearly always the problems that arise from the dysfunction, negative traits or dark side of the previous level. So even when there are problems arising at a certain level of values development this could be brewing up an upward evolutionary force or momentum. In other words when the negative characteristics inherent at each value level become inhibiting enough and stand in our own way they will often trigger a 'software upgrade' so we can transcend the negative characteristic of that level and move up the spiral. It's the negative traits of each level that ultimately create the burning platform for development.

Each level of the spiral has been given a colour which is relevant to that level and helps us remember where we are on the spiral (Figure 5.1). As we progress up the levels the focus oscillates between the individual and the collective. What's especially interesting about spiral dynamics is that regardless of scale the model still holds true. Thus we can predict the likely behaviour of an individual, a team, a division, a business, an industry, a nation, a region or the entire population of the planet based on where the gravity is on the spiral. Clearly none of us sits entirely at one level. We are a kaleidoscope with a balance between multiple levels and this changes depending on what we are paying attention to. For example, when we are *building* a strategy we may be valuing different things and be operating from a different address on the spiral compared to when we are *implementing* our strategy.

Beige: Survival (individual focus)

The journey up the spiral starts with our own evolutionary journey as a human being and what we need. At our most basic level we need food, water and shelter to survive the day.

FIGURE 5.1   Spiral dynamics

	Upside	Downside
Turquoise	missionary, compassion	baffling, appears indulgent
Yellow	innovation, big picture	over complicated
Green	caring, inclusivity	stagnation, judgementalism
Orange	wealth creation	greed, manipulation
Blue	order, stability	rigid inflexibility
Red	make it happen	ego-centricity
Purple	safety, belonging	no direction
Beige	survival	no progress

This value system can be witnessed amongst the homeless, unemployed, sick or marginalized within industrialized societies. In times of economic hardship such as bankruptcy or redundancy people can revert to a beige value system as they struggle to come to terms with the change in circumstance. If we were to visit some of the current disaster zones around the world, whether caused by natural disaster or ongoing conflict we would also see people operating from beige. They are no longer concerned with material possessions or the future, they just want to survive today.

People focused on survival tend to live in the moment. The reason they don't plan for the future is because they don't necessarily believe they have one or they simply don't think about the future. A very good friend of mine, Dr Anthony Vogelpoel, is working with a very remote aboriginal community in Northern Australia. He tells me that it is often extremely difficult to get his patients to take their diabetic medication because they don't really have any concept of preventative medicine. If diabetic complications arise they think it's because of their ancient beliefs or 'Goanna spirit' rather than their personal failure to take their Glicizide tablets.

The upside of beige is that the individual survives but the downside is there is very little progress or forward movement. Beige can be a very lonely, scary and stressful place so eventually these negative aspects push individuals operating at beige to find or connect with other people. They recognize that it will be easier to survive as part of a group and it is this insight that pushes individuals up the spiral to purple.

Purple: Belonging (collective focus)

Those operating from the purple value system realize that survival is easier in groups. Magic, superstitions and rituals are important at this level as individuals come to understand that being part of a collective is safer than being alone.

It is common to see tribal behaviour in business. Corporate tribes can be found in any business silo such as sales or IT. The tribe may be organized, not around a functional imperative, but a geographic location. Often the people in these corporate tribes will feel more loyalty to their local tribe than they will to the company itself. It is this purple value system that often reinforces silo behaviour in organizations where everyone in the silo is busy looking out for everyone else in the silo but rarely considers their impact on the rest of the business. Protectionism and defensiveness is the norm. The tribe will resist input from 'head office' and be motivated to see the 'threat' from that 'other' group. Within the tribe, members can be quite hostile to the larger business; they are often simplistic in their analysis of commercial considerations and strive not to rock the boat too much, as this could undermine the security of the group. Since safety and security is so central to them people operating from this value system are often very quick to sense a personal or commercial threat. They can react strongly to protect their own position and the security of their tribe.

Communicating with Purple

The best way to encourage those operating from a purple value system to evolve or embrace changes is to position those changes as necessary in order to protect the group in the future. Instead of focusing on what will be different focus where possible on how changes will allow the group to maintain the status quo. Speak in simple terms about what matters to this value system – tradition, ancestors, security, no change, togetherness. Allow the purple tribe to debate the suggested change with the group and reach a collective agreement. Try to identify the 'loudest' voice in the tribe, the 'elder' or most influential members as they are likely to be the closest person that is ready to make the next developmental leap. If they respond well to the suggested change immediately reward their engagement and give them increased power and status within the group.

Living your life at this level does have its upsides. There is often a very strong sense of community and belonging. Life is lived together and the 'safety in numbers' principle is felt at a personal level as shown in a fascinating BBC TV series called *Tribal Wives*, where women from comfortable

Western families were dropped into very remote tribal communities to see how they would cope. Many of the women had a profoundly emotional experience, and were overwhelmed by the affection complete strangers had for them and the sense of belonging they felt from the tribe (BBC Two, 2010).

However, this level of values development does have a downside. Namely, decisions are often reactive, poorly thought through and there is minimal long-term thinking and often no real sense of direction. This lack of direction eventually initiates an evolutionary move up the spiral to red.

Red: Power (individual focus)

Red is characterized by individuals who take charge. It is the colour of power and passion and sooner or later a red leader steps forward to take charge of the purple tribe so that things can finally get done rather than long debates, unpredictable 'group think' or decision driven by the latest 'fad' or fashion as people seek to position themselves with the latest trend of the 'in-crowd'.

The military actively flush out red leaders by dropping recruits into uncertain situations and waiting. They know that the purple lack of direction will push someone to step up and take the reins. The same happens in business, out of the group, steps a red leader who takes the reins and doesn't let go, often going all the way to the top.

Red leaders are one of the two most common value systems we see in the upper echelons of global multi-nationals. They are often energetic, charismatic 'larger than life' individuals who often have a great sense of humour. However, they can also lead by fear, intimidation or strength of will. They are great at simplifying and clarifying the priorities which can help increase action. Red leaders are known for making things happen, so they are ideal if a business is opening a new market or going into a new territory. They always want to be number one in their market. They are restless, relentless and resilient with a strong sense of urgency. They move fast to get control and use their status, power or authority to dominate. They are good in a fight, an emergency or in a turnaround where they are often perceived as the hero.

Communicating with Red

The best way to encourage those operating from the red value system to evolve and develop is to show them how, with a little more structure, they can celebrate even grander victories. The knack is to help them work smarter not harder; a little more skill and a little less speed and brute force is often what's required. Be sure to emphasize how the initiative or action will allow the red leader to contribute personally, how others will see that contribution and how it will increase their own profile or reputation. Where possible make their development seem fun and exciting so they maintain interest and always seek to communicate clearly without the hype. Red individuals prefer short to the point communications.

The real benefit of red leadership is their passion and desire to 'just do it'. However, the downside is that progress is often dependent on the individual leader themselves. The red leader can become a bottleneck for decisions and the excessive responsibility taken by a red leader can create the responsibility virus we explored in Chapter 1 (Martin, 2003). The intoxicating nature of ultimate power can fuel a sense of omnipotence in the red leader and start to drive a wide range of unhelpful behaviours or egomania. It is this thirst for power and narcissism that upsets the collective who eventually club together to curb the excesses of red leadership and blue 'order' emerges.

Blue: Order (collective focus)

Blue represents order, conservatism and loyalty and heralds a swing back to the collective. Someone operating from blue is keen to 'do the right thing'. For the first time meaning emerges and higher principles or causes become important. This is in stark contrast from a red individual who is often too busy enjoying themselves to consider what stuff means.

Blue cultures are often present in government departments, bureaucracies and public sector partnerships where order, rank and rules are imposed and adhered to. Business too usually goes through a blue phase – usually once it's grown to a certain level and the 'seat of the pants' approach becomes too chaotic. Blue pulls order and infrastructure from the chaos to create a stable platform for growth. The bigger a business gets the more structure is needed to really prosper – high quality processes can make a massive difference to most companies. The rules, regulations and accuracy imposed by blue can also bring some much needed discipline to a business and prevent red excesses from derailing the organization.

Communication must be structured, tidy and well presented. Meetings must be well managed, stick to time and follow a disciplined process. Blue people tend to be diplomatic, avoid conflict, and are efficient finishers who like to take the moral high ground.

Communicating with Blue

The best way to encourage those operating from the blue value system to evolve and develop is to encourage them to experiment and show others how the initiative or change could benefit the collective, without compromising its values. Whatever you are trying to get a blue person engaged in you need to position it as 'the right thing to do'. If the blue individual doesn't believe what they are being asked is fair and right then you will not get their cooperation. Underneath this principled stance there is a seed of self-interest. If there is a personal benefit in being different, whether it is greater freedom or self-determination or even financial then this can also be a stimulus to evolve out of blue to the next level up.

The upside of blue is stability. But too much blue and the business can become rigid and inflexible – both qualities that struggle in a VUCA world. Like all levels it is the dysfunction of blue that eventually creates the conditions for the evolutionary push up into the next level and orange emerges.

Orange: Wealth (individual focus)

Orange illustrates a swing back to an individual focus. Most businesses are run by leaders from either a red or orange value system. Essentially the orange leader is a more mature version of the red leader because they've come to appreciate the importance of process, procedure and principle. They are also less likely to make unilateral decisions and are more inclusive and considered.

Free from the stifling constraints of too many blue rules the orange leader looks to leverage the best parts of the blue infrastructure and system whilst being more flexible in order to compete, grow the business and deliver results. The ultimate goal of orange is wealth creation. Orange leaders take a pragmatic no-nonsense view of the world and they are happy to do whatever it takes to achieve their targets.

Individuals operating from an orange value system want to make money. They are highly competitive and want to win. They have a slightly more mature ambition compared to red individuals and are often better equipped to take advantage of other people's abilities to achieve their own and the business's goals.

Communicating with Orange

The best way to encourage those operating from the orange value system to evolve and develop is to be outcome focused and make it clear how the plan or initiative will work to deliver wealth and success. Orange individuals respond to the outcome not the method of getting to the outcome so if they can invent the journey and are free to work through the challenges and make changes in how they achieve that outcome they will be a lot more engaged and are much more likely to do what you want them to do. Focus too on how the changes will impact them or the business financially.

In modern society orange is often considered the pinnacle of success. Wealth is often seen as the finish line or the ultimate prize for hard work and effort. Perhaps unsurprisingly the dark side of orange is therefore greed and avarice. When we deregulate markets and sweep away too many rules then we start to create the conditions that foster extreme orange behaviour – think Enron, global financial crisis etc. People start to 'play the system' for their own personal benefit. Whilst the upside of orange is wealth creation it is polluted by the excessive greed of the few which acts as the next evolutionary stimulus and green emerges.

Green: Social (collective focus)

The excess of orange triggers a swing back to the collective and green businesses or green leaders emerge. Green is motivated to find a more inclusive way of achieving success that benefits the many not just the few. Green leaders have realized that the 'winners and losers' mindset is ultimately a zero sum game and are driven to make different choices. They take a more sensitive, people-centric approach. This care extends from people to the planet. They are interested in their carbon footprint, fair trade, local produce, sustainability and the whole green agenda. They are also much more attuned to the needs of the collective.

Green CEOs and leaders are often ambassadorial in style. They are generally more emotionally intelligent, empathic and are driven by a desire to help. They attempt to include a wide section of opinion and have an intense dislike of hierarchies.

Those operating from green want to be inclusive, provide a platform for varied views and reach a collective agreement. They take the view that there is implicit judgement in all hierarchies and hierarchies therefore promote the idea of 'good, better, best'. As a result green are often the most likely to reject the vertical nature of development. What they are really rejecting is 'dominator or power hierarchies' and they often fail to distinguish such dynamics from natural hierarchies. For example, molecules do not exist without atoms, which do not exist without electrons and protons. It would be ridiculous to suggest that atoms are better than protons. They are in a natural hierarchy with each other. If you get rid of protons you collapse everything above this level. So molecules need protons to exist – just as a leader needs followers. One is not 'better' than the other but they play different roles and make different contributions.

Green wants to bring everyone to the same level playing field. But in doing so the green value system is blind to the fact that it creates its own power hierarchy and belief that the horizontal ('we are all equal') is *better* than a vertical hierarchy. Such blindness typifies the green contradiction. On the one hand very caring and inclusive, and on the other hand myopic and judgemental.

The challenge with green, as with all the previous levels is that they believe their perspective and approach is the right one and defend their position loudly. In fact every leader in the first tier (beige to green) thinks they are right and everyone else is wrong and spiral dynamics is very similar to the maturity model in this regard. Most of the world's big problems stem from this 'I'm right, you're wrong' duality. In business this dynamic consumes a huge amount of time and effort as individuals or cliques defend their position, engage in office politics and slow initiatives because they don't agree with the party line. And considering that everyone from beige to green is making the same fundamental error – ie refusing to step into someone else's shoes – then a huge amount of wasted energy goes into this pointless dance.

Green is the last level in the first tier. And, according to Ken Wilber, it is the main stumbling block for widespread evolution and progress – especially in business (2003). Most leaders don't make it past the green consensual swamp and stay firmly rooted in the orange reality, or below.

Communicating with Green

The best way to encourage those operating from the green value system to evolve and develop is to position the change or initiative as a win-win. Take a collective position and emphasize how others will be taken with the change and it will help everyone not just the few. Green individuals respond well to sincerity and heartfelt expressed emotion moves them forward. They want to feel involved and will welcome the opportunity to participate and say their piece. They can react badly to assertive leaders with simple answers.

The upside of green is collaboration; the inclusion of diversity and care but ultimately their drive for consensus can stall them as they try to keep 'everyone on the bus'. They simple don't get enough done. The failure of the first tier value systems, of which green is the last, to adequately deal with the VUCA world has provided a stimulus to accelerate a greater emergence of the second tier value system, the first of which is yellow.

Yellow: Innovation (individual focus)

Yellow sees a move away from the collective and back to the individual. Those operating at yellow finally understand that it's not 'I'm right, you're wrong' but that all of the previous perspectives have some validity and that they are all also incomplete in some way. By evolving past the 'consensual hell' and overt inclusivity of green, yellow injects rocket fuel to green's creativity and becomes innovative.

Yellow is disruptive. Red can also be disruptive but the red approach is directive – 'my way or the high way'. Yellow is much more nuanced and sophisticated. Businesses that operate from yellow become innovation engines, constantly coming up with better, brighter, more efficient solutions to their evolving challenges. As such they often change the game, create paradigm shifts and establish 'clear blue water' from their competition (Kim and Mauborgne, 2005). Instead of competing in highly competitive markets that require ferocious defence (cut-throat red water) yellow companies simply keep innovating – thus always staying one step ahead of the competition. Yellow businesses are usually small or if not they are organized into small, highly dynamic divisions. They are competitive because they are fast, agile and able to 'hack' around older less optimal structures. The power of the yellow value system in business is beautifully described in Frederic Laloux's brilliant book *Reinventing Organizations* (2014).

Yellow leaders know that the world is not black and white and they accept that they may be simultaneously part of the problem and part of the solution but they take responsibility for inventing the solution. They see multiple perspectives and can easily handle conflicts of interest. They are drawn to complex problems and see them as a challenge. They are excited by new ideas and want to have an impact beyond their company.

Although only 1 per cent of the global population is operating at yellow (Wilber, 2001), this number increases to 10 per cent amongst the more developed population of 2,000-plus business leaders whose value systems we have assessed in the last few years. However, even at 10 per cent yellow offers a distinct competitive advantage that most businesses are simply not exploiting. What the Leadership Values Profile does is allow leaders to understand where they and their senior team are operating from and take steps to vertically develop up the spiral.

Communicating with Yellow

The best way to encourage those operating from the yellow value system to evolve and develop still further is to help them articulate their ideas.

They can over complicate things or wrongly assume that people follow the sophistication of their thought processes, when those around them, who almost certainly come from earlier levels, simply don't get it. They can appear disinterested and above the fray and this may impair their ability to connect and land their ideas or views.

To engage effectively with yellow individuals it is vital to lay out the conceptual frame for the conversation first. Then there has to be sufficient substance to the message otherwise yellow individuals will perceive it as lightweight, not serious and not worthy of consideration.

Yellow leaders take personal responsibility; they are innovative, often disruptively so and are very focused on learning and their own development. They can however be way too conceptual – especially to those operating from the first tier. Often they are considered too complex for others to understand and can appear aloof, dispassionate or even detached. And it is this disconnection that often triggers the emergence of the turquoise value system.

Turquoise: System balance (collective focus)

Those operating from turquoise swing back to the collective again. As such turquoise individuals and organizations tend to be focused on initiating movements rather than formal businesses. Their perspective is on the long term and they are interested in creating cultural and social change for the benefit of all people without falling into the trap of being too prescriptive or patronizing. A turquoise leader is therefore much more interested in the greater good.

However these leaders can appear distracted and don't necessarily engage in the daily nitty-gritty of business because they are more concerned in moulding the future. They have an ability to take in a huge amount of information, moving variables and different perspectives and make sense of it all. This allows them to dynamically steer the business which can feel too free flowing and unnerving to those in any of the first tier value systems.

A turquoise leader can and will show up from many different value systems, since turquoise transcends and includes all previous levels. They can take the role of strong commercial leader, wealth generator or social missionary depending on what's needed. This can appear fickle to others but the turquoise leader is not playing a role, they are just moving up and down the spiral depending on what the situation warrants.

Globally, only 0.1 per cent of the population operate from a turquoise value system. This means that less than 2 per cent of the global population are operating from a second tier value system of either yellow or turquoise. Even in our own population of 2,000-plus leaders we have profiled only two turquoise CEOs. For the record it has also been suggested that coral, a level above turquoise is beginning to emerge but it's still unclear (Wilber, 2001).

Communicating with turquoise

The best way to get the most out of those operating from the turquoise value system is to help them connect with the less sophisticated perspectives which they may have less familiarity with. They may also struggle with being fierce when they need to be.

Turquoise leaders prefer to be open to difference, tolerant and inclusive. Unfortunately, especially to a red or orange leader this can be interpreted as indecision and weakness. Emphasizing the social change aspect of a project can energize the turquoise leader. Although to be fair, these individuals are so rare the chances of you encountering one in your business are unfortunately very slim!

Using spiral dynamics to better understand yourself and others

Appreciating our own and others' value systems can completely change the 'WE' dimension. Having a way of understanding the difference between our perspective and that of others, being able to see the upsides and downsides of both can enable us to better reconcile our differences, reduce any conflict and improve the quality of our communication. This will almost always improve relationships. We have seen time and again that the insights gained from the LVP often help to dissolve contentious issues and discussions and negotiations become much less personal.

Disagreements between executives are often misdiagnosed as a 'personality clash' but the conflict is usually nothing to do with personality. Rather it is to do with different value systems at play. When we can see that both our different points of view have validity and are arising from our different value system then we are much better placed to shift our position and find a way to reconcile our differences. For example say two people are having an argument where one wants to make a decision and get into action and the other wants to explore more options and find the consensus. When both individuals realize that most of what they are arguing about is actually a reflection of their value system then much of the heat is taken out of the situation. When the red individual realizes they are operating from red and the green individual realizes they are operating from green and both can appreciate the other's value system then they can come to a compromise position that will facilitate a better, less fraught and more mutually agreeable way forward.

This is especially true when using the LVP because there are various sub-scales built into the tool that reveal how a person's value system varies depending on the task they are engaged in. When a leader is focused on strategy for example they may operate at the yellow values level indicating an open and innovative approach – highly desirable for strategy. That same leader may then shift into blue for implementation and seek to follow process and implement the right procedures to execute the strategy. The leader may even resort to a little autocratic red value system should implementation be too slow. Understanding which value system we tend to show up with in different circumstances can create a clear platform for how we can get the best out of ourselves and each other.

It is also possible to plot the gravity of a work group or executive team to see where most of the members operate from and therefore where the natural bias is. If there are more red individuals in a team then unless this is identified and 'called out' those red individuals may have a tendency to monopolize meetings and ride roughshod over other people. Knowing the dynamics and how this gravity shifts depending on the task can therefore allow the leader to bring the best people to the table for each type of discussion to fast track decision making and implementation. Essentially the LVP allows us to see how we show up in each of the four quadrants of the Enlightened Leadership Model. We can see how we show up when we are called on to conceptualize the business's long-range objectives in the top right, market leadership quadrant; what value is dominant when we are executing our chosen strategy in the top left commercial performance quadrant; what values are dominant when we are managing others in the bottom right, people leadership quadrant; and how we are showing up personally in the bottom left personal performance quadrant.

This understanding also offers powerful insights to why leadership breaks down and why there can be an apparent loss of authenticity in a leader. For example if a leader's profile indicates that how they show up in their personal life is significantly different from how they show up at work then this may reveal that a leader is struggling to be authentic or bring all of their personal qualities to bear at work. That disconnect may impact the leader's fulfilment, personal effectiveness and this may impact the team. By profiling around all four quadrants leaders and senior executives can appreciate their own values systems and the gravity shifts that occur depending on what quadrant they are operating in and how that impacts the team. In effect the LVP facilitates a much deeper understanding of the subtlety of our own values so we can understand ourselves more deeply and better explain ourselves, our actions and choices to others.

Once a senior team has been profiled and each individual understands how they show up in various situations this information can be touched upon at the start of important meetings to reframe the meeting and remind all the participants of the strengths and vulnerabilities they may bring to the discussion. The meeting leader could for example open by saying, 'Before we get started I appreciate that I have a tendency to get carried away with ideas and possibilities; I know from my LVP that this can be particularly irritating to at least two of you; it's also important that we follow a due process here for you John so let's agree on a process that offers a good compromise and we agree on a set time frame for strategic discussion before we get into action.' That way the other people in the meeting feel as though their values are being taken into consideration and a framework is agreed that honours the various strengths and mitigates a few of the weaknesses. This mutual understanding and value specific language alone can massively improve the quality and output of relationships and a lot of the arm wrestling and power struggles simply disappear.

The values spiral also helps improve performance and results because it allows us to work with and bring in the right people to get the various tasks done. For example turquoise and yellow are particularly useful in strategy meetings because they can appreciate multiple perspectives and may come up with 'out the box' innovations. But these perspectives play less of a driving role when it comes to implementation. Green individuals are great for including everyone and ensuring the team feel involved. Orange can bring commercial nous, blue are brilliant at process and procedure while red can be invaluable for injecting energy and getting stuff done. Everyone has a role to play that allows the group to tap into the collective strength while mitigating the collective weaknesses. These insights allow us to appreciate that many of the stumbling blocks in business could actually be avoided when we effectively blend people who have different values we don't have into the decision.

Obviously, the more sophisticated the leader the more options they have in dealing and working with their team. Remember we can move down the spiral at will in order to match the values of the people around us but we have to put the effort in to work our way up the spiral through vertical development. When we do we increase the verticality of the 'WE' dimension to facilitate 4D Leadership.

How to cultivate the inter-personal world of 'WE'

It is impossible to have good relationships without good communication. Communication is essential and yet we're never really taught how to communicate effectively.

Effective communication has two basic aspects: transmission and reception. However as children we are only ever taught half the formula – transmission. Our parents and teachers may correct us – for example, 'you can't say "more better", it's just better' – they help us to understand the correct tense, pronunciation, grammar and spelling. We are taught when to use what words and the power of linguistic tricks like analogy and metaphor and eventually we become reasonably proficient at transmission. But, we don't ever get trained in reception or how to receive information. Our parents or teacher rarely gave us instructions and asked us to repeat those instructions to make sure we understood them. Instead they probably said, 'Right now, listen up' or 'Are you listening?' Or, more usually, 'Why can't you just listen!'

Little people grow up into big people, believing that listening is simply 'waiting to speak'. To most people listening is the moment before *they* say something. For most people listening isn't even focused on what the other person was saying. As a result when someone is sitting quietly in a business meeting we assume they are listening, but they're usually not. Instead, what they are actually doing is thinking about what they are going to say next. Or worse – what they plan to have for dinner later. There is often little or no reception actually going on. This is why people constantly talk at cross purposes. In business we ask someone to do something and they seem to agree with the request and look confident. They do what we ask and yet it often bears no resemblance to what we believe we asked for. The truth is we have no idea if they were even listening to our request – they could have been simply agreeing to get out the meeting quickly, or they could have simply misinterpreted our instructions or been thinking about last night's episode of *Game of Thrones*! It's not deliberate, malicious, unprofessional or even intentional, it's just that most of us have never been taught *how* to listen. Consequently our level of connectivity is very superficial; we haven't really heard each other so there is little chance that we really understood each other.

Effective communication is about both the transmission and receipt of meaning. Unfortunately standard communication training does not teach us how to be effective receivers. Usually standard training focuses on the words, tone, and body language of the message. Yet we have known since 1972 that the actual words we use account for only 7 per cent of what we understand. Albert Mehrabian, professor emeritus of psychology at UCLA, proposed that the rest of our understanding was made up of 38 per cent vocal tonality and 55 per cent body language (1972). These component parts of basic communication are often referred to as the '3 Vs' for Verbal, Vocal and Visual. In truth we are able to gauge far more from the tone that someone uses and their body language than we are from the words they use. Anyone who has asked a subordinate to do something they really don't want to do will have experienced this. The words coming out of their mouth may be, 'Yeah sure that's fine!' But their tone and body language is screaming, 'What? You have to be kidding me!!' This is why face-to-face communication is always better than phone and phone is always better than email. Because when we are forced to only rely on the words we don't always get the full meaning and the meaning is much more open to our own interpretation.

Often leaders mistakenly believe that their job is to give people answers. Employees, managers and senior executives may come to them with problems or questions but there is often more going on. The leader's real job is to get beyond the words, tonality and body language and even go beyond the thoughts and feelings behind the words to discover the deeper truth and what that person really means. Often it's just too easy to take conversations at face value, jump to conclusions and offer up a ready-made, off the cuff, solution. When a leader can accurately understand what that individual really *means* – sometimes clarifying a point that the individual isn't fully cognizant of themselves – they can make the transmitter feel validated and heard. And making another human being feel heard is such a rare occurrence in most workplaces that it can be extremely motivating. If we don't take the time to develop the ability to do this we often end up solving the wrong problem because we are much too focused on the words, tonality and body language of the communication.

The only way to get to the meaning is to learn the other half of the communication formula. We need to get much *much* better at reception. Again we already know this and so we send our people on active listening courses or rapport building courses. But many of them don't work either. If anything they simply make someone more sophisticated at not listening! It's all artificial; relationship by numbers – nod three times, repeat the phrase, 'I hear what you are saying ...' or when the person you are talking to leans in you lean in, or when they cross their legs you cross your legs! It's insincere, and the very best outcome is that it allows people to get better at faking communication.

For most of us, when someone says something, we start thinking. Their talking usually triggers a thought in us of some sort be that, 'Oh no here he goes again', or 'Oh that reminds me I need to pick up my dry cleaning', or 'That's an interesting idea' etc.

This thinking about what the other person is saying starts almost immediately. We then start chasing our own thoughts rather than processing what the other person said. As a result, we think we are talking with someone when actually both parties are actually having an internal dialogue with themselves! Or one person is talking and the other person is waiting to speak and working out what they are going to say. We see this in TV quiz shows like *Family Fortunes* where one member of a team will give an answer and it will be wrong and then the next member of the same team will give exactly the same answer. As soon as the question was asked the second team member stopped listening to the conversation and started to think about what they were going to say when asked the same question – so much so that they didn't hear their team mate's answer and ended up looking like an idiot on national TV! We also see this in business in the form of endless circular meetings. Part of the reason meetings go on so long and little gets resolved is because no one is actually listening to each other. Everyone is just having a conversation with themselves: 'I just said that!' 'Did you? Oh I wasn't listening.' We even say that to each other!

Not only that but we are often so desperate to look smart and get our point across before someone else does or before we forget it that we interrupt the original transmission. Even if the interruption is for good reasons, to clarify the message, it's still a break in the transmission and therefore often sets up confusion, withdrawal and resentment on the part of the person who's just been interrupted.

We can create better relationships and vertically develop in the interpersonal world of 'WE', but only if we dispense with the superficial and seek to go beyond the words, tone and body language so we can access meaning and create more authentic connections with others that facilitates genuine listening or reception. And the skill that can help us achieve that outcome is called the MAP skill.

The MAP skill

The MAP skill helps us to tap into our social intuition, empathy and rapport enabling us to become more deeply aware of others. And when we learn how to appreciate others we develop positive working relationships more easily, even with those we wouldn't normally gravitate to.

In the good old days it may have been possible to rise through the ranks on IQ, business smarts and aggression alone without any real regard for emotional and social intelligence (ESQ). But in a VUCA world it is impossible to build a great company without the ability to create and nurture great relationships.

MAP is an acronym for the process we must go through to ensure that we are really listening for and understanding meaning.

Move your attention away from your own thinking and drop into the body and BREATHE;

Appreciate the speaker;

Play back the underlying meaning.

The MAP skill may initially go against everything you believe to be true about communication and listening but just try it – it will transform your communication. Don't test it out in a high stakes conversation until you have mastered the technique. Instead start small so you can be comfortable with the process.

When you are next in conversation with someone, rather than immediately focusing on what you are going to say or interrupting the other person **move** (**M**) your attention away from the noise in your own head. So consciously and deliberately move your attention away from your own thoughts, preconceived ideas and judgements about yourself, the meeting, the other person or the pile of work you need to get back to and shift your focus to the centre of your chest and your breath. Use the same BREATHE skill from Chapter 3 – **b**reathe **r**hythmically **e**venly **a**nd **t**hrough the **h**eart **e**very day. This will help you stop the thought chasing.

When I first teach this skill to executives they think they won't hear if they're not thinking or fully consciously engaged with the words. But we already know that only 7 per cent of any communication is determined by the words we use so it's actually not that necessary to 'actively listen' to every word transmitted anyway. Even when we are not actively listening our brain still processes most of the words so we really don't need to concentrate that hard. The MAP skill can therefore save us a lot of the energy we expend through intense concentration.

Next activate a state of **appreciation (A)** for the transmitter. This is the critical step. Influential psychologist Carl Rogers referred to this state as an 'unconditional positive regard' (1967). Turn on a warm glowing feeling of acceptance and support for the person transmitting the message, regardless of what they say or do. Rogers believes that unconditional positive regard is essential to healthy development and when we do this properly the transmitter feels it – they feel a sense of warmth and acceptance which can be extremely moving.

Asking seasoned business executives to turn on a warm glow of acceptance can be quite funny. Usually it's not a request they've heard before but as soon as they let go of their reservations and just try it the results are immediate and often profound. Both the individual who is transmitting the warm regard and the individual receiving it feels the shift in the communication. It becomes deeper, easier and more authentic.

Because so much of the judgement falls away the person doing the talking tends to open up and often tells the listener things they hadn't planned to tell them so the listener gets much more information. When we do this with a customer, supplier or client they will tell us all sorts of things that they had no intention of divulging. Plus when the transmitter feels encouraged and appreciated the quality of their transmission also improves. So not only do we get more information but the information we get is also transmitted much more clearly, more precisely and more succinctly. We get to the heart of the issue much faster using appreciation than we ever would with impatience, interruption or restlessness.

The next step is **play back (P)** – so play back what you've received. Until you get good at this you can't be sure that what you think is going on is actually what is *really* going on.

Often we mistakenly assume we have accurately detected the meaning but what we have actually detected is our own internal noise. For example we may listen to an employee and be immediately convinced they are having issues with their immediate supervisor but our interpretation is actually being clouded by the fact that we are having issues with our immediate boss too. One of the quirks of the human condition is that we are better able to see issues in others that we resonate with and this affinity, even if it's unconscious, can muddy the waters. As a result quality play back is absolutely vital. And quality play back is very different from just repeating or summarizing what the other person just said or providing our own view or answer. It's about playing back what we feel the other person *meant* at the deeper level.

It's important that you don't impose your views when it comes to play back. Play back from your subjective perspective so you might preface your play back with a statement such as, 'It felt to me that you ...' or, 'I get the impression that you ...'. This allows the other person to either agree or disagree and provide more information.

It is also best to present your observations as a question or suggestion and not an assertion. This approach therefore invites them into the interpersonal 'WE' space with you and your question creates a connection which they can choose to engage with or not. If your subjective sense was accurate, the transmitter will usually confirm your assertion or they will deny it and give you more information so that you can fine tune your play back. In the moment of confirmation you are suddenly aligned in the same place of understanding. The transmitter knows for certain you understand them, you've played back and they've confirmed. This can be profoundly moving for the transmitter who can feel genuinely heard and listened to – often for the first time.

The MAP skill is a deceptively powerful technique that can improve the quality and outcome of discussions while also mending bridges and strengthening ongoing relationships. It is also very effective for conflict resolution.

We used this MAP skill for an IT team who were increasingly overwhelmed with the volume of work coming their way and they were finding it difficult to keep up with all the demands from the business. They would meet every month as a team to try to get ahead of the curve only to discover they were getting further behind. They would start their day with a very long agenda, the debate would be painfully circular; decision making was slow and by 6pm they would still not have finished. Often the discussion would migrate to the bar with everyone feeling dissatisfied. We worked with this team for an entire day on the MAP skill, drilling them in how to use it effectively to speed up their understanding of each other and the issues they were facing. Investing this amount of time in developing a faster way of getting to the crucial issues was transformational. At their next month's meeting they found that they got through the entire agenda by lunchtime and in the afternoon they all went and played golf and created a powerful bonding experience. That's the power of the MAP skill.

Imagine being able to enter any meeting or situation and grasp the real meaning behind the discussions. Interactions are much more effective, usually decisions are reached faster and there is much less stress in the exchange – even for opposing viewpoints.

Plus when you play back really accurately what's going on for another person it can step change other people's perception of you. When you accurately identify the deeper meaning of someone's transmission, particularly when they did not actually say what they meant the other person often looks at you with a new found respect.

Appreciation of others' skill

Although appreciation is built into the MAP skill it is also an important tool in its own right. We explored how to use the appreciate skill on ourselves to bring our strengths and positive qualities into conscious awareness in Chapter 3. Not only is this skill important for developing verticality in the 'I' dimension, when turned outward it is also useful for developing verticality in the 'WE' dimension. Appreciation of others is a fundamental skill of social intelligence that can positively impact communication and relationships.

When we sincerely appreciate something in another human being that is also meaningful to them it can be profoundly motivational and this exchange can help unlock discretionary effort. Appreciation of others is not something that is common place in business. Something I was reminded of when I was speaking to a main Board director of a global retailer. He told me that appreciation from his CEO was so rare that he remembered the exact time and place it occurred. In the same way we always remember where we were when we heard that JFK was assassinated or when Princess Diana was killed, he remembered the rare moments of praise and appreciation during a 25 year career.

Recognizing someone's skill and contribution and calling that out publicly can be more motivational for people than a bonus. And yet it's a hugely under-utilized business tool. This skill is however especially useful when dealing with people we would not normally gravitate to. Often in our professional lives we need to be able to work with people that we don't necessarily warm to or like. The appreciation of another's skill allows us to be able to do that more effectively so that we can deliberately and consciously find things about that person to appreciate which can open the door for better communication and trust.

Highly socially intelligent leaders are able to find something to appreciate about *everyone* they meet, not just the ones they naturally resonate with. With elevated ESQ we can learn to connect with anyone and create productive relationships.

When you meet someone you don't immediately warm too, or actively dislike, take a moment to find some quality within the other person that you can sincerely appreciate. Perhaps you could appreciate their caustic wit, or their intelligence or their ability with numbers or the fact that your interaction with this person is limited to one meeting a month! Without appreciation you will never make an effective connection. And if we can't make an effective connection we will never be able to create and nurture the relationships necessary to thrive in the VUCA world.

We all need others to deliver on our objectives. Learning to notice what is special about the other people you deal with regularly can also be a very valuable habit to get into. Create a list of the people you are in regular contact with in your professional and private life and take a moment to consider what specific qualities they have that you appreciate. Think about the specific quality as well as when, where and how it shows up.

Make sure you take the time to notice at least one of these qualities every time you communicate with each person and where appropriate take the opportunity to tell the other person that you appreciate that quality.

It's a general principle that moving yourself to a more positive emotion 'planet' is generally more helpful in terms of improving your performance. This is why the SHIFT skill from Chapter 3 is so useful because it allows us to induce positive emotions and alter brain function which in turn alters the way we see things and how we interact with others. Appreciation is a powerful antidote to judgement or any negative emotion and can radically improve our ability to create strong working relationships and develop trust.

The 4D leader can work with anyone to deliver anything because they have developed verticality in the relationship crucial dimensions of 'I' and 'WE'. And that capability is going to become increasingly relevant to long-term business success in the VUCA environment.

Action steps

When it comes to extracting commercial value from the 'WE' dimension, many of the previous action steps in the dimensions of 'I' and 'IT' will have a positive, cumulative effect on the world of 'relating'. However below are some suggested action steps that can help extract the maximum value from the 'WE' dimension:

1 Consider having your own and your executive team's values assessed using the Leadership Values Profile (LVP) that clarifies the eight levels of development of the value systems.

2 Understand which of these eight levels you are personally operating from and how that changes depending on whether you are working on strategy and implementation ('IT'), people management ('WE') or just being yourself ('I'). Values levels shows up differently in each of the four quadrants.

3 Clarify the upside and downside of each value system as it shows up in each of the four quadrants so you can appreciate where you might add value but also undermine performance when operating from that level.

4 As part of your personal development plan focus on evolving your value system to the next level. This can be achieved by understanding the characteristics and behaviours of the next level and making a concerted effort to incorporate them into your daily life.

5 Having understood where you operate from on the values spiral you need to know how that relates to other people in your team so you can 'spot the difference'. Clarify the value that they bring which may be different from the value you bring and identify how you may need to change your attitude and behaviour toward others to allow them to express that value fully.

6 Take the time to practise and master the MAP skill to improve communication and build understanding. Try it initially in one-on-one discussions that are not critical so that you can build up confidence in the process.

7 Try to actively boost other people's energy and motivation through explicitly appreciating them and their efforts.

The secret of successful relationships in the 'WE' dimension

06

When it comes to relationships most people are as baffled about how to create productive successful relationships as they are about how to create consistently high performance. Like performance we are confused about what causes it and what impairs it. Certain relationship approaches work with some individuals and the same things don't work with others. In an attempt to improve performance in business or sport this inconsistency of outcome has spawned innumerable 'solutions'. Similarly the inconsistency of relationships and the unpredictable results of relationship strategies have also spawned all manner of ideas about how to improve our connectivity with others. But despite this most people remain confused and dismiss relationship failures in the 'WE' domain as a personality clash, a style difference, something to do with typology, down to nationality, creed or an even more random explanation like star sign incompatibility.

However as we've discovered performance is not a mystery and neither are relationships. Developing high performance or brilliant relationships results from cultivating increased altitude and coherence across a number of lines of development. Relationships remain a mystery for most people. This chapter will seek to unpack that mystery and the magic so we can understand the anatomy of relationships and how we can be brilliant in the interpersonal domain. We will also explore perspective taking, leadership behaviour as well as team development, effective feedback and how network analysis can increase verticality in the 'WE' dimension.

The starting point to building successful relationships is to truly understand the structural dynamics of human interaction, specifically the importance of perspectives and the distinction between 1st, 2nd and 3rd person perspective taking. You may remember from the Leadership Maturity Profile (LMP) model in Chapter 4 that there are actually at least six levels of possible perspective taking but for the purposes of really understanding what makes relationships work (and not work) then we need to focus on the first three levels – 1st, 2nd and 3rd person perspective.

Perspective taking

Over the last 20 years I have had the privilege of working with many Executive Boards in many companies all over the world, as well as many Olympic and elite sporting teams. One thing that is absolutely consistent across all these teams is how the dynamics of the conversations within these groups play out. Regardless of the agenda, group interactions frequently degrade into what we call 'Popcorn meetings'. In other words, someone in the room passionately advances their point of view, before long a second person chips in, making a separate point while effectively ignoring the first comment. This triggers a thought in a third individual who pitches in with a third point which is separate from either of the two views already aired. This can go on for some time with each new person basically advocating their own point of view and endlessly seeking opportunities to return to it and persuade the room of its validity. It is like listening to popcorn being made in a saucepan – there may be the occasional lull and then furious popping, followed by a short lull and then a flurry of popping until it's all popped out. This happens in meetings all the time.

And, the views being shared come in one of two forms, either a passionate 1st person perspective or a rational 3rd person observation. I have often seen this type of dynamic continue unchecked for 45 minutes before the executives in the room realize no progress is being made. Even after individuals have been taught the secret of successful relationships and understand the fundamental importance of perspective taking, the urge to express themselves from 1st or 3rd person perspective is so ingrained and strong that they will immediately ignore what they just learnt about perspective taking and start making a completely different point again.

When a leader is stuck in the 1st person perspective they communicate from a position of 'Me, My or I' – 'I think ...' or 'let me tell you my feelings on this ...' The compulsion to speak occurs because the sense of importance they hold for their own point of view is so strong it has 'got them'. They lose awareness so they can't see that they are being consumed by their own desire to make a noise, even when the point they feel compelled to make doesn't necessarily move the conversation forward. Often their point simply diverts the focus of the conversation in a completely different direction and even if someone immediately points out that 'we've gone off-topic', it may not stop it happening. The energy of the 1st person perspective comes from an individual's beliefs, values and convictions and is often therefore fuelled by emotion. So we hear leaders and senior executives say things like, 'Well in *my* view ...' or 'In *my* experience ...'.

There is of course, absolutely nothing wrong with taking a 1st person perspective. In fact it is very useful for leaders because power, passion and authenticity emerge from this perspective. When Martin Luther King said, 'I have a dream ...' there was strength in that message because it was delivered from the 1st person perspective. It would have been much less powerful and much less memorable if he had said, 'You have a dream ...' or 'There is a dream ...'.

When we communicate in the 1st person perspective we are often putting a stake in the ground about what we want, think or believe. As a result we tend to be very attached to what we transmit in the 1st person. We can then become instantly defensive if someone interrupts our 1st person transmission; ignores it or, worse, disagrees with it. This can feel like a personal attack and is likely to inflame the interaction or cause us to become more deeply entrenched in our 1st person perspective. We can take feedback or challenge very personally when we are stuck in the 1st person. We are seeing the world from inside our belief structure with all its attached emotion and feeling. The goal from this perspective is to 'win' the argument and impose our personal view often with force of personality. We are stuck in the dichotomy of 'I am right and you are wrong' because 'we can't both be right'.

If leaders are not stuck in the 1st person perspective then they are almost certainly stuck in the 3rd person perspective. This is less emotive and more detached, rational and objective. The 3rd person perspective involves seeing the world from a distance and taking an observer's view. Anything can be held as an object in awareness – ideas, plans, people, even relationships. The world is full of things, stuff, others, you, its.

Leaders operating from this 3rd person perspective believe there is an objective 'truth' which cannot be refuted. The world often makes more sense and therefore leaders will 'make the case', cite the 'evidence', believe in meritocracy and the 'facts'. 'If I am in possession of the facts I can't be wrong, so it must be that you are wrong'. Leaders in this perspective will say things like, 'the evidence suggests ...', or 'according to the data ...', or 'the numbers don't lie', or 'the fact of the matter is ...'. A leader can't possibly lose the argument because they are right; the facts are on their side. Senior leaders will more commonly default to 3rd person than 1st person perspective taking and many pride themselves in being able to take the 3rd person 'helicopter view' because it's not 'personal', 'it's just business'.

As a result of this dynamic, when two people are arguing they are either both stuck in 1st or 3rd person perspective or one person is stuck in 1st and the other is stuck in 3rd. If both are stuck in 1st the argument is usually louder and more heated. If both are stuck in 3rd the discussion is not so inflamed and it is much easier for people in the 3rd person to 'agree to differ', although these discussions can end in stalemate. Whether both protagonists are stuck in 1st or 3rd or one of each both parties are motivated to win. Neither can easily surrender because doing so would require the person in 1st to surrender their 'belief' or the person in 3rd to surrender their 'facts'. Both sides are equally convinced that their view is the 'truth'. In the case of the 1st person perspective the truth is based on conviction and in 3rd person the truth is based on 'objective evidence'.

When people are in dispute and making no progress they will often rapidly shift from 1st to 3rd to try and 'win' the argument. So if they perceive they are making little progress, the rationalist in 3rd will suddenly engage emotion. They can sometimes get really angry that their 'truth' is being challenged and engage in 'bulldozing' other people in the debate. If the person concerned is the leader this behaviour can be quite destructive. Likewise if someone who is full of conviction doesn't seem to be getting their own way they may disappear to track down the evidence to prove their case. Or they may use evidence and data from the 3rd person to drive home their 1st person perspective. In other words they will use the data to validate their personal opinion. The challenge here is that they will often distort or cherry pick only the evidence that supports their opinion and ignore the rest.

Generally speaking it is easier for people who naturally sit in the 3rd person perspective to flip into a 1st person view than people who are stuck in 1st to flip into 3rd. The irony in all this is when two people are locked in an argument and stuck in 1st or 3rd they actually both want the same thing – 2nd person perspective. But because very few people understand perspective taking or don't know that there is such a thing as 2nd person perspective they can't access this view so they remain stuck.

Whatever the preference or mix, the vast majority of leaders spend their life in 1st or 3rd person perspective. Very few leaders will operate from 2nd person perspective or even know what it is.

We talked in the last chapter about the fact that relationships are tough and they are tough largely because we don't really communicate. We don't listen because our idea of communication is 'waiting to speak'. But there is also something deeper at work here – we simply don't understand the anatomy of relationships.

Ego maturity and perspective taking

As we mature as human beings we become more aware of other people. When we develop from HBv1.5 ego-centricity into HBv2.0 we start to understand other people have views that are different from ours and for our own protection we may start to consider these views as important. But this does not mean we are skilled at 2nd person perspective taking. Understanding another person's interior is really bringing 3rd person objectification capability *and* 1st person empathy to their 1st person interior world. Thus we may understand they have a different view and understand their 1st person perspective but genuine 2nd person perspective taking is about creating common ground and something shared. Just because we understand an alternative 1st person perspective does not mean we have created anything shared. For our own safety we may be able to adapt our behaviour to 'fit in' but that does not mean we have developed the ability to build common ground or a shared understanding.

As we develop further into HBv2.5, where we begin to understand the rules of relationships more, we will often choose to conform. There may be some shared understanding of the social rules but this is often unexpressed, so solid 2nd person perspective taking still does not necessarily exist to any extent. HBv2.0 and HBv2.5 are still relatively unsophisticated ways of looking at the nature of reality. And whilst at these maturity levels we appreciate that there is more to the world than just 'Me, My, I', we still don't understand the anatomy of relationship to any great extent. Even as we vertically develop up the ego line this lack of understanding means that relationship largely remains a mystery and so conformity is the safest bet.

Very strong relationships at any level of maturity, cultural sophistication or geography are characterized by the ability to create common ground, even if the people doing so do not realize this is what they are doing. The secret to great relationships of any type can be found in the 2nd person perspective taking.

Often this terminology can begin to feel very abstract so to help these ideas really land I usually provide a stereotypical scenario that most people can relate to. Imagine the scene; a couple are at home eating dinner. The wife is very upset about something that has happened at work. She's actually been a bit upset for a week or so because the business is going through a re-shuffle and she has a new boss who she doesn't like. The wife proceeds to tell her husband about her terrible day and how horrible her new boss is. The husband, having listened for about two minutes, figures it's the same conversation they had last night and thinking he is being helpful interrupts his wife and says, 'Hey look, you obviously really hate it now, just resign. Go in tomorrow and hand in your notice.' Quite pleased with himself for being so helpful and supportive he then goes back to eating his dinner. He looks up from his plate a few moments later to see his wife looking very irritated. In fact he wonders if he's about to wear his dinner. Things go from bad to worse and they end up in seething silence or a slanging match.

So what happened?

The wife is angry because she didn't want a solution she just wanted her husband to listen to her and show some understanding of her dilemma. She's firmly entrenched in 1st person perspective explaining why she's upset and how terrible the situation is. Her husband has drifted into an unwillingness to actually listen to the conversation especially as they had a similar one the night before. So he immediately 'helicoptered' up to dispassionate rational 3rd person perspective and offered a perfectly valid solution.

In doing so a huge gulf emerges between them because they both feel baffled and dissatisfied with the conversation. The wife is upset because she believes her husband doesn't listen, doesn't understand and doesn't there-fore care because he's not sharing her pain. The husband is upset because *she* doesn't listen or value his opinion. After all he suggested the same answer to the same problem a week ago and if she'd just done what he suggested then they wouldn't be having this conversation at all!

Both the husband and the wife feel irritated with each other and they both start to worry that there is something deeply wrong with their relation-ship. There is actually nothing wrong with the relationship at all, they just don't appreciate that they are each taking a particular perspective that is pushing them further apart instead of pulling them closer together toward a way forward. It is this lack of awareness about the existence of 1st, 2nd and 3rd person perspective that is causing the disconnect – not some deeper dysfunction in the relationship.

Ironically what they both want can be secured in 2nd person perspective which is about what they both share. The 2nd person perspective is the *shared* perspective. The wife wants her husband to share her pain; the husband wants his wife to share his solution. So they both want something shared from the other but they don't know how to get into the 2nd person perspective so they stay stuck in 1st and 3rd respectively. And that's why relationships so often fail because we don't realize there is a 2nd person perspective that can significantly speed up interaction, resolution and strengthen the bonds of that relationship. Even if we do know 2nd person perspectives exist then it's very unlikely that we will learn to consciously communicate from that perspective. The truth is we are pretty resistant to getting into the 2nd person perspective and this resistance is at the heart of all relationship breakdowns in our professional and private lives.

Why 2nd person perspective is so rare

Second person perspective is rare because if we are stuck in 1st it can feel like we have to give up part of our identity. And if we are stuck in 3rd it feels like we have to give up the truth. This is why increasing the altitude in the ego line of development is so crucial because the more ego mature we become the more able we are to surrender our position without that surrender feeling like some sort of failure or loss of face. Surrender, like vulnerability is actually a demonstration of strength and maturity not weakness and yet surrender is very difficult for anyone operating at HBv3.5 or below. Sadly that means that surrender is almost impossible for about 85 per cent of the population. And this certainly goes a long way in explaining why the world is so full of conflict – in the West through flip flopping 'democracy' that changes little to the civil wars and escalating conflicts in the Middle East, Ukraine, Africa and beyond.

With adequate levels of ego maturity (HBv4.0 and above) we realize that we are not really giving anything up. In 1st our idea or opinion still exists but we are just choosing to park it for a moment, and in 3rd the facts are still there but we are just choosing to park them for a moment in an effort to shift into 2nd and find a shared reality.

Understanding and learning perspective taking massively improves effectiveness in the 'WE' dimension and to allow leaders and executives to experience the difference between 1st, 2nd and 3rd person perspective we often run an exercise. In groups of four, two executives are asked to take the 1st person perspective and discuss the issue in the business that is currently upsetting them. Not necessarily with each other, just in their current role. The third executive is then instructed to take on the role of facilitator and their job is to try to create a shared understanding (2nd person perspective). And then the last executive is to take the 3rd person perspective and be the reporter or witness – keeping notes on what happens. Once everyone is clear on their roles the discussion begins and it usually takes about five minutes before the whole conversation degenerates into a complete shambles. The two people in 1st normally talk over each other; they rarely make any genuine connection because they are talking at cross purposes. They are essentially talking to themselves at each other. The 3rd person observer who is watching the discussion normally finds it difficult to stay in the observer position. Instead they get frustrated because they've noticed something about the 1st person discussions that they feel compelled to share. So they eventually drop out of 3rd into 1st, interrupt the discussion and add, 'Hey, let me stop you there because I think what is going on here is ...'. This is particularly true if the facilitator is failing.

And the person who is supposed to be facilitating the discussion and shifting the two people into the shared space of 2nd normally sits silently as they increasingly realize that they don't have the skills to get the two people into the 2nd person perspective. Why? Because they don't know the anatomy of relationship dynamics so they do the only other thing they know how to and go up to dispassionate, impersonal 3rd person perspective and say something like, 'look guys what you seem to be doing here is ...'. So they will explain what's happening between the two rather than facilitate a shared space. Alternatively they may flip into 1st, wade in, take sides or express a strong view about the issue.

The results of this experiment are almost always the same – the two executives stay in the 1st person perspective and, as a result, remain profoundly disconnected. The executive who was supposed to be in 2nd flips to 3rd and the executive in 3rd flips to 1st so no one moves to the 2nd person perspective.

Very occasionally one of the protagonists in the 1st person perspective realizes the discussion is going nowhere so they park their own agenda and start to really listen to the other person. We saw this happen with a healthcare team we were working with. In one of the groups one female and one male executive who started in the 1st person perspective broke through. Stereotypically the male executive was dominating the conversation completely. The female executive, realizing they were getting nowhere decided to let go of her own issues and engage with her colleagues' problems. Whether she was consciously aware of doing it or not she surrendered her 1st person position and moved into the shared space of the 2nd person perspective. By doing so they quickly became incredibly connected because she was sharing his challenges with him, asking him questions about those challenges and he started to feel heard and appreciated. As a result he felt connected to her and automatically shifted into 2nd himself. Once they had figured out a way forward on his issues the male executive felt compelled to reciprocate and started to ask her about her challenges. And as for the facilitator and the observer – they became irrelevant because the two debating executives fixed the issues by themselves because they both moved into 2nd person perspective. What was particularly surprising was that the other two executives and in fact the rest of the room knew something very unusual was happening. Everyone could feel the energy that was created between the two debating executives. It was palpable to such an extent that when the exercise was over it felt like they wanted to share more time together and dive even deeper into each other's issues.

A lot of the magic of relationship lives in the 2nd person perspective. When we understand the anatomy of relationships and understand when we are in 1st or 2nd or 3rd person perspective then relationship is no longer a mystery and we can build trust, foster understanding and radically improve the outcome of communication.

Getting into 2nd person perspective

Getting to 2nd person perspective requires you to look for the point of connection between you and the other person. This point of connection may be contained in the detail of the discussion or you may have to pull back to higher levels of abstraction in order to find common ground. For example two people could be discussing healthcare and both parties may have passionate but opposing views on the subject. In the course of the discussion they realize how quickly their views diverge on how to prioritize the healthcare budget. If they pull back however they may agree on a higher purpose such as the goal of free healthcare at the point of delivery. Once they have found something – anything – they can agree on they can build from there. Once established the two could drop a level to identify at what point their views diverge and the enquiry shifts to why there is a disconnection. Think of it like a zip. The top part of the zip is connected at purpose – 'free healthcare at the point of delivery' – but quickly becomes disconnected when discussing how that might actually work in practice. Similarly the point of connection may be a detail but when the issue becomes more complex they disconnect.

Think of your own relationships. When you were a young adult you may have had relationships where there was a strong physical compatibility but emotionally one of you was stable and one of you was labile. The relationship ultimately broke down because of that divergence. Alternatively, you may have had a meeting of minds with a friend at university and developed a close relationship but at a simpler level – physically – you were incompatible and therefore the relationship broke down. Building 2nd person perspective is like closing the teeth of the zip so the relationship becomes strong. A zip that is fully zipped where the teeth are interlocking all the way from top to bottom is much stronger than a zip where only the top or bottom is zipped.

Remember, just sharing opinions or facts doesn't mean anything is 'shared' in the 'WE' space in the same way that if I share my pencil with you it doesn't automatically become 'our' pencil. Just having two 1st person perspectives doesn't equate to common ground in the 2nd person – it's just a collection of 1st person perspectives.

Comprehension of another person's 1st person interior can certainly improve your ability to create productive relationships in the 'WE' dimension but it is not what we mean when we talk about creating 2nd person perspective. Such observational power can occur with varying degrees or depths of understanding. Thus the first part of the MAP skill, detailed in the previous chapter, is designed to uncover the deeper level of meaning behind an individual's transmission rather than just detecting the surface tone, words and body language. The second part of the MAP skill is designed to create a powerful 2nd person experience.

As a reminder, MAP is an acronym for:

Move your attention away from your own thinking and drop into the body and BREATHE;

Appreciate the speaker;

Play back the underlying meaning.

Generating appreciation shifts the receiver out of their own 1st or 3rd person perspective and when we add in the 'play back' this lands the receiver solidly in 2nd person territory. Appreciation helps to dissolve any hostility or judgement that can prevent us accessing the shared space and the play back requires the individual to play back their 1st person perspective experience of the other person's 1st or 3rd person statement. The goal is to create common understanding between the participants. Play back allows both people to get really clear about the meaning behind the communication so they share understanding.

So a more sophisticated explanation of what's really going on when we use the MAP skill and why it's so transformative is that it provides us with a *map* of how to get to the elusive 2nd person perspective through a deeper felt sense of our interior as the receiver and match this to the transmitter's interior.

When two people get into the 2nd person perspective and the stake in the ground is not personal opinion (1st) or facts and data (3rd) but actually a shared common understanding of at least some part of the discussion then real connection occurs and real progress becomes possible.

And that's why traditional communication training so often fails to change the quality and strengths of our relationships. Participants are encouraged to say things like, 'I understand you' or 'I hear what you are saying', whether that is true or not. These statements are at best a relatively superficial 3rd person reflection of the other person's 1st person interior but they don't play back to make sure that we really do understand what they are saying. After all, it is possible to understand what another person is saying (at varying degree of sophistication) but still not develop any degree of 2nd person perspective or common ground and yet it's the common ground that is so crucial to powerful relationships and success in the 'WE' dimension.

In normal conversation play back is extremely unlikely to happen because people just fake connection and understanding by nodding occasionally and saying, 'I see where you are coming from'. Often they don't see where the other person is coming from, either because they don't actually care or because they assume they know without checking. Often all they are trying to do is to revert the conversation back to their own 1st or 3rd person perspective and drive that home.

Learning how to consciously get into the 2nd person perspective is the critical component in creating verticality in the 'WE' dimension because it builds trust, massively improves connection and develops deeper more powerful relationships.

Leadership behaviours and perspective taking

In Chapter 4 we explored the 11 leadership behaviours that when elevated to 'Strength' or 'Strategic Strength' significantly improve leadership performance and results. These behaviours are organized into the four clusters: Imagine, Involve, Ignite and Implement. Two of these clusters, Involve and Ignite, are people rather than task related behaviours and are therefore vital to the development of the 'WE' space.

The Involve and Ignite behaviours are:

1 **Empathetic Connecting** – how well do we really listen to other people's perspectives and get their 'buy in' to the concept in question?

2 **Facilitating Interaction** – how well do we support and facilitate genuine interaction and build a coherent team idea?

3 **Developing People** – how able are we to support the development of other people so as to ensure success?

4 **Influencing Others** – how well do we influence and engage the other people necessary for success?

5 **Building Confidence** – how well do we inspire and build confidence in the idea or task, ourselves and others?

6 **Transmitting Impactfully** – how clearly do we communicate with other people involved in the idea or task?

The rarest and therefore the most valuable of all these behaviours is Facilitating Interaction. The reason it is so rare is because it requires the ability (and ego maturity) to move into the 2nd person perspective and create shared understanding.

As discussed, what normally happens in a team debate, discussion or meeting is that one person tries to impose their 1st person view on everyone else or individuals use data from the 3rd person perspective to win the argument and push people into a position. Decision making often comes down to the evidence and facts, meritocracy or the individual with the most forceful autocratic 1st person perspective.

Very few leaders can sit and listen to the team debate, know they have an opinion or something to add but instead decide to park that opinion in favour of facilitating a shared view or understanding that everyone can align behind. In order to nudge the collection of 1st and 3rd person perspectives into the shared space the leader might say, 'It seems that the common ground between these different perspectives may be ...'. This 'calling out' of the shared 2nd person perspective and naming it is skilful *Facilitating Interaction* behaviour because it is offered as an invitation rather than asserted like a 3rd person fact.

Again the MAP skill gives leaders a way to change and develop the ability to become more proficient at *Facilitating Interaction* and creating shared 2nd person perspective space.

When the leader appreciates that there is a 1st, 2nd and 3rd person perspective and they can operate effectively from any perspective and knows what perspective they are taking, when they are in it they have developed 4th person perspective taking. The ability to operate from the 4th person perspective adds altitude to the interpersonal dimension and enhances a leader's 4D capability.

When we operate from the 4th person perspective we transcend and include 1st, 2nd and 3rd person perspectives. For example, in a crisis we can operate as a decisive authoritative figure (1st). Alternatively we can helicopter up to rational 3rd person perspective and draw on the data that's available to help facilitate the best decisions for the business. And if the situation demands we can also create powerful shared space, make decisions quickly, facilitate constructive interaction and drive alignment around a shared vision. When we are in 4th we can choose which perspective is going to get the best results and alter our communication accordingly. In other words we need to know what perspective we are taking, when we are taking it and that requires a sophistication that is currently lacking in modern leadership.

We hear in business all the time about the need to 'take people with us' – it's a great idea and it's absolutely true but most people have no idea how to do it. They will almost always fall back on two tried and tested approaches – either through 1st person passionate advocacy or the merit of their 3rd person argument backed by data.

By far the most effective way to take people with us is to engage them so they *want* to come along. Engage them at the 2nd person perspective and they will align behind the shared objective rather than being convinced or browbeaten into it. And this approach is always much more sustainable and reliable over the long term because it activates the followers' intrinsic motivation so they don't need to be incentivized or constantly reminded to follow. Real followership occurs when we are all in 2nd and there is enough of a shared goal and commitment around shared ground that everyone wants to get to that outcome too. Mastering the art of 2nd person perspective can mean the difference between compliance and collaboration which is essential for effective team development.

Team development

The escalating speed and complexity of business means that we need to become much better at cross-functional collaboration, partnership and developing highly connected teams. In many respects the ability to build high functioning teams is at the heart of the 'WE' dimension and will increasingly be a hallmark of brilliant leadership.

For many leaders and senior executives the issue of team development and how to get people to work together effectively is a never ending challenge. Most leaders have patchy results working with teams because they've rarely been formally trained in team development – at least not beyond clichés about 'norming, storming and performing'. As a result, off-site team building days and countless generic courses make little difference to outcome but the mere mention of team building is accompanied by a collective sigh and plenty of eye rolling.

That's not to say that team development is a waste of time. Far from it; we think it is absolutely critical if organizations want to achieve their potential or stay ahead of the market. But we have to accept that genuine team development takes time. When working with CEOs and senior executives we always advise that if a leader is not prepared to invest a minimum of two days per quarter in developing their team then they probably shouldn't even start because it's a waste of time and money. Remember the difference in results between the Operations Board and Executive Board mentioned in Chapter 3. Within a year the Ops Board (two days a quarter) were functioning at a much higher level than the Exec Board (two events a year). To their credit the Exec Board recognized the disparity and invested more time in their team journey. Within just six months they were eclipsing the effectiveness of the Ops Board and driving organizational transformation.

Like performance and relationships what makes a team work is often considered a mystery. But poorly functioning teams are often just the logical outcome of certain corporate conditions. Few leaders or employees are rewarded for working well cross-functionally or building coherent teams. Instead, rewards are more commonly based on individual contribution which hinders team emphasis and focus. This often leads to 'symptom thinking' not 'systems thinking' (Cockerill, 1989a). In addition there is little technical understanding of the levels of team development, how these levels can be measured and how to guide teams through the levels to much higher levels of performance.

Twenty-five years of research by Cockerill, Schroder and others (Bales, 1951; Cartwright and Zander, 1968; Fisher, 1999; Katzenbach and Smith, 1993; Peterson *et al*, 1998; De Dreu and Weingart, 2003) has provided the foundations for the seven distinct levels to team development. These levels are discussed in detail in *Coherence: The secret science of brilliant leadership* (Watkins, 2014):

1 Talented Individuals;

2 Battling Experts;

3 Dependent Experts;

4 Independent Achievers;

5 Interdependent Pluralists;

6 Integrated Pluralists;

7 Integrated Fellowships.

Like all the developmental models we've discussed progress is always an evolution and it's not possible to skip a level of development. Teams who put in the work can progress through the levels relatively quickly and those that don't or are poorly guided will usually slide back to a lower less productive level of functioning. Step changing team capability is not only beneficial for the business but it is a significant professional asset. Unsurprisingly the strategic decision to invest in team development is one of the most commercially significant moves a leader can make in the 'People Leadership' quadrant of the Leadership Model.

As any leader who's tried it will tell you better team work can't be mandated. Any effort to enforce team engagement will almost certainly have the opposite result. But there are certain conditions that make team engagement more likely:

1 **Create interdependency** – Ideally seek to make each team member's success dependent on another team member's to foster collaboration across functions.

2 **Identify a common purpose** – Ideally seek to unite the team behind a common objective. This could be the team's vision, purpose, ambition or strategy. A genuinely shared version of any of these concepts from the boardroom to the shopfloor can serve as a unifying force.

3 **Define authority** – Teams function better when they enjoy a degree of autonomy and have the ability to determine their own destiny within defined limits of authority.

4 **Manage team size** – Ideally seek to create smaller teams to minimize complexity and politics. The optimal size really depends on the team's purpose, longevity and capabilities. Many organizations think six is the magic number but we have seen dysfunctional teams of four people and highly effective teams of 18 people. Larger teams simply need more disciplined governance.

5 **Foster a commitment to development** – Team building initiatives can be met with justifiable scepticism; however it is important to foster a shared commitment to improving the team effectiveness and enhancing the team spirit, dynamics and interpersonal relationships of the group. But it has to be sincere and not be perceived as lip service or 'box ticking'.

6 **Engage leadership** – The single biggest determinant to team success is the leader's commitment to the team and the development of the team journey. If the leader is not on board it really doesn't matter how enthusiastic the rest of the team is, the team will not really develop.

FIGURE 6.1   Executive team – 'One Boat'

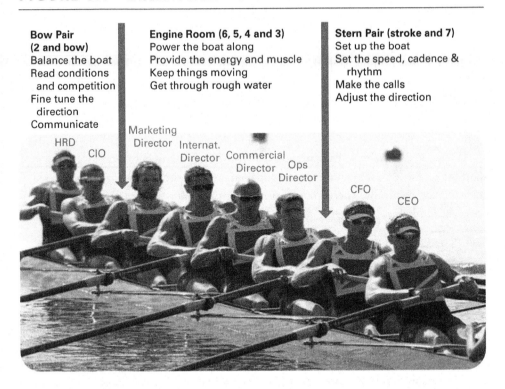

Bow Pair
(2 and bow)
Balance the boat
Read conditions
  and competition
Fine tune the
  direction
Communicate

Engine Room (6, 5, 4 and 3)
Power the boat along
Provide the energy and muscle
Keep things moving
Get through rough water

Stern Pair (stroke and 7)
Set up the boat
Set the speed, cadence &
  rhythm
Make the calls
Adjust the direction

HRD
CIO
Marketing
Director
Internat.
Director
Commercial
Director
Ops
Director
CFO
CEO

7 **One boat** – Foster a sense that we are 'all in this together' – One Team, One Boat (Figure 6.1). Using rowing as a metaphor, the rhythm, pace and direction for the boat should be set by the CEO or team leader but everyone has their role to play and no one is more significant than anyone else. In fact, if someone tries to 'be a hero' they usually slow the team down (Hunt-Davis and Beveridge, 2011). Leaders keen to exercise their own power or authority are often the primary reason teams don't develop.

If the above conditions for team development are in place then it is possible to coach and facilitate the team through the seven levels of team development. This process is not automatic so leaving teams to figure it out or engaging in 'team away days' will not facilitate this evolution. In fact such initiatives are likely to ensure the team remains stuck at level three or below (Figure 6.2). This type of unstructured approach to team development is the main reason teams fail to improve over time. Successful evolution requires a much more sophisticated understanding of the various levels of team development,

FIGURE 6.2 The levels of team development

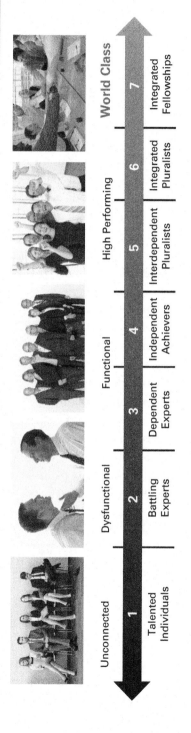

Unconnected	Dysfunctional		Functional		High Performing		World Class
1	2	3	4	5	6	7
Talented Individuals	Battling Experts	Dependent Experts	Independent Achievers	Interdependent Pluralists	Integrated Pluralists	Integrated Fellowships

how to navigate the levels, prevent backsliding and ultimately unlock the vast potential teams offer organizations (Watkins, 2014). It is highly functioning teams that separate the corporate success stories from the losers – especially in a VUCA world.

As a team develops from level three to level five the energy of team meetings changes dramatically and the level of connectivity is palpably different. This maturation is particularly characterized by a team's ability to take multiple perspectives and work freely across silos. The depth of relationship and the quality of communication between team members is also much stronger. There is also a significantly greater openness to input. These factors represent the developmental keys which unlock the greater level of performance in a level five team. Accelerating team development through these levels can be facilitated by enabling high quality effective feedback.

Effective feedback

Most leaders engage in some sort of feedback to their colleagues but few have deconstructed the nature of the feedback process to uncover what makes for *effective feedback*. As a consequence this potentially powerful motivational tool is often used badly leading to impaired relationships or disengaged colleagues. The most important thing to remember is that effective feedback is really about the person we are giving the feedback to rather than us and the message we want to transmit. Even if we have something vital to say the effectiveness of the feedback relies on our understanding of how best to deliver the message to create the desired impact on the recipient.

The overall purpose of feedback is to develop much greater levels of self-awareness that can then drive behavioural change. Self-awareness is the first step to real change. Effective feedback will 'open the window' of self-awareness penetrating the blind spots that others can see but you can't (Figure 6.3) (Luft and Ingham, 1955). Self-disclosure also opens the window and in combination such shared discovery is a rich source for learning but more importantly development.

Intention and impact

Before the feedback process even starts it is important to realize the difference between intention and impact. Many leaders assume that because they believe their intentions were clear then their impact is exactly the same as their intention. This is often far from the case. We may be clear on our

FIGURE 6.3   The Johari Window

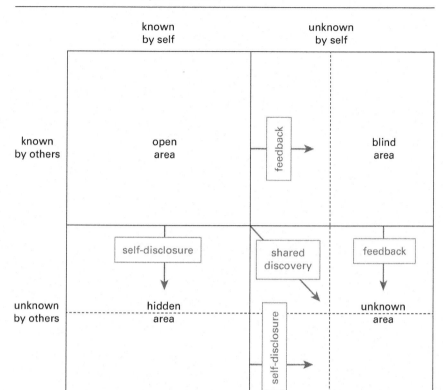

intention but our impact doesn't always match that intention. We are also aware of other people's impact on us and based on that alone we will often assume their intention. Thus when someone annoys us we often mistakenly assume that this was their intention and they were 'doing it on purpose'.

It is vital to remove the assumptions when giving people feedback and always check how the feedback has landed to ensure that it is aligned to our intention (Figure 6.4). In other words we need to solicit feedback on our feedback.

But you don't just need to test the impact that your feedback is having – you can test the receiver's intention in their response to your feedback. Thus if you feel that the receiver's response to the feedback is dismissive (that is their impact on you) then you must check whether they were intending to dismiss your feedback. Being very clear about intentions and impact is crucial to avoid the mess and miscommunication that occurs during most feedback sessions. We need to ensure that what we meant to say is exactly what was received so there is no confusion or misunderstanding.

FIGURE 6.4   Intention and impact

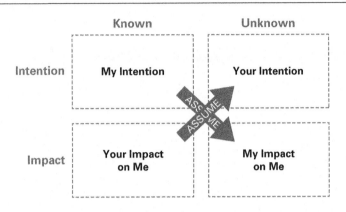

The MAP skill and relationship cache

The ability to 'MAP' someone is such a vital capability because it enables us to get to a shared understanding of what was intended and the impact of that intention so as to establish a 2nd person perspective from which we can build our relationship.

The MAP skill requires the receiver to generate a state of appreciation within their own system. This move changes the energy of the interaction. Research conducted by academic Emily Heaphy and consultant Marcial Losada demonstrated that the factor that made the greatest difference between the most and least successful teams was the ratio of positive comments to negative comments. The average ratio for the highest-performing teams was 5.6:1 (Zenger and Folkman, 2013). This ratio is also supported by research done by professor emeritus in psychology, John Gottman into happy marriages (Gottman and Silver, 2015).

So we need to work on a ratio of 5:1 positive interactions for every tough interaction if we want feedback to really land. If the only feedback we give to others is negative then our feedback is likely to be dismissed, partly because we have never built any relationship cache with the other person.

Our feedback is much more likely to be effective if the person we are giving the feedback to respects us and has an existing positive relationship with us. This is something that most bosses forget. They mistakenly assume that because they are the boss that their feedback is either right or will be well received and acted upon. But if there has been very little relationship building and very little encouragement from the boss the likelihood is that the feedback will either be ignored or its impact will be minimized because of the emotional dynamics at play.

Dimensions of feedback

In setting up the feedback it can be extremely important to signal which dimension ('I', 'WE' or 'IT') we are about to give feedback on. Without this distinction it can be very easy for people to receive feedback about some aspect of their job performance ('IT' feedback) and hear it as 'I' feedback.

For example, you may say to a colleague 'this piece of work was poorly executed and below the standard we are trying to achieve'. They hear 'you're useless ... no good at your job ... an idiot'. They convert the 'IT' feedback into 'I' feedback, usually without realizing it.

The intention of the person giving the feedback was to improve performance offering some views about quality standards and what is expected. But the feedback had the exact opposite effect because it was heard as 'I' not 'IT' – the receiver feels terrible about themselves and as a result their performance deteriorates still further. To avoid this mess we suggest that you signal which dimension you are offering the feedback in ('I', 'WE' or 'IT') and check to see how it has landed to make sure the message was received and understood to be related to the dimension it was intended.

Generally speaking 'IT' feedback is easier to give than 'WE' feedback and 'I' feedback is the trickiest of all. One way to soften the message is to offer feedback as a single insight from your 1st person perspective rather than giving the feedback as a 3rd person irrefutable fact. So you might say, 'It seems to me that something may have prevented you reaching your usual high standards on the last report', rather than 'Your last report was poor.'

Customizing the feedback

In addition to signalling the dimension of the feedback it can also help to customize the feedback according to the value system that the receiver is largely operating from. Articulating our message according to the value system can significantly enhance its effectiveness. Plus if we tune into the value system of the recipient we can set a different goal for the feedback, adjust the style and customize the language to ensure that the message lands and the feedback is optimally effective.

Table 6.1 provides insight into how to customize feedback depending on the value system of the person receiving the feedback. Remember, you need to customize to the other person's values not yours.

Before any feedback is offered take some time to prepare your message and ask yourself what is the purpose of the feedback. Is it relevant to the

TABLE 6.1   Values customization of feedback

Level of values development	Goal of feedback	Style wanted	Preferred language
Turquoise	Harmony	Unfolding	Any
Yellow	Learn	Exploration	Variety
Green	Be included	Dialogue	Sensitive
Orange	Goal progress	Data-driven	Pragmatic
Blue	Get to the truth	Follow process	Honest
Red	Cut through	Direct and fast	Simple
Purple	Feel safe	Welcoming	Friendly
Beige	Survival	Demonstration	Direct

receiver? Am I trying to change their behaviour and if so why? What is the ideal outcome I am looking for as a result of this feedback? Having checked your intentions take a few moments to ensure that your own emotional state is under control.

Too many people give 'feedback' when they are angry or frustrated. This is not feedback; it's a rant which at best will be ineffective and more likely to be destructive. One of the ways to transform the feedback process is to ask the recipient what dimension they would like feedback on ('I', 'WE' or 'IT') and maybe even what aspect of that dimension. This may not be the dimension you wanted to give feedback on but it will totally change the effectiveness of the feedback if the receiver feels in control of the focus and direction of the feedback. This switch is particularly powerful if the dimension matches the area you wanted to offer feedback in anyway.

Once you have checked your own intentions and made sure you are in an appropriate emotional state then you need to consider the receiver. Is your message customized to them? Is the timing right for this feedback? If they are particularly busy or in a rush to complete something then altering the time of the feedback can demonstrate consideration and make the huge difference as to whether it lands or not.

With all this preparation you will transform the effectiveness of the feedback and it doesn't take that much time to do so. Our relationships can also be transformed with effective, well delivered feedback. Such a high quality communication loop characterizes level five teams and mature interpersonal relationships. It creates a powerful dynamic, builds trust in a team and much greater levels of connectivity.

Network analysis revisited

In addition to embedding effective feedback into the heart of the team understanding the existing networks within an organization can facilitate a rapid evolution through the seven levels of team development.

In our work, we help senior leaders to define the current connectivity within an organization using our Leadership Network Analysis (LNA), Team Network Analysis (TNA) and Organizational Network Analysis (ONA) diagnostics. These assessments enable us to precisely define who is connected to whom, why and identify how strong those connections really are.

Although we covered network analysis in Chapter 2 as a tool to improve performance in the 'IT' dimension it is also extremely useful for creating verticality up the connection line of development which facilitates greater effectiveness in the 'WE' dimension.

Very few organizations study the connections between the people in their organization. They may create an organizational chart to conceptually illustrate how people are connected to each other but an organizational chart doesn't actually reveal how the business really works. It may illustrate hierarchies and reporting lines but even then many of those reporting lines may not actually function.

For business to succeed, especially in a VUCA environment, strong relationships and potent teams are essential if we are to deliver on objectives. Our ability to do so is largely determined by the functional, emotional and leadership networks that exist in the business.

The functional network will reveal who is important in terms of information flow. This network will identify if there are communicational blockages in the network where one person is perhaps over relied on for information. Under pressure that person can easily become a bottleneck. It is this type of network information that is so vital to security agencies that track and monitor terrorism. They know that if they can identify the key functional individuals or nodes within various terrorist cells they can seriously disrupt the functionality of the entire terrorist network. By identifying the information conduits and taking them out of the equation the information flow between the various cells collapses, therefore hampering terrorist activity.

The emotional network provides powerful insights into the developmental needs of an individual executive or leader because if an individual is highly functionally connected but doesn't have many emotional connections then people are only connecting to that person because they have to not because they want to. And that will eventually hold that person back. The emotional network can also provide powerful insights into the dysfunction of a team or why the business isn't evolving quickly enough.

We worked with one executive who had very strong emotional connectivity but was moved sideways in a corporate restructure. Unfortunately the company had not done any network analysis prior to the restructure and this move caused significant unrest in the division. It turned out that the executive was emotionally important to the community and his sideways move made many in his team and beyond very uncomfortable leading to a loss of trust in the leadership and a sudden and stark drop in performance.

The leadership network can reveal who is having the most significant directional impact on the organization or division. Again we often see situations where a leader has plenty of emotional connections but they may not be stretching people's thinking. Other executives won't go to the leader on the big issues. Conversely if there are leaders who are innovative thinkers capable of really stretching other people's thinking but they are not emotionally connected to others then that leader's capability can be squandered. They are not adding the value that they could be which again highlights areas for improvement.

For example, I worked with a global leadership team where one individual's quality of thinking and ability to come up with top notch commercially useful ideas was really strong. Unfortunately his leadership network revealed that very few of his peers turned to him for guidance on the big points where he could have added a lot of value. In addition, his emotional networks were weak despite having strong functional networks. This was an eye opener for him and caused him to significantly change his behaviour towards his peers. He realized that he did not have anywhere near the influence he hoped for or needed in order to 'land' his brilliant ideas.

Network analysis, including the Deep Network Analytics (DNA) we discussed in Chapter 2 can help us to really understand how our business works so we can be strategic about who we bring into negotiations, who is involved in strategy or who is involved in employee engagement. As such we can significantly improve relationships, reach and influence.

When considering the journey toward 4D Leadership it can be daunting to know where to start. Even if you appreciate the urgent need for vertical development across the dimensions of 'I', 'WE' and 'IT', most organizations don't have a limitless development budget. Network analysis can therefore reveal where to place that budget for maximum early impact. The insights thrown up by the process can enable the targeted spend of a limited budget and generate significant early wins which then drive a step change in relationships and performance.

A business that is suffering from poor employee engagement for example can use network analysis to identify the people in the network who are highly emotionally connected. These are the individuals who energize those around them so investing in their development could significantly impact engagement without having to put everyone through the development initiative. In other words you can figure out who to send on development programmes instead of feeling compelled to 'sheep dip' everyone into shallow areas of development. Dunking everyone in the team building course, or sales training 'just in case' is a colossal waste of time and money and deeply demoralizing for most. Network analysis allows us to identify who needs what development, therefore tailoring the developmental needs to the individual rather than attempting to find blanket solutions and engage in box ticking exercises. This approach gives us much more bang for our developmental buck.

Action steps

All the dimensions of 'I', 'WE' and 'IT' are inextricably linked. When we gain altitude in each to create 4D Leadership we create a cumulative positive impact on the business. The following actions steps will help you to maintain that positive impact in the 'WE' dimension to deliver maximum advantage:

1 Start to notice which perspective you tend to operate from – is it 1st or 3rd? Practise moving between 1st and 3rd on purpose.

2 Experiment with setting aside your own perspective (1st or 3rd) and entering the 2nd person space to broker a common understanding and shared perspective with your peers. Including using the Facilitating Interaction behaviour.

3 Ensure you are clear about the difference between Facilitating Interaction (creating 2nd person perspective) and facilitating an

answer in the room driven by one person's passionate 1st person perspective or objective 3rd person perspective.

4 Practise identifying the common ground in a conversation between two parties by either moving up to a higher level of abstraction or dropping down into greater detail.

5 Cultivate the awareness and ability to consciously step into 1st, 2nd, or 3rd, ie develop 4th person perspective.

6 Before giving anyone feedback, carefully plan what you are giving feedback on, the purpose, timing and languaging to ensure that it lands more effectively and can result in a change of behaviour.

7 Consider asking the receiver what area they would like feedback on before you offer any. Allow them to guide the focus of the feedback that *they* feel would be most useful.

8 Recognize that the intention of your feedback may not be the same as the impact it has on the other person. And the impact of other people on you may not be what they intended either, so use the MAP skill to clarify intention and impact.

9 Review the quality and strengths of your connections and appreciate the value that they bring. Seek to identify whether those connections are the right ones at the right level and use the insights to guide development.

10 Understand the various levels of team development (Watkins, 2014) and make an honest appraisal of what level your team operated from most of the time. And what the next stage of team development would be so you can actively move the team forward.

Conclusion

The need for transformational 4D Leadership is urgent. Ever since Milton Friedman wrote his landmark article, and ridiculed anyone who believed that business should be concerned with anything other than profit, business has taken a very narrow view of itself. Friedman refuted that business had any role to play in promoting desirable 'social' ends. He didn't believe business needed a 'social conscience' or should take its responsibilities seriously for issues such as eliminating discrimination, operating ethically or reducing pollution. Friedman was wrong. Business is bigger and more important than just money. And the idea that business is just about quarterly returns must be seen as a relic of the last century and rendered obsolete. Business absolutely *does* have a social responsibility to its employees, suppliers, customers, community and environment in which it operates. Too many people have assumed otherwise and this error of judgement has led us down a dark and dangerous path. However, it is possible to reverse the inequity and reinstate business as a central force for good in society. And 4D Leadership sets out the challenge for leaders if business is going to live up to its responsibility.

But this responsibility does not just mean the provision of meaningful, appropriately paid jobs and the payment of taxes. And these actions should not just be done because customers and the communities in which businesses operate in are demanding it. Businesses should embrace 4D Leadership because it will be the only way to get ahead and stay ahead in an increasingly complex and competitive world.

More and more organizations are realizing that competitive advantage does not just come from one dimension – the rational world of 'doing'. Competitive advantage comes from development in all three dimensions – 'doing', 'being' and 'relating'. Vertical development in the 'I', 'WE' and 'IT' dimensions transforms individuals, teams and organizations more effectively than any unitary focus on task and target can ever deliver. Vertical development in these three dimensions provides the crucial fourth dimension in 4D Leadership and creates a mechanism for faster adaptation to the unprecedented changes we are now facing and will continue to face in the years to come. As such 4D Leadership is a proven recipe for thriving in the volatile, uncertain, complex and ambiguous (VUCA) world of today and tomorrow.

I have outlined some of the changes in the 'IT' dimensions of modern business and the challenges they present. To date most of our efforts to address and contend with the changes in the world we see around us have been technological exterior advances that have enabled us to do significantly more. We have built more sophisticated systems and embedded more and more complicated layers in our objective world. The issue is that such progress in the objective world has not been matched by sufficient investment in the interior and interpersonal worlds of the 'I' and 'WE' dimensions. Certainly business has been slow to embrace vertical development in these traditionally undervalued dimensions.

In this book I have outlined some of the exciting frontiers in the 'I' dimension and how we can all develop as human beings. The journey of our own transformation is fascinating, deeply rewarding and holds the key to our salvation. Leaders must embrace the exploration of their inner world of 'I' – after all, genuine leadership starts from the inside out. Cultivating the interior is not only the fastest route to health and happiness it transforms our commercial capabilities. Development in the 'I' dimension enables us to understand the world and our markets and the changes sweeping through them as well as step changing our ability to invent new strategies, products or services and inspire employees and customers alike. And incredibly if we were to invest in the 'I' dimension even a fraction of what we currently invest in the 'IT' dimension we would reap significantly greater reward and future-proof competitive advantage.

That said, vertical development in the 'I' dimension gains real traction when it is coupled with concurrent vertical development in the 'WE' dimension. Ironically development in the 'WE' dimension goes right to the heart of why organizations emerged in the first place. Organizations are simply collections of people relating to each other for mutual benefit and the benefit of society. The 'WE' dimension is the organizing principle around which all businesses must ultimately function. In our rush for action, our race to deliver this quarter's dividend, profit or EBITDA and deliver on our 'to do' lists we may have lost sight of this fact. There is still so much potential to be unlocked in the 'WE' dimension for teams, across functions and in the partnerships we build with each other.

If we develop verticality in all three dimensions of 'I', 'WE' and 'IT' we set ourselves up for a much brighter future. If we develop the ability to access and leverage all of the capabilities of our mind, release the awesome power of our collective intelligence and mix this with new business models and innovative technology we are already creating, then we become the 4D Leaders of tomorrow and we can look forward with hope and excitement to the next hundred years.

REFERENCES

Babiak, P and Hare, RD (2007) *Snakes in Suits: When psychopaths go to work*, HarperBusiness, New York

Bales, RF (1951) *Interaction Process Analysis: A method for the study of small groups*, Addison-Wesley, Cambridge, MA

Banschick, M (2014) The narcissistic boss, *Psychology Today* [Online] https://www.psychologytoday.com/blog/the-intelligent-divorce/201406/the-narcissistic-boss

Bass, BM (1999) Two decades of research and development in transformational leadership, *European Journal of Work and Organizational Psychology*, 8 (1)

BBC News online (2013) Barclays' Sir Hector Sants resigns citing stress [Online] http://www.bbc.co.uk/news/business-24925872

BBC Two (2010) *Tribal Wives*

BBC Two (2013) *Horizon*, Monitor Me, narrated by Dr Kevin Fong

Boyatzis, RE (1982) *The Competent Manager: A model for effective performance*, Wiley, London

Bregman, P (2013) Why so many leadership programs ultimately fail, *Forbes* [Online] http://www.forbes.com/sites/peterbregman/2013/07/11/why-so-many-leadership-programs-ultimately-fail/

Campbell, J (2012) *The Hero with a Thousand Faces*, New World Library, Novato

The Candidate [accessed 7 January 2015] [Online] http://www.welovead.com/en/works/details/6d8wnutAe

Cartwright, D and Zander, A (1968) *Group Dynamics: Research and theory*, Harper & Row, New York

Childre, D and Martin, H (2000) *The Heartmath Solution: The Institute of Heartmath's revolutionary program for engaging the power of the heart's intelligence*, HarperCollins, London

Chorvat, VP (1994) Toward the construct validity of assessment centre leadership dimensions: a multitrait-multimethod investigation using confirmatory factor analysis, University of South Florida, Unpublished doctoral dissertation

Christensen, CM, Allworth, J and Dillon, K (2012) *How Will You Measure Your Life? Finding fulfilment using lessons from some of the world's greatest businesses*, HarperCollins, London

Clifton, J (2007) Global migration patterns and job creation, *Gallup Business Journal* [Online] http://www.gallup.com/businessjournal/101680/Global-Migration-Patterns-Job-Creation.aspx

Clifton, J (2011) *Coming Jobs War*, Gallup Press, New York

Cockerill, AP (1989a) *Managerial Competence as a Determinant of Organisational Performance*. Unpublished doctoral dissertation – sponsored by the National Westminster Bank, University of London

Cockerill, AP (1989b) The kind of competence for rapid change, *Personnel Management*, **21**, 52–56

Cockerill, AP, Hunt, JW and Schroder, HM (1995) Managerial competencies: fact or fiction? *Business Strategy Review*, Autumn

Cockerill, AP, Schroder, HM and Hunt, JW (1993) *Validation Study into the High Performance Managerial Competencies*, London Business School. Unpublished report – sponsored by National Westminster Bank, Prudential Corporation, Leeds Permanent Building Society, the Automobile Association, the UK Employment Department and the UK Civil Aviation Authority

Collins, J (2001) *Good to Great: Why some companies make the leap and others don't*, Random House, New York

Complete Coherence Ltd (2015a) The Universe of Emotions [Mobile Application Software] Available from Complete Coherence website, iTunes and Google Play

Complete Coherence Ltd (2015b) MASTERY [Mobile Application Software] Available from Complete Coherence website, iTunes and Google Play

Croghan, JH and Lake, DG (1984) Competencies of effective principals and strategies for implementation, *Educational Policy Analysis*, Southeastern Regional Council for Educational Improvement, #410 Research Triangle Park, NC

Csikszentmihalyi, C (2002) *Flow: The classic work on how to achieve happiness*, Rider, London

Cuddy, A (2012) Your body language shapes who you are [Online] http://www.ted.com/talks/amy_cuddy_your_body_language_shapes_who_you_are/transcript?language=en#t-653614]

De Dreu, CKW and Weingart, LR (2003) Task verses relationship conflict, team performance, and team member satisfaction: a meta-analysis, *Journal of Applied Psychology*, **88**, 741–49

Deepu, CJ *et al* (2012) Biomedical Circuits and Systems Conference (BioCAS)

Denning, S (2013) The origin of 'The World's Dumbest Idea': Milton Friedman, *Forbes* [Online] http://www.forbes.com/sites/stevedenning/2013/06/26/the-origin-of-the-worlds-dumbest-idea-milton-friedman/

Dowrick, S (1997) *Forgiveness and other acts of love*, Norton, New York

Duhigg, C (2012) How companies learn your secrets, *The New York Times* [Online] http://www.nytimes.com/2012/02/19/magazine/shopping-habits.html?pagewanted=1&_r=2&hp&

Dweck, CS (2007) *Mindset: The New Psychology of Success – How we can learn to fulfil our potential*, Random House, New York

The Economist (2006) A heavyweight champ, at five foot two: The legacy of Milton Friedman, a giant among economists Online Extra [Online] http://www.economist.com/node/8313925

The Economist (2009) Rolls Royce: Britain's Lonely High-Flier [Online] http://www.economist.com/node/12887368

Farbrot, A (2014) Narcissists picked as leaders [Online] http://www.bi.edu/bizreview/articles/narcissists-picked-as-leaders/

Fisher, K (1999) *Leading Self-directed Work Teams*, McGraw-Hill, New York

Fitzgerald, FS (1945) *The Crack-Up*, New Directions Publishing, New York

Friedman, M (1970) The social responsibility of business is to increase its profits, *The New York Times* [Online] http://www.colorado.edu/studentgroups/libertarians/issues/friedman-soc-resp-business.html

Fuller, RB (1981) *Critical Path*, St Martins Press, New York

Gallup (2013) *The State of the Global Workplace: Employee engagement insights for business leaders worldwide*, Gallup Press, New York

Garrard, P (2013) Dangerous link between power and hubris in politics [Online] http://theconversation.com/dangerous-link-between-power-and-hubris-in-politics-20169

Gerber, ME (2001) *The E-Myth Revisited: Why most small businesses don't work and what to do about it*, Harper Business, New York

Goleman, D and Dalai Lama (2004) *Destructive Emotions: And how can we overcome them*, Bloomsbury, London

Gottman, J and Silver, N (2015) *The Seven Principles For Making Marriage Work*, Harmony, New York

Hari, J (2015) *Chasing the Scream: The first and last days of the war on drugs*, Bloomsbury Publishing, New York

Hayward, M (2007) Hubris: bad for business, *BizEd* [Online] http://www.e-digitaleditions.com/i/57872/67

Holmes, R (2012) NASA-style mission control centers for social media are taking off, *CNN Money* [Online] http://tech.fortune.cnn.com/2012/10/25/nasa-style-mission-control-centers-for-social-media-are-taking-off/

Hunt-Davis, B and Beveridge, H (2011) *Will It Make the Boat go Faster?* Matador, Leicester

Hunter, JE, Schmidt, FL and Judiesch, MK (1990) Individual differences in output variability as a function of job complexity, *Journal of Applied Psychology*, 75, 28–42

IBM Global Technology Services (2006) *The Toxic Terabyte: How data dumping threatens business efficiency* [Online] http://www-935.ibm.com/services/no/cio/leverage/levinfo_wp_gts_thetoxic.pdf

Jensen, MC and Meckling, WH (1976) Theory of the firm: managerial behaviour, agency costs and ownership structure, *Journal of Financial Economics*, 3 (4), 305–60

Johnson, B (1996) *Polarity Management: Identifying and managing unsolvable problems*, HDR Press, Massachusetts

Katz, D, MacCoby, N and Morse, NC (1950) *Productivity, Supervision and Morale in an Office Situation*, University of Michigan

Katzenbach, JR and Smith, DK (1993) *The Wisdom of Teams*, Harvard Business School Press, Boston, MA

Kegan, R and Lahey, L (2009) *Immunity to Change: How to overcome it and unlock the potential in yourself and your organization*, Harvard Business School Press, Boston, MA

Kim, WC and Mauborgne, R (2005) *Blue Ocean Strategy: How to create uncontested market space and make the competition irrelevant*, Harvard Business School Press, Boston, MA

Kohlberg, L (1981) *The Philosophy of Moral Development: Moral stages and the idea of justice*, Harper & Row, London

Kohn, A (1993) *Punished by Rewards: The trouble with gold stars, incentive plans, A's, praise and other bribes*, Houghton Mifflin Company, New York

Kotter, JP and Heskett, JL (1992) *Corporate Culture and Performance*, Free Press, New York

Kumar, S (2002) *You are, Therefore I am: A declaration of dependence*, Green Books, Devon

Kurweil, R (2001) *The Law of Accelerating Returns* [Online] http://www.kurzweilai.net/the-law-of-accelerating-returns

Kurzweil, R (2013) *How to Create a Mind: The secret of human thought revealed*, Penguin Books, New York

Laloux, F (2014) *Reinventing Organizations: A guide to creating organizations inspired by the next stage of human consciousness*, Nelson Parker, Belgium

Langer, EJ (1975) *The Psychology of Control*, Sage Publications, Beverly Hills

Loevinger, J and, Le Xuan, Hy (1996) *Measuring Ego Development (Personality & Clinical Psychology)*, Psychology Press

Loftus, G (2012) If you're going through hell, keep going – Winston Churchill, *Forbes* [Online] http://www.forbes.com/sites/geoffloftus/2012/05/09/if-youre-going-through-hell-keep-going-winston-churchill/

Logan, D (2011) The lie of most leadership books, *CBS MoneyWatch* [Online] http://www.cbsnews.com/news/the-lie-of-most-leadership-books/

Logan, D, King, J and Fischer-Wright, H (2008) *Tribal Leadership: Leveraging natural groups to build a thriving organization*, HarperBusiness, New York

Luft, J and Ingham, H (1955) The Johari window, a graphic model of interpersonal awareness, Proceedings of the Western Training Laboratory in group development, UCLA, Los Angeles

Lyubomirsky, S (2007) *The How of Happiness*, Penguin, New York

Martin, R (2003) *The Responsibility Virus: How control freaks, shrinking violets – and the rest of us – can harness the power of true partnership*, Basic Books New York

Martin, RL (2011) *Fixing the Game: How runaway expectations broke the economy, and how to get back to reality*, Harvard Business School Press, Boston, MA

Mayer-Schönberger, V and Cukier, K (2013) *Big Data: A revolution that will transform how we live, work and think*, John Murray Publishers, London

McLennan, W (2014) Gary Barlow's 'aggressive' tax avoidance criticised by David Cameron, *The Independent* [Online] http://www.independent.co.uk/news/

people/cameron-attacks-aggressive-tax-avoidance-as-he-is-pressed-on-barlow-judgment-9353156.html

Mehrabian, A (1972) *Silent Messages: Implicit communication of emotions and attitudes*, Wadsworth Publishing Company

Muslumova, I (2003) *The Power of the Human Heart* [Online] http://hypertextbook.com/facts/2003/IradaMuslumova.shtml

NHS Choices (2014) UK's suicide rate highest among middle-aged men [Online] http://www.nhs.uk/news/2014/02February/Pages/UKs-suicide-rate-highest-among-middle-aged-men.aspx

Neville, S and Malik, S (2012) Starbucks wakes up and smells the stench of tax avoidance controversy, *The Guardian* [Online] http://www.theguardian.com/business/2012/nov/12/starbucks-tax-avoidance-controversy

Newton, I (1676) private letter sent to Robert Hooke

Nosowitz, D (2010) How many books are there in the world, *Fast Company* [Online] http://www.fastcompany.com/1678254/how-many-books-are-there-world

Ornish, D (1998) *Love & Survival: The scientific basis for the healing power of intimacy*, HarperCollins Publishers, New York

Ostrow, A (2010) Inside Gatorade's social media command center, *Mashable* [Online] http://mashable.com/2010/06/15/gatorade-social-media-mission-control/

Owen, D (2012) *The Hubris Syndrome: Bush, Blair & the intoxication of power*, Methuen Publishing, York

Peterson, RS, Owens, PD, Tetlock, PE, Fan, ET and Martorana, P (1998) Group dynamics in top management teams: Groupthink, vigilance, and alternative models of organisational failure and success, *Organisational Behavior and Human Decision Processes*, 73, 272–305

Piaget, J (1972) *The Psychology of the Child*, Basic Books, New York

Rath, T (2007) *Strengthsfinder 2.0*, Gallup Press, New York

Robertson, BJ (2015) *Holacracy: The revolutionary management system that abolishes hierarchy*, Portfolio Penguin, New York

Rogers, CR (1967) *On Becoming a Person*, Constable & Company, London

Rooke, D and Torbert, WR (2005) Seven transformations of leadership, *Harvard Business Review* [Online] http://hbr.org/2005/04/seven-transformations-of-leadership/ar/1

Rosch, P (1995) Perfectionism and poor health, *Newsletter of the American Institute of Stress*, 7

Sackett, PR and Dreher, GF (1982) Constructs and assessment centre dimensions: some troubling empirical findings, *Journal of Applied Psychology*, 67

Schilling, DR (2013) Knowledge doubling every 12 months, soon to be every 12 hours. *Industry Tap* [Online] http://www.industrytap.com/knowledge-doubling-every-12-months-soon-to-be-every-12-hours/3950

Schroder, HM (1989) *Managerial Competence: The key to excellence*, Kendall Hunt, Dubuque, IA

Sinek, S (2009) *Start with Why: How great leaders inspire everyone to action*, Penguin, New York

Steiner, S (2014) Does high-frequency trading change the game? *Bank rate* [Online] http://www.bankrate.com/finance/investing/does-high-frequency-trading-change-the-game-1.aspx

Stogdill, RM and Coons, AE (1957) *Leader Behaviour: Its description and measurement*, Bureau of Business Research Ohio State University, Columbus OH

Tappin, S (2012) *Dreams to Last*, Beijing University Press, Beijing

Tappin, S and Cave, A (2010) *The New Secrets of CEOs: 200 global chief executives on leading*, Nicholas Brealey Publishing, London

Thomas, E (2014) Mohamed El-Erian says he left job as Pimco CEO to spend more time with daughter, *The Huffington Post* [Online] http://www.huffingtonpost.com/2014/09/26/mohamed-el-erian-pimco-daughter-note_n_5883390.html

Treanor, J (2011) Lloyds chief Horta-Osório takes time off with fatigue, *The Guardian*

Wallis, C (2004) The new science of happiness, *Time Magazine*

Wallop, H (2007) £1 in every seven now spent in Tesco, *The Telegraph* [Online] http://www.telegraph.co.uk/news/uknews/1548742/1-in-every-seven-now-spent-in-Tesco.html

Watkins A (2014) *Coherence: The secret science of brilliant leadership*, Kogan Page, London

Watkins, A and Wilber, K (2015) *Wicked & Wise: How to solve the world's toughest problems*, Urbane Publications, London

Wilber, K (2001) *A Theory of Everything: An integral vision for business, politics, science and spirituality*, Gateway, Dublin

Wilber, K (2003) *Boomeritis: A novel that will set you free*, Shambhala Productions, Boston

Yerkes, RM and Dodson, JD (1908) The relation of strength of stimulus to rapidity of habit-formation, *Journal of Comparative Neurology and Psychology*, **18**, 459–82

Zenger, J and Folkman, J (2009) *The Extraordinary Leader: Turning good managers into great leaders*, New York: McGraw Hill

Zenger, J and Folkman, J (2013) The ideal praise-to-criticism ratio, *Harvard Business Review* [Online] https://hbr.org/2013/03/the-ideal-praise-to-criticism.html

Zolfagharifard, E (2014) The (almost) WATERLESS washing machine: System uses plastic beads to clean clothes – and it's more effective than detergent, *Daily Mail* [Online] http://www.dailymail.co.uk/sciencetech/article-2548677/The-washing-machine-WITHOUT-water-System-uses-tiny-plastic-beads-clean-clothes-works-better-detergent.html

INDEX

Note: The Index is filed in alphabetical, word-by-word order. Numbers and acronyms are filed as spelt out. Page locators in *italics* denote information contained within a Figure or Table.